Betty Crocker

Healthy Heart

COOKBOOK

Betty Crocker

Healthy Heart

COOKBOOK

WILEY

Wiley Publishing, Inc.

Dedication

. . . .

This cookbook is dedicated in memory of my
late father, Stanley L. Blumenthal, M.D. and
my mother Anita Blumenthal, as being early
proponents of healthy, nutritious eating.

For general information on our other products and services or to obtain technical support please contact our Customer Care Department within the U.S. at 800-762-2974, outside the U.S. at 317-572-3993 or fax 317-572-4002.

Library of Congress Cataloging-in-Publication Data:

Betty Crocker healthy heart cookbook.
    p. cm.
    Includes index.
    ISBN 0-7645-7424-8 (hardcover : alk. paper)
    1. Heart—Diseases—Diet therapy. I. Title: Healthy heart cookbook.
II. Crocker, Betty.
    RC684.D5B486 2004
    641.5'68—dc22   2004011942

Manufactured in the United States of America

10 9 8 7 6 5 4 3 2

Cover photo: General Mills Photo Studios, Sunflower © PhotoDisc.

GENERAL MILLS

Director, Book and Online Publishing: Kim Walter

Manager, Cookbook Publishing: Lois L. Tlusty

Editor: Cheri A. Olerud

Recipe Development and Testing: Betty Crocker Kitchens

Food Styling: Betty Crocker Kitchens

Photography and Food Styling: General Mills Photography Studios

WILEY PUBLISHING, INC.

Publisher: Natalie Chapman

Executive Editor: Anne Ficklen

Senior Production Editors: Jennifer Mazurkie and Michael Olivo

Cover design: Paul DiNovo

Book design: Mauna Eichner and Lee Fukui

Manufacturing Manager: Kevin Watt

Thanks go to:

- Joyce Hendley for her outstanding writing

- Bell Institute of Health and Nutrition members Eric Gugger, Lori Fromm, Jean Storlie, and Susan Crockett for their nutrition expertise

- Dr. Tim Crimmins, General Mills Medical Director, and Dr. Elizabeth Klodas, Cardiologist, for their medical advice and wisdom

- A heartfelt thanks to the following individuals who provided insightful quotes and shared the things that have worked for them in their quest to prevent heart disease: Cathy P, Cindy L, Ken B, Kevin W, Lori S, Margot & Dave C, Marilyn B, Nanci D, Pat R, Sherry L, Timothy C, Wanda S.

Our Betty Crocker Kitchens seal guarantees success in your kitchen. Every recipe has been tested in America's Most Trusted Kitchens™ to meet our high standards of reliability, easy preparation and great taste.

Find more great ideas and
shop for name-brand housewares at

BettyCrocker.com

The good news about heart disease? About 80% of the factors that increase your risk are within your power to change. How you live your life now can make a major difference in what happens to your heart later. Experts agree: incorporating a few simple healthy habits can help protect you against heart disease. In fact, we now know that the connection between what you eat, your exercise habits and the other things you do to stay healthy is stronger than ever.

As an added plus, using these guidelines benefits not only your heart, but can also help you reduce your chance of developing cancer, diabetes and digestive disorders. And you'll look better, feel better and have more energy to enjoy life to its fullest.

Another bit of good news—making even small positive changes and sticking with them, over time, can add up to big results. And, the best news of all—you don't have to give up the foods you love or the activities you enjoy most—the secret to keeping them is balance and moderation.

So, turn the page and come on, eat to your heart's content!

Roger S. Blumenthal

Dr. Roger S. Blumenthal

Contents

Perhaps you or someone you care for has been diagnosed with a heart problem. Maybe heart disease runs in your family; your goal may be to do all you can to stay healthy, or you just want to help your family eat more heart-healthy. However you came to this cookbook, you'll find what you need to get started: information on how the heart works and how heart disease develops; the latest news about nutrition and exercise; tips for maintaining a healthy weight. Also included are suggestions for stocking

Eat to Your ....
Heart's Content!

your pantry with heart-healthy foods, menus to get you started—and, most importantly, easy, delicious kitchen-tested Betty Crocker recipes you can prepare and serve with confidence to family and friends. ❤ While making lifestyle changes can be challenging at first, they can soon become lifetime habits. As you read on, you'll see that a heart-smart lifestyle is well within your reach—and that it can be joyful and satisfying, too. ❤ Here's to living well, in every sense of the word!

Playing the Game of Heart-Health

Keeping our hearts healthy is like playing a card game: We begin with whatever we're dealt, but the game's outcome is influenced by the skills we employ and the choices we make—as well as a little luck. Learn the ground rules of the healthy-heart game: how the heart works, how heart disease can harm, and how our lifestyles can change the outcome. You'll find that at every stage of the game, there's a lot you can do to keep your heart at its healthiest. **While 20 percent are risks you cannot control, a whopping 80 percent are risks you can control.**

Your Trump Card: Your Heart

Although it's only about the size of your fist, your heart is a very powerful, hardworking muscle. With every beat, it pumps blood at a rate of about five quarts per minute throughout your body. In a single day, your heart will beat more than 100,000 times, and pump about 2,000 gallons of blood. It works without a break and usually without repairs for upwards of seventy years. Few man-made machines could match that performance record!

Your heart, along with your lungs, is the vital center of your **circulatory system**, the network of tubes, called **blood vessels**, which carry blood throughout your body. Blood travels from the heart to the lungs, where it picks up oxygen. Then it passes through the heart again, through blood vessels called **arteries**, to deliver the oxygen and other nutrients to all your body's cells.

From there, the deoxygenated blood is carried by another set of blood vessels, the **veins**, to the heart and lungs. Blood also carries waste products from your cells to your liver and kidneys, which filter them out. After the veins return the blood

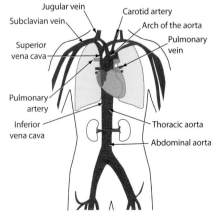

Jugular vein
Subclavian vein
Carotid artery
Arch of the aorta
Superior vena cava
Pulmonary vein
Pulmonary artery
Inferior vena cava
Thoracic aorta
Abdominal aorta

to the heart, it circulates back to the lungs to pick up oxygen, beginning the cycle all over.

Your pumping heart propels the blood throughout this complex system—and with each beat, the blood travels far. To give you an idea of how hard your heart works, imagine that all your blood vessels were laid end-to-end. They'd stretch for 60,000 miles—long enough to circle the world twice!

Knowing Your Cards: Risk Factors for Heart Disease

Though heart disease is a major killer, great progress in fighting it is being made. In fact, the death rate from coronary heart disease declined by 25 percent from 1990 to 2000. Part of that success can be attributed to people recognizing the risk factors that make heart disease more likely, and working to reduce those risks.

The 20 Percent Hand You're Dealt: Risk Factors You Can't Change

Some risk factors are simply a matter of circumstance—you don't have any control over them. But knowing about them can help you make decisions that can influence your health. The factors include:

Increased age. Men over age forty-five and women over age 55 are at greater risk of developing coronary heart disease than are younger people.

Gender. At least until they reach menopause, women have a lower risk of heart disease than men. This gender difference may be due to the effects of the female hormone estrogen. After menopause, when natural estrogen levels wane, the differences lessen. By age seventy, men's and women's risk of cardiovascular disease (CVD) are about equal. See "A Heart-to-Heart Talk with Women" page 90.

Family History. If one or both of your parents (or a sibling, aunt or uncle) had heart problems at an early age, the likelihood of your developing heart disease is greater than that of people with no family history of the disease. Heart disease and stroke run higher in African-Americans and Hispanics. In fact, heart disease and stroke are the No. 1 and No. 3 killers of Hispanics/Latinos and African-Americans as well as whites.

The Five Spades: Diseases of the Heart

When you consider that your heart is part of such an exquisitely tuned, complex system, it's amazing more things don't go wrong. Many of us go through our lives without any problems with our hearts—but others aren't so lucky. In fact, nearly 62 million Americans have some form of **cardiovascular disease** (CVD), the catch-all term for diseases of the heart and blood vessels. CVD is our nation's number one killer, causing more than 40 percent of all deaths in 2000. Here, a quick introduction to the five most common cardiovascular diseases in the United States:

1. Coronary Heart Disease. (CHD) This is the most common heart disease affecting Americans—and the cause of one out of every five deaths each year. CHD is sometimes called "coronary artery disease," because it begins in the coronary arteries, those that lead to the heart. If these arteries become clogged with plaques—deposits containing a waxy substance

called **cholesterol**—it becomes harder for the blood to get to the heart. Without treatment, the plaques can build up, making the artery walls thicker and less flexible. This is called **atherosclerosis** (hardening of the arteries), sometimes called atherosclerosis.

Plaque-clogged coronary arteries inhibit the flow of oxygen-rich blood to the heart. A warning signal that the heart isn't getting enough oxygen is **angina pectoris**, a disease characterized by brief attacks of crushing pain in the chest. Angina attacks are painful, but they usually only last a few minutes. The only good that can come from angina pectoris is if the person heeds the body's warning and seeks medical treatment.

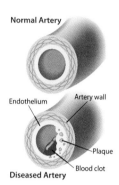

Normal Artery

Endothelium

Artery wall

Plaque

Blood clot

Diseased Artery

If plaques keep building up in a coronary artery, they can eventually burst or tear, causing a blood clot to form. The clot can clog the artery completely, cutting off blood flow to the heart. The affected parts of the heart muscle start to die, resulting in a heart attack. A **heart attack** can be disabling or life-threatening, depending on how much heart muscle is irreversibly damaged and how quickly treatment can be started. About 1.1 million Americans suffer heart attacks each year.

Stroke. Some experts refer to a stroke as a "brain attack," because it occurs when blood flow to part of the brain is reduced, depriving it of the oxygen it needs. Strokes often occur when part of a blood clot travels through the bloodstream and gets lodged in a blood vessel that brings blood to the brain. Some strokes occur when the arteries serving the brain become clogged and hardened by fatty deposits, or are damaged by high blood pressure. Another type of stroke, called a **hemorrhagic stroke**, is caused by bleeding in the brain.

Whatever its cause, a stroke can be devastating. The affected part of the brain can become injured or even shut down, resulting in paralysis, numbness, or speech defects. Strokes can also be fatal: of the half-million Americans who have a stroke each year, about one quarter do not survive. Luckily, new treatments and promising research continue to improve the odds.

Don't Delay, Get Help Right Away! Know the Signs of Heart Attack and Stroke

A heart attack occurs when one or more of the heart's arteries are blocked. The blood supply to the heart muscle is severely reduced or stopped; if the blood supply is cut off for more than a few minutes, the heart's muscle cells suffer permanent injury or die. Depending on how much of the heart is damaged, this can kill or disable someone.

Heart attack and stroke are life-threatening emergencies, so **every second counts**. If you notice any of the warning signs below, dial 9-1-1 immediately. Today there are new, clot-busting medications and treatments available that can stop some heart attacks and strokes while they are happening, saving lives and reducing disabilities.

Not all the signs below will occur in every heart attack or stroke. They may go away for a while and then return.

Signs of Heart Attack

Some heart attacks are sudden and intense—with these "movie heart attacks," no one is in any doubt about what's happening. More often, though, heart attacks start slowly, with only mild pain or discomfort. The person affected may wait too long before getting help because he or she isn't sure what's wrong. Know the signs:

- **Chest pain.** Most heart attacks involve pain in the center of the chest; it lasts more than a few minutes or it may go away and come back. It can feel like uncomfortable pressure, squeezing or fullness.

- **Discomfort in other areas of the upper body.** Symptoms may also include pain or discomfort in one or both arms, the back, neck, jaw or stomach.

- **Shortness of breath.** This feeling often accompanies chest pain, but it can occur beforehand.

- **Other signs:** Breaking out in a cold sweat, nausea or lightheadedness.

The American Heart Association and the National Heart, Lung and Blood Institute have launched a new "Act in Time" campaign to increase awareness of heart attack symptoms and the importance of calling 9-1-1 immediately. Their motto: Don't delay, get help right away!

Signs of Stroke

A stroke occurs when a blood vessel that brings oxygen and nutrients to the brain bursts or is clogged by a blood clot or other particle. Because of this blockage or rupture, part of the brain doesn't get the blood and oxygen it needs. Deprived of oxygen, the nerve cells in the affected area of the brain die within minutes.

These are the warning signs of stroke, as identified by the American Stroke Association:

- Sudden numbness or weakness of the face, arm or leg, especially on one side of the body

- Sudden confusion, trouble speaking or trouble understanding speech

- Sudden trouble seeing out of one or both eyes

- Sudden trouble walking, feeling of dizziness, a loss of balance or coordination

- Sudden, severe headaches with no known cause

If you or someone you're with has one or more of these signs, call 9-1-1 immediately. **Check the time so you know when the first symptoms appeared.** For the most common type of stroke, a clot-busting drug can reduce long-term disability if it's administered within three hours of the start of symptoms.

2. Heart Failure. (HF) Formerly known as Coronary Heart Failure, having heart failure doesn't mean that your heart has "failed." Rather, it's the result of your heart working too hard, usually for too long. HF develops when the heart becomes damaged by heart diseases, heart attacks or other problems.

The damaged heart is less able to pump blood through the body, limiting the blood supply to vital organs like the kidneys. Without enough blood, the kidneys can't do their job (making urine) as well, so the body retains too much fluid. When fluids build up in the lungs, it can cause shortness of breath and a persistent cough—some of the most common symptoms of HF. These excess fluids add to the load the already weakened heart has to pump, straining it further.

Because HF is a disease that develops over time, the likelihood of developing it increases as you get older. As the average age of Americans has risen, so has the incidence of HF; at last count, two or three out of every 100 Americans—about 4 million—were living with some degree of HF.

3. High Blood Pressure (Hypertension). When the force of a heartbeat pushes blood into your arteries, it exerts pressure on the walls of your blood vessels: Picture it like water flowing through a garden hose. Some pressure is needed to keep the blood flowing, but if the blood vessels are constricted for any reason, the pressure rises—just as the force of water increases if you squeeze the hose. Hypertension is like keeping the faucet turned up too much: the increased workload strains your heart, and your blood vessels, just like the hose, get damaged over time.

It's estimated that one out of every four Americans has high blood pressure. Because the disease rarely causes symptoms that can be felt, many of them don't know it. But the consequences of letting this "silent killer" go untreated are serious. Having high blood pressure greatly increases your chances of developing heart failure, stroke, and kidney failure—especially if you have other risk factors, such as obesity, smoking, diabetes, or high cholesterol. That's why your blood pressure is checked at every doctor visit—and why, if it's high, it's so important to keep it under control. Staying on top of your treatment for high blood pressure—which usually involves managing your weight, exercise and medications—can help prevent these problems from developing.

4. The Lipids (Fats) In Your Blood. When you have your cholesterol measured by a blood test, you'll get a **Total Cholesterol** reading: the amount of cholesterol circulating in your blood. Most cholesterol is made in the body, though the amount is influenced by the amounts and kinds of fats we eat. A high total cholesterol reading, of course, is a risk factor for heart disease—but alone, it doesn't tell the whole story. That's why your cholesterol test includes a **lipid profile**, an analysis of the fats (lipids) present in your blood. Besides total cholesterol, a lipid profile will report your level of **triglycerides (TG)**—a transportable form of fat. While triglycerides are used as a source of energy by the body, persistently high blood triglyceride levels add to your risk of developing coronary heart disease.

Since your blood is mostly water—and water and fat don't mix—these lipids need to attach to proteins in order to travel through the blood. The combination of lipids and proteins is called a **lipoprotein**. Determining the levels of certain types of lipoproteins in your blood can provide important clues about your heart health. Your lipid profile will likely include measures of:

High-Density Lipoprotein (HDL), or "good" cholesterol. HDL carries cholesterol to the liver where it is broken down and removed from the body. The higher your HDL, the lower your risk of cholesterol building up in your arteries, and the lower your risk of developing coronary heart disease.

Low-Density Lipoprotein (LDL), or "bad" cholesterol. LDL carries cholesterol through the bloodstream to your cells. The higher your LDL, the higher your risk of cholesterol building up in your arteries, and the greater your risk of developing coronary heart disease.

5. Congenital Heart Disease. These are heart defects present at birth. They can include improperly formed blood vessels, heart valves or the walls between different sections of the heart. Six to eight of every 1,000 babies born each year have congenital heart defects. Although it's rare, adults are occasionally diagnosed with a congenital heart disease that wasn't noticed in childhood. Most congenital problems, if they are caught early enough, can be repaired with surgery and other treatments.

Aneurysms. Sometimes the arteries and blood vessel walls can become damaged and, in response, develop **aneurysms.** An aneurysm is a bulge in a blood vessel, much like a bulge on an over-inflated inner tube. Aneurysms are dangerous because they may burst, but they can be surgically removed. More than 90 percent of abdominal aortic aneurysms are associated with atherosclerosis. Other risk factors include smoking, high blood pressure and family history.

Playing Your Aces: Controlling the Risk Factors You Can Change

When it comes to heart disease, *about 80 percent of the factors that increase your risk are within your power to change. How you decide to live your life now can make a major difference in what happens to your heart later.* What's more, since many of the risk factors are interrelated, reducing one risk factor can improve your heart health in other areas. Begin exercising regularly, for example, and you're likely to lower your blood pressure, reduce your weight and improve your cholesterol profile. You can make a powerful difference! Here are some of the most important things you can do:

1. Quit Smoking.

While every vital organ of your body suffers when you smoke, it is especially hard on your heart. Depending on how often they light up, cigarette smokers double, triple, or even quadruple their risks of heart disease compared to nonsmokers.

Smoking hurts your heart by damaging artery walls and promoting the buildup of fatty deposits within those arteries' walls. It also increases the tendency of blood to clot, setting the stage for a heart attack or a stroke. With every puff you take, nicotine (the chemical most responsible for making smoking so addictive) increases blood pressure and heart rate, and it causes the coronary arteries to constrict, adding to the stress on your heart.

The good news about smoking-related heart disease is that it's preventable: Quit now, and your health risks start to drop right away. Many of the 1.2 million ex-smokers who quit each year do it with the help of nicotine-containing patches, gum, nasal sprays or inhalers that help ease the symptoms of nicotine withdrawal. Nicotine-containing patches and gum are available without a prescription. Your doctor can also put you in touch with organizations for group support, problem-solving and counseling.

2. Aim for a Healthy Weight.

Studies show our notions of the "ideal" weight change with the times. A century ago, people wanted to be "pleasingly plump"; today, the majority of people long for a sleek look. But for most of us, the reality is far from ideal: nearly two-thirds of adult Americans are overweight, according to estimates.

Being overweight strains your heart—it has to pump more blood to reach a greater amount of body tissue. Extra pounds increase your risk of developing high blood pressure and high cholesterol, as well as diabetes. The more you weigh, the greater your risk: **People who are considered "obese"**—they weigh more than 20 percent over their ideal weight—**double their risk of developing heart disease.**

Because excess weight is linked to so many problems, *reaching or maintaining a healthy weight can have a major impact.* In fact, few other changes in your lifestyle will have such a dramatic, positive effect on your health. Some of the improvements you'll realize by reaching a healthy weight:

- Added energy

- Reduced blood pressure, if it's high (on average, every 2 pounds you lose can lower your readings by 1 to 2 points)

- Better control of your blood sugar, if you have diabetes

- Lower blood cholesterol levels

- Reduced risk of coronary heart disease, stroke and cancers

How can you tell if your weight is healthy? Just getting on the scale is a start, but health experts prefer to use a more accurate measurement that takes both your weight and height into account: your **body mass index**, or BMI.

Body Mass Index (BMI)

Body mass index, or BMI, is the measurement of choice for many physicians and researchers studying obesity. BMI uses a mathematical formula that takes into account both a person's height and weight. BMI equals a person's weight in kilograms divided by height in meters squared. $(BMI = kg/m^2)$

Determining Your Body Mass Index (BMI)

The table below has already done the math and metric conversions. To use the table, find the appropriate height in the left-hand column. Move across the row to the given weight. The number at the top of the column is the BMI for that height and weight.

BMI (kg/m²)	Normal							Overweight				Obese		
	19	20	21	22	23	24	25	26	27	28	29	30	35	40
Height (in.)	Weight (lb.)													
58	91	96	100	105	110	115	119	124	129	134	138	143	167	191
59	94	99	104	109	114	119	124	128	133	138	143	148	173	198
60	97	102	107	112	118	123	128	133	138	143	148	153	179	204
61	100	106	111	116	122	127	132	137	143	148	153	158	185	211
62	104	109	115	120	126	131	136	142	147	153	158	164	191	218
63	107	113	118	124	130	135	141	146	152	158	163	169	197	225
64	110	116	122	128	134	140	145	151	157	163	169	174	204	232
65	114	120	126	132	138	144	150	156	162	168	174	180	210	240
66	118	124	130	136	142	148	155	161	167	173	179	186	216	247
67	121	127	134	140	146	153	159	166	172	178	185	191	223	255
68	125	131	138	144	151	158	164	171	177	184	190	197	230	262
69	128	135	142	149	155	162	169	176	182	189	196	203	236	270
70	132	139	146	153	160	167	174	181	188	195	202	207	243	278
71	136	143	150	157	165	172	179	186	193	200	208	215	250	286
72	140	147	154	162	169	177	184	191	199	206	213	221	258	294
73	144	151	159	166	174	182	189	197	204	212	219	227	265	302
74	148	155	163	171	179	186	194	202	210	218	225	233	272	311
75	152	160	168	176	184	192	200	208	216	224	232	240	279	319
76	156	164	172	180	189	197	205	213	221	230	238	246	287	328

Body weight in pounds according to height and body mass index.

Risk of Associated Disease According to BMI and Waist Size

BMI	Waist less than or equal to 40 in. (men) or 35 in. (women)	Waist greater than 40 in. (men) or	35 in. (women)
18.5 or less	Underweight	N/A	N/A
18.5–24.9	Normal	N/A	N/A
25.0–29.9	Overweight	Increased	High
30.0–34.9	Obese	High	Very High
35.0–39.9	Obese	Very High	Very High
40 or greater	Extremely Obese	Extremely High	Extremely High

Adapted with permission from Bray, G.A., Gray, D.S., Obesity, Part I, Pathogenesis, West J. Med. 1988: 149: 429-41.

Federal guidelines define a BMI of 18.5 to 24.9 as normal. That means if your BMI falls within these boundaries, your weight is probably at a healthy level, and there's no health advantage to changing it. (If your BMI is less than the number 18.5 on the chart, you may be severely underweight; talk to your doctor about your health risks.)

If your BMI is between 25 and 29.9, you're considered "overweight;" if it's 30 or above, you are in the "obese" category. The higher your BMI within these ranges, the greater your risk of heart problems and other weight-related health issues—and the more you'll benefit from losing weight! Talk to your doctor about your BMI; occasionally some people are fit and muscular yet they fall into the overweight category.

Pear or Apple?

Carrying excess fat is a known health risk, but *where* you carry it on your body matters, too. Studies show that people with "apple" shapes—those who tend to accumulate fat around their waists—have an increased risk of coronary heart disease, high blood pressure, stroke, diabetes and even some cancers, when compared with their "pear"-shaped counterparts—those who tend to carry fat around their hips and thighs. This connection between weight and body shape leads some health experts to feel that taking a waist measurement is important to assess health risks.

To determine whether you're carrying too much fat around your middle, place a tape measure around your waist just above your hipbones. A reading of more than 40 inches in a man, or 35 inches in a woman, is considered a health risk—especially if your BMI places you in the "overweight" range or above.

Healthy Ways to Lose

As tempting as it sounds to "lose ten pounds in one week" (as some diet programs boast), most experts agree that slow, steady weight loss—about one to two pounds per week—is the safest and most effective strategy. The best diet, in fact, isn't a diet that

The 10-Percent Solution

If you're overweight, losing just a few pounds may seem like a drop in the bucket, but from your heart's point of view, it's a major improvement. Studies show that a weight loss of just 5 to 10 percent of body weight can significantly lower your blood pressure, improve cholesterol readings, and, if you are diabetic, improve your ability to control your diabetes.

What does 5 to 10 percent amount to? If you weigh 160 pounds now, it's a weight loss of just 8 to 16 pounds.

you "go on" or "go off," but a way of living your life more healthfully. If you work at making changes gradually, you'll allow yourself the time to adopt new ways of thinking that result in new behaviors and improved, sustainable habits.

Another reason to avoid crash diets is that they are so hard to stay on: no one can tolerate feeling constantly hungry and deprived for long. A crash diet also makes it harder for you to keep weight off; the diet makes your body believe it is starving, and it reacts by slowing the rate at which you burn calories. Crash dieters almost always regain the weight they lost, and often gain even more.

The best strategies for losing weight also include increasing your level of activity. Exercise helps people lose weight more easily and keep it off longer than if they were merely adjusting their diets. Among the successful "losers" tracked by the National Weight Control Registry—a database of more than 2,000 people who lost more than 30 pounds and kept it off for more than a year—the most common element in their weight loss success was regular exercise. Other key factors in successful weight loss include setting realistic goals, keeping a food and/or exercise diary, rewarding yourself for weight-loss accomplishments, acknowledging and accepting setbacks, and enlisting support of families and friends, support groups or organized weight-loss programs. Your health care provider can help you find a weight-loss strategy that works for you.

3. Get Moving!

The benefits of exercise really sound too good to be true, don't they? "Lose weight!" "Have more energy!" "Cut your risk of heart disease in half!" In fact, exercise is so important to good health that the lack of it—a sedentary lifestyle—is considered a major risk factor for coronary heart disease. Unfortunately, most Americans—over 60 percent of us—don't get the exercise we need, and that's bad news for our hearts. By staying sedentary, we *double* our risks of developing heart disease.

Why is exercise so important? Remember, your heart is made of muscle—and like any muscle, it benefits from a good workout. Regular activity makes your heart a more efficient pump, and it helps lower your blood pressure and blood cholesterol levels—all while boosting your levels of "good" HDL

cholesterol. Regular activity also helps you lose weight and keep it off, which decreases your heart-disease risks even more. As far as your body is concerned, the old adage is true: "Motion is lotion."

Step-Starters

Before you get started, the American Heart Association recommends that men over the age of 50, and women aged 55 or older, who have previously been sedentary should have a physician-supervised exercise tolerance test before they begin a new exercise program.

To keep your heart healthy, start by exerting yourself just a little more than usual—and do it regularly. Many health guidelines suggest a goal of 60 minutes of activity, most days of the week. That might seem like a lot if you're inactive now, but, for starters, any activity is better than nothing. Housework, gardening, and yard-work qualify, especially if you approach them with zest.

You can ease yourself into an exercise routine by first aiming for 30 minutes of daily activity, then working your way up. If you can't spare a block of time, start with smaller sessions that can be squeezed into your day. You might try a 15-minute brisk morning walk and another walk at lunchtime, for example. Gradually increase the frequency and intensity of your activity as your fitness improves.

Aerobic Exercise

The best exercises for strengthening your heart are **aerobic** activities—those that involve continuous, rhythmic use of your muscles. These include:

Walking briskly (3-4 mph)	Jumping rope	Swimming
Jogging or running	Cycling	Dancing

Whatever activity you choose, be sure it's something you enjoy, and you'll stick with it longer. Your workout should be intense enough to feel like you're working, but not so strenuous that you can't pass "the talk test": you should always be able to have a conversation with someone during the activity (except swimming, of course). In fact, having an exercise buddy is a great way to get and stay motivated.

To further support your success, try to work out at the same time each day so that it becomes a regular part of your life. Consider thinking about it as the one meeting in your day you can*not* miss. Prevent boredom by varying your activities; ride your bike on one day, walk briskly around in a shopping mall on another. And don't be too hard on yourself if you miss a day or two. Instead, acknowledge that we all have lapses—and get right back into your routine the following day.

Get the Kids Moving, Too!

When kids are physically active every day, they reap the same physical, psychological and social benefits you do. To achieve and maintain a good level of heart and lung fitness, the American Heart Association recommends:

- Children age 2 and older participate in at least 30 minutes of fun, *moderate-intensity* activities every day.

- Children age 2 and older participate in at least 30 minutes of *vigorous* physical activities at least 3 to 4 days per week.

Be a role model: Adopt an active lifestyle yourself, and provide your children with opportunities to have fun being active and growing strong. It's the best way to help kids develop a lifelong exercise habit. It doesn't have to be fancy: Get everyone out for a game of tag, go for a bike ride, toss a baseball, kick a soccer ball or football around or take a walk together. Get moving and have fun with your kids!

You're It. Get Fit!

Many fitness programs have been developed to make becoming—and staying—active easy and fun. Some are aimed at kids, some at adults. Programs such as 10,000 Steps, The President's Council on Fitness, Jump Ropes for Heart, Hoops for Heart and Fitness Fever have become popular. The simple message of each is the same: Get moving and stay moving; it makes a difference in your overall health, and in turn, for your heart.

It's Never Too Late

Pioneering work at Tufts University School of Nutrition, in Massachusetts, proves that you're never too old to benefit from exercise. In their landmark study, researchers introduced strength-training techniques to a group of six nursing home residents whose average age was 90 years. At the beginning of the study, most were so frail they needed help getting out of a chair, and used walkers or canes to get around. But within two months of a supervised weight-lifting program, the residents had more than doubled their strength, on average—and their performance on walking and balance tests improved dramatically. Two of the residents even got rid of their canes!

4. Stay in Charge

Perhaps the most important way you can reduce your risk of heart disease is to take an active role in managing your health. That means treating your body with respect and love, and giving it the nutritious foods, exercise, and regular rest it needs. It also means staying in touch with your doctor for regular checkups, recognizing that you are the most important member of your health-care team.

If you have any of the risk factors such as atherosclerosis, high cholesterol or diabetes, staying in charge of your health is even more important. Even if you take medications for these conditions, taking risk-reducing steps such as eating a nutritious diet and getting regular exercise can make these medications more effective, allow you to reduce your dosage level or even eliminate your need for them.

5. Eat Heart-ily

The *Dietary Guidelines for Americans*, the most recent recommendations from the U.S. Department of Health and Human Services and Agriculture, reflect science and medicine's current thinking on nutrition and health. They are designed to help you make sound food choices so you get enough, but not too much, of the nutrients you need to stay healthy. They outline a way of eating that is inherently heart-smart: moderate in calories, and based mostly on foods of plant origin rather than animal foods.

The *Dietary Guidelines* recommend we:

- Eat a variety of grains every day, especially whole grains.

- Eat a variety of vegetables and fruits every day.

Think of how much your heart pounds when you're nervous or anxious; being "stressed out" certainly feels like it's straining your heart. Some studies show that extreme stress—especially when it's triggered by events over which we have little control, such as the death of a loved one—can take a toll on our hearts. Heart attacks occur more often in the six months following a traumatic life event than they do in the six months prior to the event.

While you can't make your life stress-free, you *can* make a big difference by changing the way you react in stressful situations. This is especially important if you have a "Type A" personality: aggressive, competitive and easily frustrated by setbacks. If you feel overwhelmed by the stress in your life, talk with your doctor—who can recommend stress-management techniques, such as yoga, relaxation exercises, meditation, and biofeedback. Other techniques:

- *Get plenty of rest* so you're better able to handle what life throws you.

- *Get regular exercise;* it will lift your spirits, boost your energy and help you sleep more soundly.

- *Focus on the present,* rather than spending too much time reliving past events or dreading the future.

- *Talk about your concerns* and seek support from someone you're close to.

- Keep fat intake moderate. Choose unsaturated fats more often and limit foods that contain saturated fats, trans fatty acids and cholesterol.

- Choose a lifestyle combining sensible calorie intake with exercise to aim for a healthy body weight.

- Choose beverages and foods to decrease our intake of sugars.

- Use less salt in the foods we prepare and eat.

- Drink alcoholic beverages only in moderation, if at all.

As the deliciously satisfying recipes in this book show, eating more healthfully isn't complicated—and it doesn't mean giving up your favorite foods, feeling deprived or having to eat "special" meals. In fact, a heart-healthy diet is good for virtually everyone, whether they have heart disease or not!

The True Winning Hand: The Preventative Heart-Smart Plan

Using the *Dietary Guidelines*, above, to re-form your eating plan will benefit not only your heart, but can also help you reduce your chance of developing cancer, diabetes and digestive disorders. In addition, you'll feel and look better, and you'll have more energy to enjoy your life. The following sections take a look at the key components of a healthy diet in more detail.

Fat Facts

The fats we eat make food more satisfying and delicious; just think of what dressing does for a salad. Having some fat in our diets helps us feel full. And fat performs vital functions in the body, too, supplying it with essential fatty acids and fat-soluble vitamins, maintaining the integrity of all your body's cells and playing a key role in your immune and nervous systems. Getting adequate amounts of some types of fats may even help reduce your risk of heart disease.

But most Americans consume too much dietary fat. Health organization recommendations vary for fat, ranging from 20 percent to 35 percent of our daily calories. Our fat consumption averages 34 percent of the calories we eat, which means many Americans are above that level. High-fat diets are associated with the development of high blood cholesterol, obesity and diabetes—all known risk factors for heart disease.

FAT FACTS TABLE

Type of Fat	Suggested Level (% of total calories)	Description	Effect on Heart Disease	Risk
Saturated	Less than 10% combined saturated and trans fat	Found in high-fat animal products, tropical oils like palm and coconut, cocoa butter, shortening and certain nuts.	Solid at room temperature, this fat increases your LDL "bad" cholesterol. **Eating less saturated fat is the most important step you can take to lower your blood cholesterol.**	Increases
Trans		Created when hydrogen is added to liquid oil and turned into a solid fat. Found in shortening, stick margarine (stick margarine is more hydrogenated than soft tub margarine), baked goods like doughnuts and muffins and French fries.	Increases your LDL "bad" cholesterol and may decrease HDL "good" cholesterol. In 2006, food labels will include trans fat information in the "Nutrition Facts" statement.	
Monounsaturated	Up to 15%	A "good" fat found in olive oil, canola oil, peanuts and almonds.	Experts believe the bulk of the fats we eat should be monounsaturated.	Decreases
Polyunsaturated	Up to 10%	A class of "good" fats found in vegetable oils such as corn, sunflower, and their products, and in many nuts.	Known to reduce LDLs when substituted for saturated fats—a plus. At high intakes they may cause some reductions in triglycerides in some people—but may also reduce heart-protective HDLs and triglycerides in some people.	Decreases
Omega-3 fatty Acids	0.8%	A type of polyunsaturated fat found in cold-water fish like salmon and sardines; it remains liquid even at very cold temperatures. Other sources: vegetable oils like canola and soybean, flaxseed, and walnuts.	Populations with diets that include significant amounts of fish regularly have lower rates of heart disease than do populations with diets that feature other kinds of meats.	Decreases

What's more, eating lots of fat can be fattening. At 9 calories per gram, fat contains more than twice the calories as the other types of food we eat: protein and carbohydrates both contain 4 calories/gram. That's key to understanding why many Americans are overweight. If you're trying to lose weight, cutting some fat in your diet is one of the easiest ways to cut calories. The foods we eat contain several different types of fats; each causes different reactions in the body. The table on page 19 contains the most important fats in our diets, along with experts' recommendations on their consumption.

Cholesterol. A waxy substance used by the body to make hormones and acids, cholesterol is a component in all our cells. It's so vital, our bodies manufacture all we need, but we also get it from eating meat, poultry, eggs, and dairy products.

When there's too much cholesterol in your blood, it builds up on the walls of your arteries, setting the stage for coronary heart disease. Compared with saturated and trans fats, the cholesterol we eat doesn't have as much of an effect on our blood cholesterol levels: most of us compensate for the excess cholesterol in our diets by manufacturing less of it in our bodies.

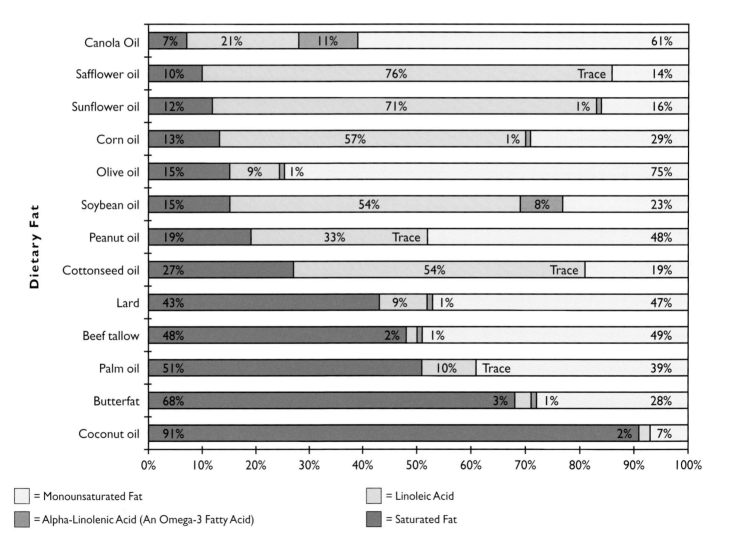

Dietary Fat	Saturated Fat	Alpha-Linolenic Acid	Linoleic Acid	Monounsaturated Fat
Canola Oil	7%	11%	21%	61%
Safflower oil	10%	Trace	76%	14%
Sunflower oil	12%	1%	71%	16%
Corn oil	13%	1%	57%	29%
Olive oil	15%	1%	9%	75%
Soybean oil	15%	8%	54%	23%
Peanut oil	19%	Trace	33%	48%
Cottonseed oil	27%	Trace	54%	19%
Lard	43%	1%	9%	47%
Beef tallow	48%	1%	2%	49%
Palm oil	51%	Trace	10%	39%
Butterfat	68%	1%	3%	28%
Coconut oil	91%		2%	7%

☐ = Monounsaturated Fat   ☐ = Linoleic Acid
▒ = Alpha-Linolenic Acid (An Omega-3 Fatty Acid)   ▓ = Saturated Fat

Nonetheless, it's important to stay on top of your cholesterol intake, especially when you consider that most cholesterol-rich animal foods also contain saturated fat. *The American Heart Association recommends healthy Americans limit their intake of cholesterol to less than 300 milligrams (mg) per day.*

Fishing for Omega-3s

While fish is the richest source of Omega-3 fatty acids, you don't have to be a fish lover to benefit. Some plant foods contain another type of Omega-3 fatty acid, called alpha-linolenic acid, which has similar, heart-healthy benefits. Flaxseeds and walnuts, along with the oils made from them are concentrated sources. Soybean and canola oils are also good sources, and they are the major contributors of Omega-3s in the American diet. Some supermarkets sell eggs that contain Omega-3s; if you can find them, try using them in your favorite recipes.

Choosing Heart-Healthy Fats

To reduce the saturated fat in your diet, think "liquid": use oils instead of butter and shortening. Since all the fats we eat are a combination of different types, even oils have some saturated fat, and some have more than others. You can use the chart on the previous page to help you choose the heart-healthiest fats.

Fiber: A "Royal Flush" of Health Benefits

Protecting your heart doesn't always mean you have to eat less. Nutrition experts wish Americans would eat much more of one nutrient: **fiber**. Fiber is simply the part of plant foods that the body cannot digest. There are two main types, each with important health benefits:

- **Insoluble fiber** doesn't dissolve in water. It helps add bulk to stools and keeps the bowels moving regularly. It's found primarily in whole-grain cereals and bread, bran and in the skins of fruits and vegetables.

- **Soluble fiber** can dissolve in water. It helps lower cholesterol in the blood. In the small intestine, where most of our food is digested, soluble fiber combines with water to form a gel. The gel binds with cholesterol particles, preventing them from being absorbed, and ushers them out of the body. Studies show that regularly consuming soluble-fiber rich foods, including ready-to-eat whole-grain oat cereal, oatmeal or oat bran, can help reduce blood cholesterol levels.

- Soluble fiber also slows the absorption of carbohydrates, so it may help control blood sugar levels in people with diabetes. Best sources of soluble fiber: whole-grain oats, barley and rye, as well as beans, seeds, nuts, brown rice, fruits and vegetables.

Since most fiber-rich foods contain both types of fiber, the benefits multiply when you eat them regularly. Foods rich in any type of fiber can also help you control your weight because they're digested more slowly, which helps you feel satisfied longer. For all these reasons, many health organizations, including the American Heart Association, recommend we get at least 25 grams of fiber daily in our diets. Unfortunately, most of us average less than half that: about 12 grams.

It's easy to boost the fiber in your diet. Following the *Dietary Guidelines for Americans*, pages 17–18, will put you on the right track; that eating plan is based primarily on fiber-rich plant foods: whole grains, vegetables and fruits, and legumes (beans and peas). To boost your intake of whole grains, eat at least half of your grain-based foods each day from whole-grain sources. See "Getting to the Heart of the Matter with Whole Grains," page 160.

The Whole Package

Because whole-grain foods include all parts of the grain, they include all the grain's nutrients, too. Foods made with refined grains lack the nutritious bran and germ components—and even if the grains are enriched later, only some of these nutrients are restored. By choosing the "whole" food, you get the whole package of health benefits.

Remember, if one of the pieces of the grain is missing, it's not whole-grain. See "Getting to the Heart of the Matter with Whole Grains," page 160.

Fruits and Vegetables: Stack the Deck in Your Favor

While it's catchy, the slogan, "Five a Day for Better Health"—a campaign urging Americans to get at least five daily servings of fruits and vegetables—hasn't proved to be very persuasive: At last count, nearly three-quarters of the population, or about 135 million people, fell short of the campaign's "five-a-day" goal.

But research continues to uncover the benefits of eating a vegetable- and fruit-rich diet. The findings have persuaded many experts to believe the five-a-day recommendation may be too small. Here are just a few of the benefits:

Folic acid. Even its name, which sounds like "foliage," is a clue that vegetables, especially leafy green ones, are excellent sources of this important B vitamin. (It's also found in fruits—especially citrus—legumes, and other plant foods, as well as in fortified cereals.) Folic acid has long been known to be important in protecting against birth defects. More recent studies suggest, but have not proven, that it protects the heart by helping to lower the body's levels of homocysteine—a substance produced when the body breaks down proteins. High blood levels of homocysteine are associated with increased risk of coronary artery disease, and folic acid may be one reason why fruit-and-vegetable-rich diets are so heart-healthy.

Phytonutrients. These beneficial substances, found in plant foods, help strengthen our bodies' defenses against heart disease and cancer. Some phytonutrients that are attracting attention as possible heart-disease fighters are the carotenoids, vegetables like carrots that are high in beta-carotene. (See "Color Them Healthy," page 197.)

Antioxidants. These substances may help prevent cholesterol from damaging arteries by preventing "bad" LDL cholesterol from changing to a form that's readily absorbed by arterial cells. Antioxidants include vitamin C, vitamin E, beta-carotene—all found in many fruits and vegetables.

Fiber. Fruits and vegetables are good sources of both soluble and insoluble fiber, making them an important weapon against heart disease and other illnesses. Since much of the fiber is contained in the skins of fruits and vegetables, avoid peeling edible skins whenever possible.

Fewer Calories. Even though they'll fill you up as well as take up lots of room on your plate, fresh fruits and vegetables won't set you back much on a calorie count. On average, a half-cup serving of vegetables provides just 25 calories, while fresh fruit provides 60 calories. And, with very few exceptions (avocadoes, coconuts) fresh produce is fat-free.

A Tricky Card: Salt

If you have high blood pressure, or if it runs in your family, reducing the sodium in your diet by cutting down on salt may help. While our bodies only need about 500 milligrams (mg) of sodium per day to function, the average American consumes about 3,300 mg.

For many people, all that salt isn't a problem; our kidneys divert the excess salt to be excreted in the urine and sweat. But others who are "salt-sensitive" may find that their bodies can't handle any excess salt. It causes them to retain water, increasing their blood volume and placing additional strain on their hearts. Eating a low-salt diet—plus losing excess weight and getting regular exercise—can fight this process.

Since there's no easy way to tell if you're salt-sensitive, many health experts consider it safe and reasonable for everyone to keep their salt intake moderate: The American Heart Association suggests we limit our sodium intake to less than 2,400 mg per day, about the amount in 1 teaspoon of salt. One great way to cut salt is to eat more fresh foods—preferably home-cooked, so you can control the salt, and sprinkle salt on only at the table (tasting the food first, of course). Be sure to read the labels to find foods that are lower in sodium. Look for

Instead of Salt, Sprinkle On:

Lemon juice

Vinegar (try herbal varieties, sherry or rice wine vinegar, or balsamic vinegar)

Chopped fresh or dried herbs

Salt-free seasoning blends

Grated lemon, lime or orange zest

Chopped fresh chili peppers

Sautéed chopped onions, garlic and/or minced fresh ginger root

reduced-sodium and low-sodium versions of your favorite foods; there are many.

A Helpful Card: A DASH of Good News

Can diet really make a difference in managing high blood pressure? Findings from the recent DASH Study (Dietary Approaches to Stop Hypertension) indicate it can. When people ate more fruits, vegetables and low-fat dairy products—and less saturated fat—than a typical American diet, their blood pressures dropped significantly. In some cases, the effects were similar to those achieved by taking medications! A later study found the DASH diet was even more effective if salt was also reduced; the less sodium was consumed, the more blood pressures dropped.

Even if you don't have high blood pressure, DASH is a heart-healthy way to eat; other studies have found the diet can help lower LDL ("bad") cholesterol levels, too. For more information about the DASH diet, check out the National Heart, Lung, and Blood Institute's Web site at www.nhlbi.nih.gov.

A Wild Card: A (Moderate) Toast to Alcohol

You've probably heard that a daily drink or two is good for your heart. Indeed, several studies suggest that light to moderate drinkers have a lower risk of heart disease, and perhaps a lower risk of death following heart attacks, than do teetotalers. Moderate amounts may even protect against certain types of strokes. When taken in moderation, alcohol seems to exert its heart-healthy effects by boosting blood levels of HDL ("good") cholesterol, as well as reducing the tendency of blood to clot.

But these benefits have to be considered within the context of how alcohol addiction can damage lives. Further, excessive amounts of alcohol can raise your blood pressure—that's why most health experts agree: If you're not a drinker now, don't start just to protect your heart. There are so many other ways to lower your heart-disease risks, it's not worth it.

If you do drink, keep your intake moderate: no more than two drinks daily for men, and one for women. One "drink" equals 12 ounces of beer, or 4 to 5 ounces of wine or 1 1/2 ounces (3 tablespoons) 80-proof spirits. The recommendations for women are lower because they tend to be smaller and to metabolize alcohol more slowly than men. Elderly people ages 65 or over should halve those amounts, since they don't metabolize alcohol as efficiently as younger people. The kind of drink isn't as important as how you enjoy it: Drink your alcohol with food to help slow its absorption—and take time to savor the pleasure it adds to the meal. Spread your drinks throughout the week, rather than consuming large amounts at one sitting and abstaining on other days.

Moderation, the Wisest Play of the Game

By now, you're familiar with the components of a heart-healthy way of eating, but equally important is making sure you're eating an amount that's right for you. In our food-abundant society, where eating opportunities are plentiful and portions are often "super-sized," it's easy to lose track of what "eating in moderation" means. Many health experts believe that eating too much is at the heart of our country's obesity epidemic.

How much should you eat? You can determine the calories your body needs daily with the formula below; individuals' results will vary, depending on how active people are. The formula will give you a rough estimate, but be sure to consult with your doctor or a registered dietitian to find a calorie range that's best for you.

Fighting "Portion Distortion"

Americans are eating more calories than they did a decade ago, and one reason is that we're eating larger portions. According to a recent study, most marketplace food portions are much bigger—sometimes two to eight times larger—than normal portion sizes. Consider that a typical bowl of spaghetti in an Italian restaurant is about three cups, or six standard servings. With the advent of mega-sized meals, jumbo muffins and extra-big drink cups, it's easy to lose touch with what proper portions look like.

Use the chart below to help you visualize the correct portion sizes of the foods you eat most often. Make an effort to measure your portions, and you'll soon be able to "eyeball" them accurately.

1 teaspoon	=	About the size of your fingertip (tip to middle joint)
1 tablespoon	=	About the size of your thumb tip (tip to middle joint)
1/2 cup	=	A fruit or vegetable that fits into the palm of your hand—about the size of a tennis ball
1 ounce nuts	=	Fits into the cupped palm of a child's hand
1 cup	=	About the size of a woman's fist; cereal that fills half of a standard cereal bowl
1 ounce	=	About the size of a standard slice of processed cheese or 2 dominoes
3 ounces meat	=	About the size of a deck of cards or a cassette audiotape

Daily Calories: What's Your Number?

This formula will help you estimate the amount of calories you need to hold your current weight steady. If you want to lose weight, eat fewer calories or increase your activity level.

Multiply your current weight by one of the activity factors:

If you're sedentary (inactive most of the time): Multiply by 12

If you're moderately active (exercise a few times a week): Multiply by 14

If you're very active (participate regularly in heavy exercise): Multiply by 16 to 18

Example:
For a sedentary woman who weighs 140 pounds:
140 (pounds) x 12 (activity factor) = 1680 calories/day
To maintain her current weight, she will need to take in about 1,680 calories per day

Stacking the Deck in Your Favor

Eating a variety of foods in moderation, getting regular exercise, staying on top of your health—each one of these healthy lifestyle decisions is like adding another valuable card to your hand. Each one makes an impact in reducing your risk of heart disease—and they all work together to keep you healthy and feeling great.

Taking steps to improve your health can have a trickle-down effect on the rest of your life: Once you start, you'll find that other positive changes will be easier to make. Think of someone you know who has made a big change for the better in his or her health recently. Chances are, that person made other healthy moves along the way—becoming a regular mall walker, say, after losing a few pounds. Positive changes have a way of building on each other—and they can for you, too.

Cards You Can Draw On: The Recipes in this Cookbook

As you start cooking and eating with your heart in mind, the Pantry Planner for Heart Health, page 239, will help you select and keep on hand the best heart-smart foods. The recipes in this cookbook have been chosen for great taste, all-family appeal and ease; best of all, they are low in saturated fat and cholesterol and high in fiber. So you can make the best choice possible, each recipe also lists the calories, calories from fat, fat, saturated fat, cholesterol, sodium, carbohydrate, dietary fiber and protein per serving. To calculate the nutrition content of the recipes, these guidelines were followed:

- The first ingredient is used whenever a choice is given (such as 1/3 cup plain yogurt or sour cream).

- The first ingredient amount is used whenever a range is given (such as 2 to 3 teaspoons).

- The first serving number is used whenever a range is given (such as 4 to 6 servings).

- "If desired" ingredients are not included in the nutrition calculations, whether mentioned in the ingredient list or in the recipe directions as a suggestion (such as "top with sour cream if desired").

- Only the amount of a marinade or frying oil that is absorbed during preparation is calculated.

Ask the Doctor

Dr. Roger Blumenthal, Chief of Ciccarone Preventive Cardiology Center, recent spokesperson of the American Heart Association and a cardiologist at Johns Hopkins, answers frequently asked questions about heart disease.

Q. What is Metabolic Syndrome?

A. Some people have a cluster of conditions that place them at greater risk of heart disease, including insulin resistance (decreased effectiveness of the hormone insulin), high blood pressure, high blood levels of triglycerides, lower levels of "good" HDL cholesterol and a greater tendency for blood to clot. Because these symptoms tend to occur together in some people, researchers have recently dubbed the condition "Metabolic Syndrome" or "Metabolic Syndrome X." People with an "apple" body shape, who tend to accumulate fat around their waists, may be more likely to develop manifestations of Metabolic Syndrome.

Treatment for Metabolic Syndrome includes developing the heart-healthy lifestyle habits discussed in this chapter, but because insulin resistance plays an important role, some researchers recommend carbohydrates be generally lower than in a typical "heart-healthy" eating plan—and they recommend a slightly higher intake of unsaturated fats. If you or someone you care for has been diagnosed with Metabolic Syndrome, a registered dietitian can help you put together a healthy eating plan.

Q. I have high blood pressure. Is it safe for me to lift weights?

A. Most experts agree that to build fitness and to strengthen your heart, aerobic exercise should be the core focus of your exercise program. However, as you become more physically fit, and if your doctor agrees, you may add strength training to your workout. Strength training, which involves using weight machines or hand-held weights, helps make muscles stronger and more efficient, boosts energy and helps prevent weight gain. But people with heart problems should approach vigorous strength training with caution, because it can cause temporary increases in blood pressure.

Some people with heart conditions can benefit from "cardio-friendly" strength training workouts designed by experts with experience in cardiac rehabilitation. These typically employ lower weights and more frequent repetitions. Ask your doctor to recommend such a program.

Q. How can food labels help me find heart-healthy foods?

A. Today's "Nutrition Facts" labels make it easy to compare different foods and make sure you're getting the best health "deal" for your money. You can also use them to get a clearer understanding of proper portion sizes. Label terms most relevant to heart health:

Serving Size/Servings Per Container: Know the standard single serving of the particular food is—especially if it's different from what you were planning to eat.

Calories: Reflects the calories in one portion; if you eat more or less of the listed serving size, you'll need to adjust the numbers.

Total Fat: Keep your total fat intake to between 20 percent to 35 percent or less of your daily calories. If your daily intake is 1,600 calories, that means about 53 grams per day [(1,600 x 30%)/9 = 53].

Saturated Fat: This fat can raise your level of LDL ("bad") cholesterol; it should comprise only 7 to 10 percent of your daily calories or less. If your daily intake is 1,600 calories, that means no more than 12 to 18 grams daily.

Trans Fat: Keep your intake of this fat as low as possible; the number to aim for is zero.

Sodium: Keep your sodium intake to 2,400 milligrams (mg).

Fiber: Choose foods with the most dietary fiber and (if it's indicated on the label) soluble fiber. A food is considered to be high in fiber if it has 5 or more grams per serving.

Percent Daily Value: This provides a snapshot of how the food meets the needs of someone consuming a diet that provides 2,000 calories per day. Your calorie needs may be different, so "adjust the picture" accordingly.

Q. Should I eat soy foods or take soy supplements to protect my heart?

A. It's worth a try. Research suggests, but isn't conclusive, that when people replace some of the animal-protein foods they eat with about 25 grams of soy protein daily from soy foods, their blood cholesterol levels tend to drop. In fact, some soy foods containing a significant amount of soy protein are allowed to advertise on their labels that soy protein, in the context of a low-fat, low-cholesterol diet, can help reduce the risk of heart disease.

Soy foods like tofu, soy milk and yogurt, tempeh and soy-based meat substitutes are excellent sources of low-fat, high-quality protein; they deliver a fair amount of fiber, Omega-3 fatty acids and calcium. Soy foods also contain isoflavones, hormone-like substances that may have heart-protective and cancer-preventing effects. What's more, using soy foods as occasional meat substitutes can help you lower your intake of saturated fat—and that alone will help your heart. For recipes, see pages 118, 144 and 178.

When it comes to soy supplements, however, the answers aren't as clear. Many health experts recommend eating soy foods, such as roasted soy nuts or soy milk, rather than soy's isolated components. Eating the actual food ensures you get all the beneficial nutrients—including those that may yet be discovered—that come in the whole soybean "package."

Q. I've been hearing about C-reactive protein. What does it have to do with heart disease and how can I find out if I have it?

A. C-reactive protein (CRP) is one of the proteins that increases during inflammation (the process by which the body responds to injury). No one knows for sure what causes the low-grade inflammation that puts otherwise healthy people at risk for heart disease; one hypothesis is that a bacteria or virus is to blame. We also know that high blood cholesterol, high blood pressure and high blood sugars also increase inflammation. Studies show that high levels of CRP consistently predict new and recurrent coronary events in patients with unstable angina and heart attack. Higher CRP levels are also associated with a lower survival rate of these people, so it is useful as a risk predictor. Testing CRP levels in the blood may be a new way to assess cardiovascular risk, and a sensitivity test for high CRP levels in the blood is now available. If your cardiovascular risk overall is low, there is probably no need to be tested. However, if your cardiovascular risk is average to high, ask your doctor about it.

Q. Some of my friends take an aspirin a day to reduce their risk of heart attack. Is this a good thing for everyone to do?

A. The American Heart Association does recommend aspirin use for patients who've had a myocardial infarction (heart attack), unstable angina, ischemic stroke (caused by blood clot) or transient ischemic attacks (TIA's or "little strokes"). This is based on evidence from clinical trials showing that aspirin helps prevent the recurrence of such events as heart attack, hospitalization for recurrent angina, second strokes, etc. Studies show that aspirin also helps prevent these events from occurring in people at high risk. The risks for aspirin therapy vary for each person, so I recommend consulting your physician first before just taking aspirin on your own.

Start Your Day with Breakfast

Providing your body with vital fuel first thing in the morning gives it energy and provides valuable nutrients for your brain.

Watermelon-Kiwi-Banana Smoothie

a note from Dr. B

At 3 grams per serving, this smoothie is a good source of fiber—all in a food you can drink! The soluble fiber you eat binds with fat and cholesterol to remove what your body doesn't need. Besides keeping you regular, eating foods containing fiber gives you a sense of fullness that lasts through the morning.

2 SERVINGS (1 CUP EACH)

1 cup coarsely chopped seeded watermelon

1 kiwifruit, peeled and cut into pieces

1 ripe banana, frozen, peeled and cut into chunks

2 ice cubes

1/4 cup chilled apple juice

1 Place all ingredients in blender. Cover and blend on high speed about 30 seconds or until smooth.

2 Pour mixture into glasses. Serve immediately.

"I love this smoothie for breakfast with half a toasted bagel and reduced-fat peanut butter. It's a great start to the day with enough energy to keep me going for hours. Who needs bacon and eggs?"

CINDY L.

1 Serving: Calories 115 (Calories from Fat 10); Fat 1g; Saturated Fat 0g (0% of Calories from Saturated Fat); *Trans* Fat 0g; Cholesterol 0mg; Omega-3 0g; Sodium 5mg

Carbohydrate 29g (Dietary Fiber 3g); Protein 1g

% Daily Value: Vitamin A 10%; Vitamin C 84%; Calcium 2%; Iron 2%; Folic Acid 6%

Exchanges: 2 Fruit

Carbohydrate Choices: 2

Sugar 'n Spice Green Tea

4 SERVINGS (ABOUT 1 CUP EACH)

4 cups boiling water

4 tea bags green tea

1/4 teaspoon ground cinnamon

6 whole cloves, broken into pieces

1/4 cup sugar

1/4 cup orange juice

2 tablespoons lemon juice

2 orange slices, cut in half

1 Pour boiling water over tea bags in heatproof container. Add cinnamon and cloves. Cover and let steep 3 to 5 minutes.

2 Remove tea bags; strain tea to remove cloves. Stir sugar, orange juice and lemon juice into tea. Serve hot with orange slice half in each cup.

a note from Dr. B

Current research findings make a strong case for tea's positive contribution to healthy living. Green tea contains antioxidants, which may help keep your heart healthy. In many cultures, drinking tea also has long been thought of as a great way to relax.

Flax Facts

Flax, a tiny, shiny brown seed that grows in North Dakota and Canada, is the highest plant source of Omega-3 fatty acids. Recent studies have shown that about 1 teaspoon of ground flaxseed* per day gives you enough heart-protective benefits to help reduce cholesterol and triglyceride levels.

You can find flaxseed in the grains or natural-foods section of the grocery store. For greater freshness and less expense, buy whole flaxseed and grind it with your coffee grinder, food processor or blender just before using. Because flaxseed is high in good fat and does not keep very long, grind only the amount you need and keep it covered in the refrigerator for up to two weeks or freeze for up to three months.

A good way to begin using ground flaxseed is in place of some of the flour, tablespoon for tablespoon, in muffins, breads, cookies or other baked goods; or you can sprinkle it over cereals, smoothies, salads and casseroles.

These 10 recipes were developed to use at least 1 teaspoon ground flaxseed per serving:

Berry-Banana Smoothie, page 38
Flaxseed Morning Glory Muffins, page 34
Granola-Whole Wheat Waffles with Double-Berry Sauce, page 47

"Pear-fect" Rhubarb Bread, page 50
Lemon Muesli, page 52
Oatmeal-Cranberry Muffins, page 78
Old-Fashioned Spiced Fruit Cookies, page 226

Chewy Chocolate-Oat Bars, page 220
Orchard Date-Apricot Bars, page 227
Molasses Lover's Carrot-Raisin Cookies, page 228

You do need to grind flaxseed because the whole seeds will pass right through your system and you won't get all of the health benefits.

1 Serving: Calories 6 (Calories from Fat 0); Fat 0g; Saturated Fat 0g (0% of Calories from Saturated Fat); *Trans* Fat 0g; Cholesterol 0mg; Omega-3 0g; Sodium 10mg

Carbohydrate 15g (Dietary Fiber 0g); Protein 0g

% Daily Value: Vitamin A 0%; Vitamin C 6%; Calcium 0%; Iron 0%; Folic Acid 4%

Exchanges: 1 Fruit

Carbohydrate Choices: 1

Berry-Banana Smoothie

2 SERVINGS (ABOUT 1 CUP EACH)

a note from Dr. B

Besides being very refreshing, this smoothie contains cholesterol-lowering oats and flaxseed— so beneficial for heart health—and is a good source of both soluble and insoluble fiber. What more could you ask of any breakfast food?

1 cup vanilla, plain, strawberry or raspberry fat-free yogurt

1/2 cup Cheerios® or another round oat cereal

2 tablespoons ground flaxseed or flaxseed meal

1/2 cup fresh strawberry halves or raspberries, or frozen whole strawberries

1/2 cup fat-free (skim) milk

1 to 2 tablespoons sugar

1/2 banana

1 Place all ingredients in blender. Cover and blend on high speed 10 seconds; stop blender to scrape sides. Cover and blend about 20 seconds longer or until smooth.

2 Pour mixture into glasses. Serve immediately.

1 Serving: Calories 245 (Calories from Fat 35); Fat 4g; Saturated Fat 1g (2% of Calories from Saturated Fat); *Trans* Fat 0g; Cholesterol 5mg; Omega-3 0g; Sodium 150mg

Carbohydrate 42g (Dietary Fiber 4g); Protein 10g

% Daily Value: Vitamin A 6%; Vitamin C 44%; Calcium 28%; Iron 20%; Folic Acid 24%

Exchanges: 2 Fruit, 1 Milk, 1 Fat

Carbohydrate Choices: 3

"I've always been a breakfast eater, and I generally eat Cheerios for breakfast, but I like them even better in this great-tasting smoothie."

KEVIN W.

Best Beverages for Heart Health

Choosing good, heart-smart drinks goes hand in hand with choosing good, heart-healthy foods. As well as quenching your thirst, beverages replenish the fluids lost through your daily activities. Experts recommend you drink at least 8 to 10 glasses of water and other liquids per day to keep your body running smoothly. There are many beverages to choose from, but which are the most beneficial for heart health?

Water is the very best liquid for our bodies. Our cells thrive in a fluid environment, so drink plenty of fresh water. To flavor plain water, squeeze a little lemon juice into it, or place a slice of lime or lemon in your water. Plain or flavored mineral water also makes a refreshing drink.

Eating several kinds of **fresh whole fruits and vegetables every day, including the water they contain,** ensures your body gets enough liquid as well as other healthful nutrients. Fruits and vegetables are convenient little packages of fiber, minerals and water all rolled into one.

Fresh-squeezed fruit or vegetable juices. Carrot juice, tomato juice, apple juice and orange juice are all good choices. Make sure they are 100 percent fruit juice and not labeled fruit drinks. If you have a juicer, whip up a batch of refreshing carrot or apple juice daily. Or, experiment with a combination of several juices.

Fat-free milk and yogurt drinks provide calcium, protein and other essential nutrients. Look for fat-free chocolate milk; it also contains calcium and protein.

Soy milk and other soy beverages are excellent sources of low-fat, high-quality protein, Omega-3 fatty acids and calcium. Soy also contains isoflavones, hormone-like substances that may have heart-protective effects. Health experts recommend drinking soy milk to ensure you get all the beneficial nutrients of the whole soybean.

Alcoholic beverages, in moderation. Research shows there may be some benefit to drinking wine, especially red wine, in moderation. The best-known effect of alcohol is a small increase in HDL (good) cholesterol. Though alcohol may provide heart-saving benefits, many doctors say: If you don't drink now, don't start. If you do drink, do so in moderation. Moderate alcohol consumption for women is an average of 1 to 2 drinks per day, and 2 drinks per day for men. Since too much alcohol can damage the heart muscle, the AHA recommends you discuss the benefits/hazards of drinking alcohol with your doctor.

Green Tea. The health benefits of this ancient beverage w have now been confirmed in scientific studies. According to recent studies, antioxidants contained in green tea have been shown to fight viruses, slow aging and have positive effects on the entire body. In addition, these antioxidants have been shown to reduce high blood pressure, boost the immune system and lower blood sugar, aiding in weight loss.

Low-sodium broth and low-sodium bouillon are good low-calorie choices, especially if you are salt sensitive or have high blood pressure. You can use them as a base for soup or to make a refreshing warm drink.

PREP: **30 MIN**

BAKE: **25 MIN**

Flaxseed Morning Glory Muffins

12 MUFFINS

1 cup Fiber One® cereal

2/3 cup fat-free (skim) milk

1 cup all-purpose flour

3/4 cup ground flaxseed or flaxseed meal

3/4 cup chopped apple

1/2 cup packed brown sugar

1/2 cup finely shredded carrot

1/4 cup granulated sugar

1/4 cup flaked coconut

1 tablespoon canola or soybean oil

3 teaspoons baking powder

2 teaspoons ground cinnamon

1 teaspoon vanilla

1/2 teaspoon salt

4 egg whites or 1/2 cup fat-free cholesterol-free egg product

1 Heat oven to 375°. Line 12 medium muffin cups, 2 1/2 x 1 1/4 inches, with paper baking cups and spray bottoms with nonstick baking spray.

2 Place cereal between waxed paper, plastic wrap or in plastic bag; crush with rolling pin (or crush in blender or food processor). Mix cereal and milk in large bowl; let stand about 5 minutes or until cereal is softened. Stir in remaining ingredients. Divide batter evenly among muffin cups.

3 Bake 22 to 25 minutes or until toothpick inserted in center comes out clean. Immediately remove muffins from pan. Serve warm.

1 Muffin: Calories 160 (Calories from Fat 35); Fat 4g; Saturated Fat 1g (5% of Calories from Saturated Fat); *Trans* Fat 0g; Cholesterol 0mg; Omega-3 1g; Sodium 280mg

Carbohydrate 31g (Dietary Fiber 5g); Protein 5g

% Daily Value: Vitamin A 16%; Vitamin C 2%; Calcium 12%; Iron 12%; Folic Acid 12%

Exchanges: 2 Starch

Carbohydrate Choices: 2

"I love muffins, but a bakery muffin can have more than double the calories and fat of a homemade one. These muffins have flaxseed and fruit that I need to include in my diet. I bake them once a week, and keep them on hand."

MARILYN B.

Lemon-Date Muffins

PREP: **15 MIN**

BAKE: **22 MIN**

12 MUFFINS

1 1/2 cups whole wheat flour

3/4 cup all-purpose flour

3 teaspoons baking powder

1/2 teaspoon salt

1/4 cup packed brown sugar

2 teaspoons grated lemon peel

1 cup fat-free (skim) milk

1/3 cup canola or soybean oil

1 egg

1/2 cup chopped dates

1 Heat oven to 400°. Grease bottoms only of 12 muffin cups with shortening (do not use paper baking cups).

2 Mix flours, baking powder and salt in large bowl; set aside. Beat brown sugar, lemon peel, milk, oil and egg in medium bowl with fork or wire whisk until well mixed. Stir into flour mixture just until flour is moistened. Fold in dates. Divide batter evenly among muffin cups.

3 Bake 18 to 22 minutes or until toothpick inserted in center comes out clean and tops begin to brown. Run knife around edge of cups; remove muffins from pan to wire rack. Serve warm.

a note from Dr. B

When you start exercising, you'll be replacing fat with muscle. Because muscle weighs more than fat, your weight may not drop much at first. Instead of using the scale to measure whether you've lost or gained, go by how much more energy you have, how well your clothes fit or most importantly, by how well you feel overall.

1 Muffin: Calories 195 (Calories from Fat 65); Fat 7g; Saturated Fat 1g (3% of Calories from Saturated Fat); *Trans* Fat 0g; Cholesterol 20mg; Omega-3 1g; Sodium 240mg

Carbohydrate 28g (Dietary Fiber 3g); Protein 4g

% Daily Value: Vitamin A 0%; Vitamin C 0%; Calcium 10%; Iron 6%; Folic Acid 0%

Exchanges: 1 1/2 Starch, 1/2 Fruit, 1 Fat

Carbohydrate Choices: 2

PREP: 15 MIN

BAKE: 45 MIN

Baked Apple Oatmeal

8 SERVINGS

2 2/3 cups old-fashioned oats

1/2 cup raisins

1/3 cup packed brown sugar

1 teaspoon ground cinnamon

1/4 teaspoon salt

4 cups fat-free (skim) milk

2 medium apples or pears, chopped (2 cups)

1/2 cup chopped walnuts

Additional fat-free (skim) milk, if desired

1 Heat oven to 350°. Mix oats, raisins, brown sugar, cinnamon, salt and 4 cups milk and the apples in 2-quart casserole.

2 Bake uncovered 40 to 45 minutes or until most liquid is absorbed. Sprinkle walnuts over top. Serve with additional milk.

1 Serving: Calories 270 (Calories from Fat 65); Fat 7g; Saturated Fat 1g (3% of Calories from Saturated Fat); *Trans* Fat 0g; Cholesterol 0mg; Omega-3 1g; Sodium 140mg

Carbohydrate 47g (Dietary Fiber 5g); Protein 10g

% Daily Value: Vitamin A 6%; Vitamin C 2%; Calcium 18%; Iron 10%; Folic Acid 6%

Exchanges: 1 Starch, 1 Fruit, 1 Milk, 1 Fat

Carbohydrate Choices: 3

Canadian Bacon and Potato Frittata

4 SERVINGS

a note from the Nutritionist

Try egg substitutes, and you'll be in for a pleasant surprise. They can replace whole eggs in nearly any breakfast dish without a loss of flavor or texture. If you are watching your cholesterol, they make a tasty alternative to eggs!

1 1/2 cups fat-free cholesterol-free egg product or 6 eggs

2 tablespoons chopped fresh chives or 1 tablespoon freeze-dried chopped chives

2 tablespoons fat-free (skim) milk

1/4 teaspoon salt

1/8 teaspoon dried thyme leaves

1/8 teaspoon pepper

1/4 cup chopped red or green bell pepper

2 cups refrigerated southern-style hash-brown potatoes

1/2 cup coarsely chopped Canadian bacon or cooked ham

2 tablespoons shredded Cheddar cheese

1 Beat egg product, chives, milk, salt, thyme and pepper in medium bowl; set aside.

2 Spray 10-inch nonstick skillet with cooking spray. Add bell pepper; cook and stir over medium heat 1 minute. Add potatoes; cover and cook 8 to 10 minutes, stirring frequently until potatoes begin to brown. Stir in Canadian bacon; cook and stir 1 to 2 minutes or until thoroughly heated.

3 Add egg mixture to skillet; cover and cook over medium-low heat until set, 6 to 9 minutes, lifting edges occasionally to allow uncooked egg mixture to flow to bottom of skillet.

4 Sprinkle with cheese. Cover; cook until cheese is melted, about 1 minute longer. Cut into wedges.

1 Serving: Calories 215 (Calories from Fat 25); Fat 3g (Saturated 1g); *Trans* Fat 0g; Cholesterol 15mg; Omega-3 0g; Sodium 610mg

Carbohydrate 30g (Dietary Fiber 3g); Protein 17g

% Daily Value: Vitamin A 22%; Vitamin C 24%; Calcium 6%; Iron 12%; Folic Acid 16%

Exchanges: 2 Starch, 2 Very Lean Meat

Carbohydrate Choices: 2

"I've been trying to work exercise and stretching into my morning. Nothing gets my heart started in the morning like a great breakfast, especially this frittata that is hearty and heart-friendly."

KEVIN W.

French Toast with Gingered Applesauce

PREP: 10 MIN
COOK: 16 MIN

4 SERVINGS

1/2 to 1 teaspoon grated gingerroot or 1/8 teaspoon ground ginger

1/2 cup unsweetened applesauce

1/4 cup sugar-free maple-flavored syrup

3/4 cup fat-free cholesterol-free egg product or 2 eggs plus 1 egg white

3/4 cup fat-free (skim) milk

1 teaspoon vanilla

1/4 teaspoon salt

8 slices whole-wheat sandwich bread or 1-inch-thick slices French bread

1 Mix gingerroot, applesauce and syrup in small microwavable bowl. Microwave uncovered on Medium (50%) about 1 minute or until very warm; set aside.

2 Beat egg product, milk, vanilla and salt in small bowl with fork or wire whisk until well mixed; pour into shallow bowl.

3 Spray griddle or 10-inch skillet with cooking spray; heat griddle to 375° or heat skillet over medium heat. Dip bread into egg mixture, coating both sides; place in skillet. Cook about 2 minutes on each side or until golden brown. Serve with applesauce mixture.

a note from the Nutritionist

An easy way to get at least three servings of whole grains a day is to make sure that all the bread and cereal you eat is from whole grains. Check the labels of bread and cereal packages; if they contain whole grain, it will be listed in the ingredient listing.

"The ginger, apple and maple mix is the perfect topping for this heart-healthy French toast."

WANDA S.

1 Serving: Calories 205 (Calories from Fat 25); Fat 3g; Saturated Fat 1g (2% of Calories from Saturated Fat); *Trans* Fat 0g; Cholesterol 0mg; Omega-3 0g; Sodium 590mg

Carbohydrate 38g (Dietary Fiber 5g); Protein 12g

% Daily Value: Vitamin A 6%; Vitamin C 0%; Calcium 10%; Iron 16%; Folic Acid 14%

Exchanges: 2 Starch, 1/2 Fruit, 1/2 Very Lean Meat

Carbohydrate Choices: 2 1/2

PREP: 15 MIN
BAKE: 33 MIN
COOL: 10 MIN

Mixed-Berry Coffee Cake

8 SERVINGS

1/3 cup packed brown sugar

1/2 cup buttermilk

2 tablespoons canola or soybean oil

1 teaspoon vanilla

1 egg

1 cup whole wheat flour

1/2 teaspoon baking soda

1/2 teaspoon ground cinnamon

1/8 teaspoon salt

1 cup mixed berries, such as blueberries, raspberries and blackberries

1/4 cup low-fat granola, slightly crushed

1 Heat oven to 350°. Spray round pan, 8 x 1 1/2 or 9 x 1 1/2 inches, with cooking spray.

2 Mix brown sugar, buttermilk, oil, vanilla and egg in large bowl until smooth. Stir in flour, baking soda, cinnamon and salt just until moistened. Gently fold in half of the berries. Spoon into pan. Sprinkle with remaining berries and the granola.

3 Bake 28 to 33 minutes or until golden brown and top springs back when touched in center. Cool in pan on wire rack 10 minutes. Serve warm.

1 Serving: Calories 150 (Calories from Fat 45); Fat 5g; Saturated Fat 1g (4% of Calories from Saturated Fat); *Trans* Fat 0g; Cholesterol 25mg; Omega-3 0g; Sodium 150mg

Carbohydrate 25g (Dietary Fiber 3g); Protein 4g

% Daily Value: Vitamin A 2%; Vitamin C 2%; Calcium 4%; Iron 6%; Folic Acid 8%

Exchanges: 1 Starch, 1/2 Fruit, 1 Fat

Carbohydrate Choices: 1 1/2

"The best thing I can do for my heart is to relieve stress that comes up during the day. I take a deep breath, step back and think good thoughts—a peaceful river flowing, a calm countryside, children playing in the park—they all do the heart good."

SHERRY L.

PREP: 10 MIN
COOK: 15 MIN

Peach Melba Pancakes

9 SERVINGS (18 FOUR-INCH PANCAKES)

a note from Dr. B

Adding fruit to your pancakes adds flavor, color, variety and most of all, extra nutrition. Experts now recommend at least 5 servings of fruits and vegetables per day, and scientists are still uncovering important benefits of those nutrient powerhouses.

2 eggs

2 cups all-purpose flour

2 tablespoons sugar

3 teaspoons baking powder

1/2 teaspoon salt

1 1/2 cups milk

1/4 cup canola or soybean oil

1/2 cup chopped canned (drained) or frozen (thawed and drained) sliced peaches

1/2 cup fresh or frozen (thawed and well drained) raspberries

Additional peaches and raspberries, if desired

Raspberry syrup, if desired

1 Heat griddle to 375° or heat 10-inch skillet over medium heat; grease with shortening if necessary (or spray with cooking spray before heating).

2 Beat eggs in medium bowl with wire whisk until well beaten. Beat in flour, sugar, baking powder, salt, milk and oil just until smooth. Stir in 1/2 cup each peaches and raspberries.

3 For each pancake, pour slightly less than 1/4 cup batter onto hot griddle. Cook pancakes until bubbly on top, puffed and dry around edges. Turn; cook other sides until golden brown. Serve with additional peaches and raspberries and syrup.

"This is a great way to start the day and get my fruit servings in. I love the fact that the recipe is low is sugar, and I can use the raspberries that I grow in my own garden."
LORI S.

1 Serving: Calories 205 (Calories from Fat 70); Fat 8g; Saturated Fat 1g (4% of Calories from Saturated Fat); *Trans* Fat 0g; Cholesterol 45mg; Omega-3 0g; Sodium 330mg

Carbohydrate 29g (Dietary Fiber 1g); Protein 63g

% Daily Value: Vitamin A 4%; Vitamin C 2%; Calcium 14%; Iron 8%; Folic Acid 12%

Exchanges: 2 Starch, 1 Fat

Carbohydrate Choices: 2

Oatmeal Pancakes

4 SERVINGS (9 PANCAKES)

a note from Dr. B

The American Heart Association recommends keeping dietary cholesterol to 300 milligrams or less per day, especially for people who already have elevated blood cholesterol or high triglycerides. This recipe makes a great choice, because there is virtually no cholesterol.

1/2 cup quick-cooking or old-fashioned oats

1/4 cup all-purpose flour

1/4 cup whole wheat flour

1 tablespoon sugar

1 teaspoon baking powder

1/2 teaspoon baking soda

1/2 teaspoon salt

3/4 cup buttermilk

1/4 cup fat-free (skim) milk

1/4 cup fat-free cholesterol-free egg product, thawed or 2 egg whites

2 tablespoons canola or soybean oil

1 Beat all ingredients in large bowl with hand beater or wire whisk just until smooth. (For thinner pancakes, stir in additional 2 to 4 tablespoons milk.)

2 Spray griddle or 10-inch nonstick skillet with cooking spray; heat griddle to 375° or skillet over medium heat. (To test griddle, sprinkle with a few drops of water. If bubbles skitter around, heat is just right.)

3 For each pancake, pour slightly less than 1/4 cup batter onto hot griddle. Cook pancakes until puffed and dry around edges. Turn; cook other sides until golden brown.

1 Serving: Calories 200 (Calories from Fat 70); Fat 8g; Saturated Fat 1g (4% of Calories from Saturated Fat); *Trans* Fat 0g; Cholesterol 0mg; Omega-3 0g; Sodium 660mg

Carbohydrate 25g (Dietary Fiber 2g); Protein 7g

% Daily Value: Vitamin A 2%; Vitamin C 0%; Calcium 14%; Iron 8%; Folic Acid 6%

Exchanges: 1 1/2 Starch, 1 1/2 Fat

Carbohydrate Choices: 1 1/2

Rise-and-Shine Waffles

PREP: 10 MIN

BAKE: 5 MIN PER WAFFLE

8 SERVINGS

3/4 cup old-fashioned oats

1/4 cup packed brown sugar

1 cup fat-free (skim) milk

Maple-Yogurt Topping (below)

1/4 cup fat-free cholesterol-free egg product, thawed or 2 egg whites, slightly beaten

3 tablespoons canola or soybean oil

2/3 cup all-purpose flour

2 tablespoons wheat germ or ground flax

2 teaspoons baking powder

1 teaspoon grated orange peel

1/4 teaspoon baking soda

1 Mix oats, brown sugar and milk in large bowl; let stand 10 minutes. Meanwhile, make Maple-Yogurt Topping; set aside. Spray nonstick waffle iron with cooking spray; heat waffle iron.

2 Stir egg product and oil into oat mixture. Stir in remaining ingredients until blended.

3 For each waffle, pour 1 cup batter onto center of hot waffle iron; close lid. Bake 4 to 5 minutes or until steaming stops and waffle is golden brown. Carefully remove waffle. Serve with topping. Garnish with additional grated fresh orange peel and chopped cranberries, if desired.

a note from the Nutritionist

These yummy waffles add a whole bunch of "grain-y" and good-for-you ingredients, and they offer up great taste as well. A good habit to get into is to add oats, wheat germ, flaxseed and other heart-healthy grains to your baked goods.

Maple-Yogurt Topping

1 cup plain nonfat yogurt

1/4 cup maple syrup

Mix ingredients until well blended.

1 Serving: Calories 200 (Calories from Fat 55); Fat 6g; Saturated Fat 1g (3% of Calories from Saturated Fat); *Trans* Fat 0g; Cholesterol 0mg; Omega-3 1g; Sodium 220mg

Carbohydrate 31g (Dietary Fiber 2g); Protein 6g

% Daily Value: Vitamin A 2%; Vitamin C 0%; Calcium 18%; Iron 8%; Folic Acid 8%

Exchanges: 2 Starch, 1 Fat

Carbohydrate Choices: 2

"My husband and I both have elevated cholesterol. The, oats, flax and soy oil in this recipe all are recommended for lowering cholesterol; besides these waffles are delicious first thing in the morning."

CATHY P.

Buckwheat-Orange Waffles

6 SERVINGS

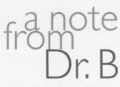

a note from Dr. B

Try experimenting with different grains to round out your whole-grain experiences. Buckwheat is a popular flour for waffles and pancakes; it's a great choice because it contains phosphorus, iron, potassium and vitamins E and B, so it's good for your heart.

1 egg

1/2 cup fat-free (skim) milk

1/2 cup plain nonfat yogurt

2 teaspoons grated orange peel

1 cup orange juice (about 2 medium oranges)

1 cup buckwheat flour

3/4 cup all-purpose flour

2 teaspoons baking powder

1 teaspoon baking soda

1/4 teaspoon ground cloves

1 | Spray nonstick waffle iron with cooking spray; heat waffle iron. Place all ingredients in blender or food processor. Cover and blend until smooth.

2 | For each waffle, pour 1/2 cup batter onto center of hot waffle iron; close lid. Bake 4 to 5 minutes or until steaming stops. Carefully remove waffle.

"I always have a banana or other fruit for breakfast.
That way, I start off eating right.
My morning fruit is a great addition to these good-for-me waffles."

NANCI D.

1 Serving: Calories 180 (Calories from Fat 20); Fat 2g; Saturated Fat 0g (3% of Calories from Saturated Fat); *Trans* Fat 0g; Cholesterol 35mg; Omega-3 0g; Sodium 410mg

Carbohydrate 33g (Dietary Fiber 3g); Protein 7g

% Daily Value: Vitamin A 2%; Vitamin C 26%; Calcium 18%; Iron 10%; Folic Acid 12%

Exchanges: 2 Starch, 1/2 Fat

Carbohydrate Choices: 2

Granola–Whole Wheat Waffles with Double-Berry Sauce

PREP: 10 MIN

BAKE: 3 MIN PER WAFFLE

7 SERVINGS

Double-Berry Sauce (below)

1 cup Original Bisquick® mix

3/4 cup ground flaxseed or flaxseed meal

1/2 cup whole wheat flour

1/2 cup low-fat granola cereal

1 1/2 cups fat-free (skim) milk

3 tablespoons canola or soybean oil

2 eggs or 1/2 cup cholesterol-free fat-free egg product

1 container (6 ounces) strawberry low-fat yogurt (2/3 cup)

1 Make Double-Berry Sauce; keep warm.

2 Heat nonstick waffle iron; spray with cooking spray before heating. Mix remaining ingredients in large bowl until blended.

3 For each waffle, pour 1 cup batter onto center of hot waffle iron; close lid. Bake 2 to 3 minutes or until steaming stops and waffle is golden brown. Carefully remove waffle. Serve with sauce.

Double-Berry Sauce

1/3 cup maple-flavored syrup

1/3 cup raspberry jam or preserves

1 cup strawberries, cut into fourths

Heat syrup and jam to boiling in 1 1/2-quart saucepan, stirring occasionally. Stir in strawberries; remove from heat.

"It is always hard to indulge my sweet tooth with something good for me. That's why I like these satisfying and refreshing pancakes with a sweet berry sauce—they are more like a treat than a breakfast."

PAT R.

a note from the Nutritionist

If you've never used flaxseed before, purchase it in the grains section of the grocery store, and store it in the refrigerator. To get the most benefit, grind it just before using with a coffee grinder. Only about 1 teaspoon per day is what's needed to lower cholesterol, so substitute a teaspoon of flaxseed for each serving for that amount of flour in your muffins, bread and cookies.

1 Serving: Calories 385 (Calories from Fat 135); Fat 15g; Saturated Fat 2g (5% of Calories from Saturated Fat); *Trans* Fat 0mg; Cholesterol 60mg; Omega-3 3g; Sodium 350mg

Carbohydrates 58g (Dietary Fiber 6g); Protein 10g

% Daily Value: Vitamin A 6%; Vitamin C 12%; Calcium 18%; Iron 12%; Folic Acid 32%

Exchanges: 3 Starch, 1 Fruit, 2 Fat

Carbohydrate Choices: 4

PREP: 18 MIN

BAKE: 60 MIN

Blueberry-Orange Bread

1 LOAF (24 SLICES)

2 cups Total® cereal, crushed

3/4 cup water

1 tablespoon grated orange or lemon peel

1/4 cup orange or lemon juice

1/2 teaspoon vanilla

2 cups all-purpose flour

1 cup sugar

1 1/2 teaspoons baking powder

1/2 teaspoon baking soda

1/2 teaspoon salt

2 tablespoons canola or soybean oil

1 egg

1 cup fresh or frozen (thawed) blueberries

Vanilla Glaze (below)

1 Heat oven to 350°. Grease bottom only of loaf pan, 9 x 5 x 3 inches, with shortening.

2 Mix cereal, water, orange peel, orange juice and vanilla in large bowl; let stand 10 minutes. Stir in remaining ingredients except blueberries and Vanilla Glaze. Gently stir in blueberries. Pour into pan.

3 Bake 50 to 60 minutes or until toothpick inserted in center comes out clean. Cool 10 minutes. Loosen sides of loaf; remove from pan to wire rack. Cool completely, about 1 hour.

4 Make Vanilla Glaze; drizzle over loaf. Wrap tightly and store at room temperature up to 4 days or refrigerate up to 10 days.

Vanilla Glaze

1/2 cup powdered sugar

1/4 teaspoon vanilla

2 to 3 teaspoons milk

Mix all ingredients until smooth and thin enough to drizzle.

a note from the Nutritionist

Besides eating cereal for breakfast, adding cereal to recipes is a good way to get the extra nutrition that the fortification, fiber and whole grain cereals provide.

1 Slice: Calories 120 (Calories from Fat 20); Fat 2g; Saturated Fat 2g (2% of Calories from Saturated Fat); *Trans* Fat 0g; Cholesterol 0mg; Omega-3 0g; Sodium 130mg

Carbohydrate 23g (Dietary Fiber 1g); Protein 2g

Daily Value: Vitamin A 0%; Vitamin C 6%; Calcium 12%; Iron 14%; Folic Acid 14%

Exchanges: 1 Starch, 1/2 Fruit

Carbohydrate Choices: 1 1/2

"As a person with a very strong family history of heart disease, I thought tasty sweet breads were off limits. This yummy low-fat bread changed my mind."

NANCI D.

PREP: **20 MIN**

BAKE: **60 MIN**

"Pear-fect" Rhubarb Bread

2 LOAVES (12 SLICES EACH)

a note from Dr. B

Studies confirm that about 1 teaspoon of ground flaxseed per day is enough to help keep triglyceride and cholesterol levels reduced. One serving of this delicious fruit bread delivers more than that. Flaxseed must be ground to have the most benefit. Using a coffee grinder does the trick.

1 1/2 cups finely chopped rhubarb (about 1/2 pound)

1 1/2 cups chopped peeled or unpeeled pears (1 1/2 medium)

1 1/2 cups sugar

1/3 cup canola or soybean oil

1 teaspoon vanilla

4 eggs

2 cups all-purpose flour

1 1/2 cups ground flaxseed or flaxseed meal

1/2 cup chopped walnuts

3 1/2 teaspoons baking powder

1 teaspoon salt

2 teaspoons ground cinnamon

1 Move oven rack to low position so that tops of pans will be in center of oven. Heat oven to 350°. Lightly spray bottoms only of 2 loaf pans, 8 1/2 x 4 1/2 x 2 1/2 or 9 x 5 x 3 inches, with cooking spray.

2 Mix rhubarb, pears, sugar, oil, vanilla and eggs in large bowl. Stir in remaining ingredients. Pour into pans.

3 Bake 50 to 60 minutes or until toothpick inserted in center comes out clean. Cool 10 minutes. Loosen sides of loaves; remove from pans to wire rack. Cool completely before slicing, about 1 hour. Wrap tightly and store at room temperature up to 4 days or refrigerate up to 10 days.

"Since my cholesterol is high, I've been trying different things and have found that flaxseed does help lower my cholesterol.

It's so great to find foods that provide a heart-health benefit."

CINDY L.

1 Slice: Calories 185 (Calories from Fat 70); Fat 8g; Saturated Fat 1g (5% of Calories from Saturated Fat); *Trans* Fat 0g; Cholesterol 35mg; Omega-3 2g; Sodium 180mg

Carbohydrate 25g (Dietary Fiber 3g); Protein 4g

% Daily Value: Vitamin A 0%; Vitamin C 0%; Calcium 8%; Iron 6%; Folic Acid 10%

Exchanges: 1 Starch, 1/2 Fruit, 1 1/2 Fat

Carbohydrate Choices: 1 1/2

Plum Pudding Parfait

4 SERVINGS

1 package (4-serving size) vanilla fat-free sugar-free instant pudding and pie filling mix

1 1/4 cups fat-free (skim) milk

1 cup plain fat-free yogurt

1/2 cup low-fat granola

4 medium plums, pitted and chopped (about 2 cups)

1 Make pudding mix as directed on package except use 1 1/4 cups fat-free (skim) milk. Fold in yogurt.

2 Place about 1/4 cup pudding mixture in bottom of each of 4 parfait glasses. Layer each glass with 1 tablespoon of the granola and about 1/4 cup of the plums; repeat layers. Top with remaining pudding mixture. Refrigerate until ready to serve.

a note from **Dr. B**

Jump-start your day by eating breakfast. Studies show that people who eat breakfast get a head start on their daily nutrition goals and are better prepared to face the challenges of the day.

"I'm not much of a morning person, so I do as much as I can the night before. For this breakfast treat, I make the pudding and chop the plums (or other fruit) the night before, then do the layering right before I eat it. This also makes a great light dessert."

CINDY L.

1 Serving: Calories 170 (Calories from Fat 10); Fat 1g; Saturated Fat 0g (2% of Calories from Saturated Fat); *Trans* Fat 0g; Cholesterol 0mg; Omega-3 0g; Sodium 410mg

Carbohydrate 32g (Dietary Fiber 2g); Protein 8g

% Daily Value: Vitamin A 8%; Vitamin C 6%; Calcium 22%; Iron 2%; Folic Acid 28%

Exchanges: 1 Fruit, 1 Milk

Carbohydrate Choices: 2

Lemon Muesli

3 SERVINGS (2/3 CUP EACH)

1/2 cup fat-free (skim) milk

1 cup old-fashioned oats

1/2 cup lemon or orange
fat-free yogurt

1 tablespoon packed brown sugar

2 tablespoons raisins or chopped
dried fruit

1/2 medium banana, chopped

3 tablespoons ground flaxseed or
flaxseed meal

1 Pour milk over oats in medium bowl. Let stand
overnight, at least 8 hours but no longer than 12
hours.

2 Just before serving, stir in yogurt, brown sugar,
raisins and banana. Spoon into individual serving
bowls; sprinkle with flaxseed.

a note from the Nutritionist

*Here's a great way to
get all the goodness
of oatmeal, yogurt
and flaxseed in a
make-ahead breakfast.
Besides adding it to
recipes, another
ideal way to eat more
ground flaxseed is to
sprinkle it over the top
of cereal, smoothies,
salads and casseroles.*

1 Serving: Calories 215 (Calories
from Fat 35); Fat 4g; Saturated Fat 1g
(3% of Calories from Saturated Fat);
Trans Fat 0g; Cholesterol 0mg;
Omega-3 1g; Sodium 45mg

Carbohydrate 42g (Dietary
Fiber 6g); Protein 9g

% Daily Value: Vitamin A 2%;
Vitamin C 4%; Calcium 14%;
Iron 12%; Folic Acid 10%

Exchanges: 2 1/2 Starch, 1/2 Fruit

Carbohydrate Choices: 3

*"A great breakfast! I
make it with my favorite
whole-grain oatmeal."*

PAT R.

Peanut Butter–Raisin Breakfast Bars

12 BARS

1/2 cup packed brown sugar

1/3 cup light corn syrup or honey

1/4 cup peanut butter

1/2 teaspoon ground cinnamon

4 cups Total® Raisin Bran cereal

1/2 cup chopped peanuts or sliced almonds

1 Butter square pan, 8 x 8 x 2 inches. Heat brown sugar and corn syrup just to boiling in 3-quart saucepan over medium heat, stirring frequently. Remove from heat; stir in peanut butter and cinnamon until smooth.

2 Stir in cereal and peanuts or almonds until evenly coated. Press firmly in pan. Let stand about 1 hour or until set. Cut into 4 rows by 3 rows. Store loosely covered at room temperature.

"It's nice to have something homemade for breakfast, and these bars are tasty, quick and nutritious!"

MARILYN B

a note from Dr. B

If you don't have time in the morning to eat your cereal in a bowl with milk, this whole-grain breakfast is a healthy, on-the-go way to begin your day. Whole grains supply fiber and B vitamins and may help to reduce the risk of heart disease.

1 Bar: Calories 200 (Calories from Fat 55); Fat 6g; Saturated Fat 1g (5% of Calories from Saturated Fat); *Trans* Fat 0g; Cholesterol 0mg; Omega-3 0g; Sodium 170mg

Carbohydrate 32g (Dietary Fiber 3g); Protein 4g

% Daily Value: Vitamin A 2%; Vitamin C 0%; Calcium 34%; Iron 34%; Folic Acid 36%

Exchanges: 2 Starch, 1 Fat

Carbohydrate Choices: 2

Harvest Bread (page 75), Cornmeal-Berry Scones (page 77), and Wild Rice–Corn Muffins (page 76)

Smart Snacks and Breads

Snacking, rather than eating large meals, is a good way to add nutrients and spread out calories and fat over the course of the day.

PREP: 15 MIN

COOK: 2 MIN

Spinach Quesadillas with Feta Cheese

16 APPETIZERS

a note from Dr. B.

Finding good-tasting, low-fat appetizers to serve when entertaining can be a challenge because many are very high in fat and calories. This one, low in calories and fat, is a tasty, heart-healthy choice.

4 fat-free flour tortillas (8 inches in diameter)

1/4 cup soft reduced-fat cream cheese with roasted garlic

2 cups frozen chopped spinach, thawed and squeezed to drain

1 tablespoon finely chopped red onion

1/4 cup crumbled feta cheese (1 ounce)

16 cherry tomatoes

2 tablespoons fat-free sour cream

1/4 cup sliced ripe olives

1 Spread 2 tortillas with cream cheese. Layer spinach, onion and feta cheese over cream cheese. Top with remaining 2 tortillas; press lightly.

2 Spray 12-inch nonstick skillet with cooking spray; heat over medium heat. Cook each quesadilla in skillet 2 to 3 minutes on each side or until light golden brown.

3 Cut each quesadilla into 8 wedges. Cut cherry tomatoes in half; top with sour cream, tomato halves and olives. Secure with toothpicks. Serve warm.

1 Appetizer: Calories 50 (Calories from Fat 10); Fat 1g; Saturated Fat 1g (12% of Calories from Saturated Fat); *Trans* Fat 0g; Cholesterol 5mg; Omega-3 0g; Sodium 115mg

Carbohydrate 8g (Dietary Fiber 1g); Protein 2g

% Daily Value: Vitamin A 26%; Vitamin C 8%; Calcium 4%; Iron 4%; Folic Acid 8%

Exchanges: 1/2 Starch

Carbohydrate Choices: 1/2

Roasted Red Pepper Bruschetta

PREP: 10 MIN
BAKE: 8 MIN

12 APPETIZERS

4 slices hard-crusted Italian or French bread, 1/2 inch thick

1 jar (7 ounces) roasted red bell peppers, drained and cut into 1/2-inch strips

1 or 2 medium cloves garlic, finely chopped

2 tablespoons chopped fresh parsley or 1 teaspoon parsley flakes

2 tablespoons shredded Parmesan cheese

1 tablespoon olive, canola or soybean oil

1/4 teaspoon salt

1/4 teaspoon pepper

1 tablespoon capers, drained

1 Heat oven to 450°. Place bread on ungreased cookie sheet. Mix remaining ingredients except capers in small bowl. Spoon onto bread, spreading evenly.

2 Bake 6 to 8 minutes or until edges of bread are golden brown. Cut each slice lengthwise into thirds. Sprinkle with capers.

"Bruschetta is a popular appetizer and can be fat laden. This version is low in fat and high in flavor."

WANDA S.

a note from Dr. B

Regular, moderate exercise has been shown to boost immunity, increasing the body's ability to ward off colds and other illnesses. More is not always better, though, because long, intense exercise may actually depress immunity.

1 Appetizer: Calories 40 (Calories from Fat 20); Fat 2g; Saturated Fat 0g (8% of Calories from Saturated Fat); *Trans* Fat 0g; Cholesterol 0mg; Omega-3 0g; Sodium 125mg

Carbohydrate 5g (Dietary Fiber 0g); Protein 1g

% Daily Value: Vitamin A 20%; Vitamin C 48%; Calcium 2%; Iron 2%; Folic Acid 2%

Exchanges: 1/2 Starch

Carbohydrate Choices: 0

Black Bean–Corn Wonton Cups

36 APPETIZERS

36 wonton wrappers
(3 1/2-inch squares)

2/3 cup chunky-style salsa

1/4 cup chopped fresh cilantro

1/2 teaspoon ground cumin

1/2 teaspoon chili powder

1 can (15 1/4 ounces) whole kernel corn, drained

1 can (15 ounces) black beans, rinsed and drained

1/4 cup plus 2 tablespoons fat-free sour cream

1 Heat oven to 350°. Gently fit 1 wonton wrapper into each of 36 small muffin cups, 1 3/4 x 1 inch. Bake 8 to 10 minutes or until light golden brown. Remove from pan; cool on wire racks.

2 Mix remaining ingredients except sour cream in medium bowl. Just before serving, spoon bean mixture into wonton cups. Top each with 1/2 teaspoon sour cream.

"I often remind myself that I changed my eating habits for me and my family. I've found that there really are a lot of great foods and recipes, if I just take the time to look for them. This is a fantastic appetizer with a lot of good-for-me ingredients."

NANCI D.

1 Appetizer: Calories 45 (Calories from Fat 0); Fat 0g; Saturated Fat 0g (1% of Calories from Saturated Fat); *Trans* Fat 0g; Cholesterol 5mg; Omega-3 0g; Sodium 100mg

Carbohydrate 10g (Dietary Fiber 1g); Protein 2g

% Daily Value: Vitamin A 0%; Vitamin C 2%; Calcium 2%; Iron 4%; Folic Acid 8%

Exchanges: 1/2 Starch

Carbohydrate Choices: 1/2

Easy Salmon Spread

16 SERVINGS (2 TABLESPOONS DIP AND 4 CRACKERS)

1 package (8 ounces) fat-free cream cheese, softened

1 can (14 3/4 ounces) red or pink salmon, drained and flaked

3 tablespoons finely chopped red onion

2 tablespoons chopped fresh or 1/4 teaspoon dried dill weed

1 tablespoon Dijon mustard

2 tablespoons capers

64 reduced-fat whole-grain crackers

1 Line 2-cup bowl or mold with plastic wrap. Beat cream cheese in medium bowl with electric mixer on medium speed until smooth. Stir in salmon, 2 tablespoons of the red onion, 1 tablespoon of the dill weed and the mustard.

2 Spoon into bowl lined with plastic wrap, pressing firmly. Cover and refrigerate at least 2 hours but no longer than 24 hours.

3 Turn bowl upside down onto serving plate; remove bowl and plastic wrap. Garnish with remaining 1 tablespoon red onion, 1 tablespoon dill weed and the capers. Serve with crackers.

"This is a great way to eat more fish. Salmon has all those great Omega-3's!
The fat-free cream cheese keeps calories and fat low. I eat organic whole-grain crackers with this super-easy spread, a delicious combination."

LORI S.

1 Serving: Calories 115 (Calories from Fat 25); Fat 3g; Saturated Fat 1g (8% of Calories from Saturated Fat); *Trans* Fat 0g; Cholesterol 15mg; Omega-3 0g; Sodium 380mg

Carbohydrate 13g (Dietary Fiber 1g); Protein 9g

% Daily Value: Vitamin A 2%; Vitamin C 0%; Calcium 8%; Iron 4%; Folic Acid 6%

Exchanges: 1 Starch, 1 Very Lean Meat

Carbohydrate Choices: 1

Hummus–Olive Spread

10 SERVINGS (2 TABLESPOONS SPREAD AND 4 PITA WEDGES EACH)

1 container (7 ounces) plain hummus, or Hummus (below)

1/2 cup pitted Kalamata and/or Spanish olives, chopped or 1 can (4 1/4 ounces) chopped ripe olives, drained

1 tablespoon Greek vinaigrette or zesty fat-free Italian dressing

7 pita breads (6 inches in diameter), each cut into 6 wedges

1 Spread hummus on 8- to 10-inch serving plate.

2 Mix olives and vinaigrette in small bowl. Spoon over hummus. Serve with pita bread wedges.

Hummus

1/2 can (15 to 16 ounces) garbanzo beans, drained and 2 tablespoons liquid reserved

2 tablespoons lemon juice

1/4 cup sesame seed

1 small clove garlic, crushed

1/2 teaspoon salt

Place all ingredients including reserved bean liquid in blender or food processor. Cover and blend on high speed, stopping blender occasionally to scrape sides if necessary, until uniform consistency

"All our friends are watching what they eat. This recipe is a wonderful exception to a heavier spread and something I can serve to them."

PAT R.

a note from Dr. B

Making dips, especially healthy ones like this, is great when getting together with friends and family. Surround yourself with others to keep your spirits lifted. Your mental health is as important as your physical health.

1 Serving: Calories 154 (Calories from Fat 28); Fat 4g; Saturated Fat 0g (1% of Calories from Saturated Fat); *Trans* Fat 0g; Cholesterol 0mg; Omega-3 0g; Sodium 340mg

Carbohydrate 25g (Dietary Fiber 2g); Protein 6g

% Daily Value: Vitamin A 0%; Vitamin C 0%; Calcium 4%; Iron 8%; Folic Acid 14%

Exchanges: 1 1/2 Starch, 1/2 Fat

Carbohydrate Choices: 1 1/2

PREP: 15 MIN
COOK: 10 MIN

Parmesan–White Bean Dip

14 SERVINGS (2 TABLESPOONS AND 1/2 CUP VEGETABLES EACH)

1 tablespoon canola or soybean oil

2 cloves garlic, finely chopped

2 teaspoons chopped fresh or
1 teaspoon dried rosemary leaves, crumbled

1 can (19 ounces) cannellini beans, rinsed and drained

1/4 to 1/3 cup chicken broth or white wine

2 tablespoons chopped fresh Italian parsley

1 cup shredded Parmesan cheese (4 ounces)

7 cups assorted cut-up fresh vegetables

1 Heat oil in heavy 2-quart saucepan over medium heat. Cook garlic and rosemary in oil 1 to 2 minutes, stirring constantly, until garlic is light golden. Remove from heat.

2 Add cannellini beans and broth to saucepan. Partially mash beans with potato masher. Stir in parsley. Heat over medium-low heat, stirring occasionally, until bean mixture is thoroughly heated. Stir in cheese until melted. Serve warm with vegetables.

"Yoga has been very good for me; I've become stronger and more flexible from it. Best of all, it has a comforting effect on my mind and is a comfort to my soul. Another thing that's important for me is to have a creative outlet, and preparing this easy recipe does it for me."

SHERRY L.

PREP: 15 MIN

BAKE: 25 MIN

Hot Crab-Artichoke Dip

15 SERVINGS (2 TABLESPOONS DIP AND 4 CRACKERS)

1/3 cup plain fat-free yogurt

3 tablespoons reduced-fat mayonnaise

1/4 cup grated Parmesan cheese

2 cloves garlic, finely chopped

6 ounces imitation crabmeat, chopped

1 can (14 ounces) artichoke hearts, drained and coarsely chopped

1 can (4 1/2 ounces) chopped green chiles, drained

Dash of paprika

60 water crackers

1 Heat oven to 350°. Spray 1-quart casserole with cooking spray. Mix yogurt, mayonnaise, cheese and garlic in medium bowl. Stir in crabmeat, artichoke hearts and chiles. Spoon into casserole.

2 Bake uncovered about 25 minutes or until golden brown and bubbly. Sprinkle with paprika before serving. Serve with crackers.

"Keeping my weight down is always a challenge, and I'm watching my calories, but I can enjoy this dip and not worry."

CATHY P.

1 Serving: Calories 95 (Calories from Fat 20); Fat 2g; Saturated Fat 1g (6% of Calories from Saturated Fat); *Trans* Fat 0g; Cholesterol 5mg; Omega-3 0g; Sodium 320mg

Carbohydrate 14g (Dietary Fiber 2g); Protein 5g

% Daily Value: Vitamin A 2%; Vitamin C 8%; Calcium 4%; Iron 6%; Folic Acid 8%

Exchanges: 1 Starch, 1/2 Very Lean Meat

Carbohydrate Choices: 1

Smart Snacks

Snacking can provide you with an extra energy boost. Try these great heart-healthy snacks:

Whole-grain granola bars, fruit-and-grain bars, cereal snack mixes, ready-to-eat cereal and light popcorn. Remember, with whole grains, "three are key!" Select three or more servings of whole-grain foods each day.

Fresh fruits and vegetables provide important nutrients and antioxidants. Keep baby carrots, celery sticks, salsa, frozen grapes, bananas, apples, kiwifruit or other favorites on hand.

Cereal and yogurt together are a nutritious combination. Choose a high-fiber, whole-grain cereal and a light yogurt. Try layering the two for a parfait!

Peanuts, roasted soy nuts, almonds, walnuts and other nuts are great for munching and contain beneficial types of fats. For variety, mix them with low-fat popcorn, whole-grain cereal or sprinkle them with your favorite savory herb blends.

Dried plums, cranberries, apricots, dates and raisins are the ultimate convenience food, and contain important vitamins and fiber. Stretch them by mixing with pretzels, low-fat popcorn or ready-to-eat cereal.

Yogurt smoothies with fruit can be a delicious treat as well as an excellent source of calcium, vitamins and other important nutrients. Simply put your favorite light yogurt and cut-up fresh fruit in the blender, whirl and enjoy!

Sandwiches made with lean turkey, beef, ham, tuna or low-fat cheese and whole-grain bread work well for more substantial snacks. Load them up with your favorite raw veggies for a hearty mini-meal.

Lower fat cheeses, like **string cheese, mozzarella cheese slices or chunks,** eaten with or without fresh fruit, provide calcium. To minimize the amount of saturated fat, choose the low-fat or nonfat versions.

Tortilla chips, bagel chips and pretzels come in many varieties, including low fat. Dip them in roasted vegetable dip, guacamole or salsa. Or, enjoy them with low-fat cheese or peanut butter. Pay attention to the sodium content of these snacks if your doctor has recommended that you follow a low-sodium diet.

Reduced-fat crackers, cookies and breads, are good choices. Especially good are animal crackers, graham crackers, rye crackers, oyster crackers, saltines, matzo, ginger snaps, molasses cookies, bread sticks and flatbread. Look for whole-grain varieties.

PREP: 10 MIN
BAKE: 45 MIN
COOL: 30 MIN

Roasted Sesame and Honey Snack Mix

20 SERVINGS (1/2 CUP EACH)

a note from Dr. B

Nuts contain a type of fat that is good for your heart and make a great snack if you keep an eye on portion size. As long as you keep the total amount of fat you eat low and keep an eye on portion sizes, you can also combine nuts with whole-grain cereal and low-fat popcorn.

3 cups Wheat Chex® cereal

3 cups checkerboard-shaped pretzels

2 cups popped light microwave popcorn

1 cup sesame sticks

1 cup mixed nuts

1/4 cup honey

3 tablespoons canola or soybean oil

2 tablespoons sesame seed, toasted, if desired*

*To quickly toast sesame seed, cook in a small nonstick skillet over medium heat 1 to 3 minutes, stirring frequently, until light golden brown.

1 Heat oven to 275°. Mix cereal, pretzels, popcorn, sesame sticks and nuts in ungreased jelly roll pan, 15 1/2 x 10 1/2 x 1 inch.

2 Mix remaining ingredients in small bowl. Pour over cereal mixture, stirring until evenly coated.

3 Bake 45 minutes, stirring occasionally. Spread on waxed paper; cool about 30 minutes. Store in tightly covered container up to 1 week.

"I started out with the goal of eating better to reduce my cholesterol and to make my diabetes easier to deal with. I've been really committed to my health, and an added bonus has been that I've lost weight. Snacks like this one make it easier!!"

SHERRY L.

1/2 Cup: Calories 165 (Calories from Fat 35); Fat 4g; Saturated Fat 0g (3% of Calories from Saturated Fat); Trans Fat 0g; Cholesterol 0mg; Omega-3 0g; Sodium 440mg

Carbohydrate 29g (Dietary Fiber 2g); Protein 3g

% Daily Value: Vitamin A 2%; Vitamin C 2%; Calcium 2%; Iron 18%; Folic Acid 24%

Exchanges: 1 Starch, 1 Other Carbohydrates, 1/2 Fat

Carbohydrate Choices: 2

Hiker's Trail Mix

12 SERVINGS (1/2 CUP EACH)

1 1/2 cups roasted soy nuts

1 cup Multigrain or Honey Nut Cheerios® cereal

3/4 cup raisins

1/2 cup candy-coated chocolate candies or chocolate chips

Mix all ingredients. Store in resealable plastic bag or tightly covered container.

a note from the Nutritionist

Soybeans have the highest-quality vegetable protein, considerably more than other legumes or nuts. Look for roasted soy nuts in the bulk-foods section at your local supermarket or food cooperative.

"Now retired, we still have a very active lifestyle. This is a great snack to indulge that sweet tooth and still watch the calories and fat. We take it hiking, biking and anytime we are on the go. A healthy gorp!"

MARGOT C.

1/2 Cup: Calories 145 (Calories from Fat 45); Fat 5g; Saturated Fat 2g (11% of Calories from Saturated Fat); *Trans* Fat 0g; Cholesterol 0mg; Omega-3 0g; Sodium 40mg

Carbohydrate 20g (Dietary Fiber 3g); Protein 5g

% Daily Value: Vitamin A 0%; Vitamin C 0%; Calcium 4%; Iron 12%; Folic Acid 14%

Exchanges: 1 Starch, 1/2 Other Carbohydrates, 1 Fat

Carbohydrate Choices: 1

Campfire Popcorn Snack

ABOUT 20 SERVINGS (1/2 CUP EACH)

6 cups popped light butter-flavor
microwave popcorn

4 cups Wheat, Corn or
Rice Chex® cereal

1 jar (7 ounces) marshmallow creme

1 Heat oven to 350°. Spray cookie sheet with
cooking spray. Mix popcorn and cereal in large
bowl; set aside.

2 Microwave marshmallow creme in medium
microwavable bowl uncovered on High 1 minute;
stir. Microwave about 1 minute longer or until melted;
stir. Pour over popcorn mixture, stirring until evenly
coated. Spread mixture on cookie sheet.

3 Bake 5 minutes; stir. Bake about 5 minutes longer
or until coating is light golden brown. Spread on
waxed paper or aluminum foil to cool. Store in tightly
covered container up to 2 weeks.

*"This reminds me quite a bit
of a trail mix snack,
but it's a lower-fat alternative."*

KEN B.

a note from the Nutritionist

*The marshmallow
creme adds sweetness to
the popcorn and cereal
without adding fat. The
key to heart-healthy
snacking is to find the
best snacks with
healthy types of fat and
low calories that still
satisfy, and this snack
does those things.*

1/2 Cup: Calories 65 (Calories
from Fat 0); Fat 0g; Saturated Fat 0g
(3% of Calories from Saturated Fat);
Trans Fat 0g; Cholesterol 0mg;
Omega-3 0g; Sodium 90mg

Carbohydrate 15g (Dietary
Fiber 1g); Protein 1g

% Daily Value: Vitamin A 2%;
Vitamin C 0%; Calcium 2%;
Iron 12%; Folic Acid 12%

Exchanges: 1 Other
Carbohydrates

Carbohydrate Choices: 1

Jeweled Fruit Dip

8 SERVINGS

1 cup vanilla low-fat yogurt

1 tablespoon mayonnaise or salad dressing

1/4 teaspoon grated orange or lemon peel

2 tablespoons orange or lemon juice

1 pint strawberries (2 cups), sliced

1 1/2 cups seedless green grapes, cut in half

1 medium kiwifruit, peeled and chopped

1 can (11 ounces) mandarin orange segments, drained

3 tablespoons dried cranberries

1 Mix yogurt, mayonnaise, orange peel and orange juice in small bowl; set aside.

2 Mix remaining ingredients in large bowl. Serve with yogurt mixture.

"This is a delicious alternative to high-fat fruit dips made with whipping cream. The yogurt mixture is great in the fall
with crisp, tart apples—instead of dipping those apples in caramel."

CINDY L.

a note from Dr. B

Research hasn't yet defined the role stress plays in the development of heart disease, but we know that individuals respond differently to stressful situations. Try to keep your stress level in check by participating in activities you enjoy and that are relaxing, like reading a book, gardening, writing in a journal, talking with a friend or anything that makes you feel good.

1 Serving: Calories 90 (Calories from Fat 20); Fat 2g; Saturated Fat 0g (4% of Calories from Saturated Fat); *Trans* Fat 0g; Cholesterol 0mg; Omega-3 0g; Sodium 30mg

Carbohydrate 22g (Dietary Fiber 2g); Protein 2g

% Daily Value: Vitamin A 4%; Vitamin C 76%; Calcium 6%; Iron 2%; Folic Acid 4%

Exchanges: 1 1/2 Fruit, 1/2 Fat

Carbohydrate Choices: 1 1/2

Guacamole and Chips

II SERVINGS (I/4 CUP DIP WITH 5 TORTILLA CHIPS EACH)

a note from the Nutritionist

For an even lighter "guacamole" with no fat and 5 calories per serving, substitute a 15-ounce can of asparagus cuts, drained then blended or processed in a food processor until smooth, for the avocados. Stir in 1/4 cup fat-free mayonnaise.

2 jalapeño chilies*

2 ripe large avocados

2 tablespoons lime or lemon juice

2 tablespoons finely chopped fresh cilantro

1/2 teaspoon salt

Dash of pepper

I clove garlic, finely chopped

2 medium tomatoes, finely chopped (1 1/2 cups)

I medium onion, chopped (1/2 cup)

1/2 bag (13 1/2 ounces) baked tortilla chips

2 tablespoons canned chopped green chiles can be substituted for the jalapeño chilies.

1 Remove stems, seeds and membranes from chilies; chop chilies. Cut avocados lengthwise in half; remove pit and peel. Place avocados in medium glass or plastic bowl; mash.

2 Stir in chilies and remaining ingredients except tortilla chips. Cover and refrigerate at least 1 hour to blend flavors. Serve with tortilla chips.

"A healthy dip—now that's an important part of snacking. I love chips but stay away from dips because they are so high in fat. But with this dip, I don't have to worry about fat."

MARILYN B.

I Serving: Calories 135 (Calories from Fat 45); Fat 5g; Saturated Fat 1g (6% of Calories from Saturated Fat); *Trans* Fat 0g; Cholesterol 0mg; Omega-3 0g; Sodium 240mg

Carbohydrate 19g (Dietary Fiber 3g); Protein 3g

% Daily Value: Vitamin A 6%; Vitamin C 14%; Calcium 0%; Iron 6%; Folic Acid 12%

Exchanges: I Starch, I Fat

Carbohydrate Choices: I

Marinated Olives

12 SERVINGS (ABOUT 6 OLIVES EACH)

1 pound Kalamata or other
Greek olives

1/4 cup canola or soybean oil

2 tablespoons chopped fresh parsley

2 tablespoons chopped fresh cilantro

1 tablespoon lemon juice

1/2 teaspoon crushed red pepper

2 cloves garlic, finely chopped

1 Rinse olives with cold water; drain. Place olives in 1-quart jar with tight-fitting lid.

2 Mix remaining ingredients in small bowl; pour over olives. Cover tightly and refrigerate at least 48 hours but no longer than 2 weeks, turning jar upside down occasionally. Serve at room temperature.

a note from Dr. B

The best diet is not one that you "go on" and "go off" but is a way of living your life more healthfully. If you work at making changes gradually, you'll allow yourself the time to adopt new ways of thinking that result in new behaviors and improved habits.

1 Serving: Calories 55 (Calories from Fat 45); Fat 5g; Saturated Fat 1g (10% of Calories from Saturated Fat); *Trans* Fat 0g; Cholesterol 0mg; Omega-3 0g; Sodium 280mg

Carbohydrate 2g (Dietary Fiber 1g); Protein 0g

% Daily Value: Vitamin A 2%; Vitamin C 0%; Calcium 2%; Iron 6%; Folic Acid 0%

Exchanges: 1 Fat

Carbohydrate Choices: 0

Gingered Fruit Salsa with Crispy Cinnamon Chips

24 SERVINGS (2 TABLESPOONS SALSA AND 3 CHIPS EACH)

a note from the Nutritionist

This is a fabulous, low-fat appetizer. Use a pizza cutter to easily cut the tortillas into wedges. You can make the chips up to one week ahead of time and store in a tightly covered container at room temperature. To change the flavor to a refreshing pineapple salsa, use 3 cups of pineapple and omit the papaya and mango.

1 tablespoon sugar

2 teaspoons ground cinnamon

6 flour tortillas (8 to 10 inches in diameter)

3 tablespoons canola or soybean oil

1 cup finely diced pineapple

1 cup finely diced papaya

1 cup finely diced mango

1/4 cup chopped fresh cilantro

1 tablespoon finely chopped crystallized ginger

1 tablespoon lemon juice

1/8 teaspoon salt

1 Set oven control to broil. Mix sugar and cinnamon in small bowl. Brush both sides of each tortilla with oil; sprinkle with sugar-cinnamon mixture. Cut each tortilla into 12 wedges.

2 Place tortilla wedges in single layer in 2 ungreased jelly roll pans, 15 1/2 x 10 1/2 x 1 inch, or on 2 cookie sheets. Broil 2 to 4 minutes, turning once, until crispy and golden brown. Cool completely, about 15 minutes.

3 Mix remaining ingredients in medium bowl. Serve salsa with chips.

"Finding party food that is right for my heart and also fun can be a challenge. These crispy chips are a sweet way to entertain and feel great about what I am serving and eating!"

KEVIN W.

1 Serving: Calories 65 (Calories from Fat 25); Fat 3g; Saturated Fat 0g (5% of Calories from Saturated Fat); *Trans* Fat 0g; Cholesterol 0mg; Omega-3 0g; Sodium 65mg

Carbohydrate 9g (Dietary Fiber 1g); Protein 1g

% Daily Value: Vitamin A 2%; Vitamin C 12%; Calcium 2%; Iron 2%; Folic Acid 4%

Exchanges: 1/2 Starch, 1/2 Fat

Carbohydrate Choices: 1/2

Harvest Bread

PREP: 15 MIN
BAKE: **55 MIN**
COOL: 1 HR
10 MIN

1 LOAF (16 SLICES)

1 can (8 ounces) crushed pineapple in juice, drained and juice reserved

1/4 cup fat-free cholesterol-free egg product or 1 egg

2 tablespoons canola or soybean oil

1 1/2 cups all-purpose flour

3/4 cup packed brown sugar

1/2 cup raisins

1 teaspoon baking powder

1/2 teaspoon baking soda

1/2 teaspoon salt

1/2 teaspoon ground cinnamon

1 cup shredded carrots (1 1/2 medium)

1 cup walnuts, chopped

1 Heat oven to 350°. Spray loaf pan, 8 1/2 x 4 1/2 x 2 1/2 inches, with cooking spray. Discard 3 tablespoons of the pineapple juice. Mix remaining juice, pineapple, egg product and oil in medium bowl. Stir in remaining ingredients until blended. Spread batter in pan.

2 Bake 50 to 55 minutes or until toothpick inserted in center comes out clean. Cool 10 minutes. Remove from pan to wire rack. Cool completely, about 1 hour, before slicing.

"This is a healthy version of a quick bread, packed with flavorful fruit, vegetables and nuts."

WANDA S.

a note from Dr. B

Breakfast eaters tend to have better overall nutritious diets than those who skip morning meals. Even when you're in a hurry, you can fuel up with a good breakfast. If you don't have time for a leisurely breakfast, grab a slice of quick bread, a carton of yogurt and a handful of berries on your way out the door.

1 Slice: Calories 185 (Calories from Fat 65); Fat 7g; Saturated Fat 1g (3% of Calories from Saturated Fat); *Trans* Fat 0g; Cholesterol 0mg; Omega-3 1g; Sodium 160mg

Carbohydrate 27g (Dietary Fiber 1g); Protein 3g

% Daily Value: Vitamin A 26%; Vitamin C 2%; Calcium 4%; Iron 6%; Folic Acid 6%

Exchanges: 1 Starch, 1 Other Carbohydrates, 1 Fat

Carbohydrate Choices: 2

PREP: **10 MIN**

BAKE: **25 MIN**

Wild Rice–Corn Muffins

12 MUFFINS

a note from Dr. B

This is a great muffin to serve with dinner. After dinner, relax and unwind with a cup of herbal tea or other noncaffeinated drink. Encourage your body to fall asleep at night by slowing down before bedtime and by limiting caffeine late in the day.

3/4 cup fat-free (skim) milk

1/4 cup canola or soybean oil

1/4 cup fat-free cholesterol-free egg product, 2 egg whites or 1 egg

1 cup all-purpose flour

1/2 cup sugar

1/2 cup whole-grain yellow cornmeal

2 1/2 teaspoons baking powder

1/4 teaspoon salt

3/4 cup cooked wild rice

1/2 cup chopped fresh or frozen cranberries

1 Heat oven to 400°. Spray 12 medium muffin cups, 2 1/2 x 1 1/4 inches, with cooking spray, or line with paper baking cups. Mix milk, oil and egg product in large bowl.

2 Stir in flour, sugar, cornmeal, baking powder and salt all at once just until flour is moistened. Fold in wild rice and cranberries. Divide batter evenly among muffin cups.

3 Bake 20 to 25 minutes or until golden brown. Immediately remove from pan. Serve warm.

"As a person with high cholesterol even on medication, I've become a label reader. So I really try to control my cholesterol by making good food choices, and this wonderful muffin has no cholesterol at all."

PAT R.

1 Muffin: Calories 155 (Calories from Fat 45); Fat 5g; Saturated Fat 0g (2% of Calories from Saturated Fat); *Trans* Fat 0g; Cholesterol 0mg; Omega-3 0g; Sodium 170mg

Carbohydrate 25g (Dietary Fiber 1g); Protein 3g

% Daily Value: Vitamin A 0%; Vitamin C 0%; Calcium 8%; Iron 6%; Folic Acid 6%

Exchanges: 1 Starch, 1/2 Other Carbohydrates, 1 Fat

Carbohydrate Choices: 1 1/2

Cornmeal-Berry Scones

PREP: 15 MIN
BAKE: 15 MIN

12 SCONES

1 cup all-purpose flour

1 cup whole-grain yellow cornmeal

2 tablespoons sugar

2 teaspoons baking powder

1/2 teaspoon baking soda

1/4 teaspoon grated orange or lemon peel

1/4 teaspoon salt

6 tablespoons firm butter, cut into cubes

1/2 cup vanilla soy milk

1 tablespoon orange juice

1 1/2 cups strawberries, coarsely chopped*

1 tablespoon vanilla soy milk

1 to 2 tablespoons sugar

*1 1/2 cups frozen strawberries, thawed, drained and coarsely chopped, can be substituted. Toss with an additional 1/4 cup flour before adding to batter.

1 Heat oven to 425°. Spray cookie sheet with cooking spray, or line with cooking parchment paper.

2 Mix flour, cornmeal, 2 tablespoons sugar, the baking powder, baking soda, orange peel and salt in large bowl. Cut in butter using pastry blender, just until mixture looks like coarse crumbs. Stir in 1/2 cup soy milk and the orange juice just until flour is moistened. Fold in strawberries.

3 Place dough on floured surface. Knead 6 to 8 times to form a ball. Divide in half; shape into two 6 x 1/2-inch rounds on cookie sheet. Brush rounds with 1 tablespoon soy milk and sprinkle with 1 to 2 tablespoons sugar. Cut each round into 6 wedges.

4 Bake 12 to 15 minutes or until tops are lightly browned. Separate wedges; serve warm.

a note from the Nutritionist

Look for whole-grain cornmeal to make certain you are getting all the benefits of the whole grain. As tempting as it may be to eat these scones right away, they taste even better after cooling for at least 10 minutes. The extra cooling time allows the scones to become set, making them more tender.

1 Scone: Calories 150 (Calories from Fat 55); Fat 6g; Saturated Fat 4g (21% of Calories from Saturated Fat); *Trans* Fat 0g; Cholesterol 15mg; Omega-3 0g; Sodium 230mg

Carbohydrate 22g (Dietary Fiber 2g); Protein 2g

% Daily Value: Vitamin A 4%; Vitamin C 8%; Calcium 6%; Iron 6%; Folic Acid 8%

Exchanges: 1 Starch, 1/2 Fruit, 1 Fat

Carbohydrate Choices: 1 1/2

"I drink soy milk every day, and this is the only thing better—adding it to a scone! Berries from my garden that I've frozen, low sugar and heart-healthy cornmeal! What a great warm breakfast or snack."

LORI S.

PREP: **20 MIN**

BAKE: **25 MIN**

Oatmeal-Cranberry Muffins

12 MUFFINS

1 cup buttermilk or sour milk

1 cup old-fashioned oats

3/4 cup packed brown sugar

1/3 cup canola or soybean oil

1/4 cup fat-free cholesterol-free egg product, 2 egg whites or 1 egg

3/4 cup all-purpose flour

3/4 cup ground flaxseed or flaxseed meal

1 1/2 teaspoons baking powder

1 teaspoon salt

1 teaspoon ground cinnamon

1 cup fresh or frozen cranberries, chopped

1 Heat oven to 400°. Pour buttermilk over oats in small bowl. Line 12 medium muffin cups, 2 1/2 x 1 1/4 inches, with paper baking cups.

2 Mix brown sugar, oil and egg product in large bowl. Stir in flour, flaxseed, baking powder, salt and cinnamon just until flour is moistened. Stir in oat mixture. Fold in cranberries. Divide batter evenly among muffin cups (about 3/4 full).

3 Bake 20 to 25 minutes or until toothpick inserted in center comes out clean. Immediately remove from pan. Serve warm.

"I've found that it's all about making good choices. Healthy eating is a choice I'm making for myself, and it helps me feel in control. These muffins with flaxseed are not only terrific tasting, they are good for me."

CINDY L.

1 Muffin: Calories 215 (Calories from Fat 80); Fat 9g; Saturated Fat 1g (4% of Calories from Saturated Fat); *Trans* Fat 0g; Cholesterol 0mg; Omega-3 2g; Sodium 300mg

Carbohydrate 29g (Dietary Fiber 3g); Protein 5g

% Daily Value: Vitamin A 0%; Vitamin C 0%; Calcium 8%; Iron 8%; Folic Acid 8%

Exchanges: 2 Starch, 1 1/2 Fat

Carbohydrate Choices: 2

Carrot-Zucchini Muffins

PREP: 10 MIN
BAKE: 21 MIN

12 MUFFINS

2 cups all-purpose flour

1 cup quick-cooking or
old-fashioned oats

3/4 cup packed brown sugar

3 teaspoons baking powder

1/2 teaspoon cinnamon

1/4 teaspoon salt

2/3 cup fat-free (skim) milk

3 tablespoons canola or soybean oil

2 egg whites, 1/4 cup fat-free
cholesterol-free egg product or 1 egg

1 cup finely shredded carrots
(1 1/2 medium)

1/2 cup shredded unpeeled zucchini
(1 small)

1 Heat oven to 400°. Spray 12 medium muffin cups, 2 1/2 x 1 1/4 inches, with cooking spray, or line with paper baking cups and spray paper cups with cooking spray.

2 Mix flour, oats, brown sugar, baking powder, cinnamon and salt in large bowl. Stir in milk, oil and egg whites all at once just until flour is moistened. Fold in carrots and zucchini. Divide batter evenly among muffin cups.

3 Bake 16 to 21 minutes or until golden brown and toothpick inserted in center comes out clean. Immediately remove from pan. Serve warm.

a note from Dr. B

Scientific research shows that oats can help reduce blood cholesterol when eaten as a regular part of a low-fat, low-cholesterol plan. The carrots and zucchini in these muffins add extra fiber, vitamins and minerals.

"Watching our cholesterol is just a habit in our home. Using the egg whites, oats and skim milk makes these muffins healthier so you don't feel guilty eating them. They are great for an afternoon snack to tide you over until dinner."

CATHY P.

1 Muffin: Calories 170 (Calories from Fat 10); Fat 1g; Saturated Fat 0g (1% of Calories from Saturated Fat); *Trans* Fat 0g; Cholesterol 0mg; Omega-3 0g; Sodium 200mg

Carbohydrate 36g (Dietary Fiber 2g); Protein 4g

% Daily Value: Vitamin A 36%; Vitamin C 0%; Calcium 10%; Iron 10%; Folic Acid 8%

Exchanges: 1 Starch, 1 Other Carbohydrates, 1 Vegetable

Carbohydrate Choices: 2 1/2

Grilled Halibut with Tomato-Avocado Salsa (page 93)

Pleasing-to-Your-Heart Fish

Fishing for great flavor and easy recipes? No doubt about it, you'll be pleased with the "catches" found here.

Lemon and Herb Salmon Packets

4 SERVINGS

2 cups uncooked instant rice

1 can (14 ounces) fat-free or low-sodium chicken broth

1 cup matchstick-cut carrots (from 10-ounce bag)

4 salmon fillets (4 to 6 ounces each)

1 teaspoon lemon pepper seasoning salt

1/3 cup chopped fresh chives

1 medium lemon, cut lengthwise in half, then cut crosswise into 1/4-inch slices

1 Heat coals or gas grill for direct heat. Spray four 18 x 12-inch sheets of heavy-duty aluminum foil with cooking spray.

2 Mix rice and broth in medium bowl. Let stand about 5 minutes or until most of broth is absorbed. Stir in carrots.

3 Place salmon fillet on center of each foil sheet. Sprinkle with lemon pepper seasoning salt; top with chives. Arrange lemon slices over salmon. Spoon rice mixture around each fillet. Fold foil over salmon and rice so edges meet. Seal edges, making tight 1/2-inch fold; fold again. Allow space on sides for circulation and expansion.

4 Cover and grill packets 4 to 6 inches from low heat 11 to 14 minutes or until salmon flakes easily with fork. Place packets on plates. Cut large X across top of each packet; carefully fold back foil to allow steam to escape.

1 Serving: Calories 400 (Calories from Fat 70); Fat 8; Saturated Fat 2g (5% of Calories from Saturated Fat); *Trans* Fat 0g; Cholesterol 75mg; Omega-3 2g; Sodium 870mg

Carbohydrate 51g (Dietary Fiber 2g); Protein 31g

% Daily Value: Vitamin A 100%; Vitamin C 4%; Calcium 4%; Iron 18%; Folic Acid 26%

Exchanges: 3 1/2 Starch, 3 Very Lean Meat

Carbohydrate Choices: 3 1/2

"As I'm getting older, I find it's important to adjust my attitude about exercise. Even if I can't work out at the same level that I used to, I tell myself that any exercise is better than being sedentary. It's okay to walk rather than run."

CINDY L.

Potato-Crusted Salmon

4 SERVINGS

1 pound salmon, artic char or other medium-firm fish fillets, about 3/4 inch thick

1 egg white

2 tablespoons water

1/3 cup plain mashed potato mix (dry)

2 teaspoons cornstarch

1 teaspoon paprika

1 teaspoon lemon pepper seasoning salt

1 tablespoon canola or soybean oil

1 Remove and discard skin from fish. Cut fish into 4 serving pieces. Beat egg white and water slightly with fork in shallow dish.

2 Mix potato mix, cornstarch, paprika and lemon pepper in another shallow dish. Dip just the top sides of fish into egg white mixture, then press into potato mixture.

3 Spray 12-inch nonstick skillet with cooking spray. Heat oil in skillet over high heat. Cook fish, potato sides down, in oil 3 minutes. Carefully turn fish, using wide slotted spatula. Reduce heat to medium. Cook about 3 minutes longer or until fish flakes easily with fork.

"We eat fish at least once a week and are trying to work it in two times a week.
This is a great, low-fat way to cook salmon."

MARGOT C.

1 Serving: Calories 190 (Calories from Fat 80); Fat 9g; Saturated Fat 2g (9% of Calories from Saturated Fat); *Trans* Fat 0g; Cholesterol 65mg; Omega-3 2g; Sodium 420mg

Carbohydrate 6g (Dietary Fiber 0g); Protein 22g

% Daily Value: Vitamin A 10%; Vitamin C 4%; Calcium 0%; Iron 4%; Folic Acid 0%

Exchanges: 1/2 Other Carbohydrates, 3 Lean Meat

Carbohydrate Choices: 1/2

Caribbean Swordfish with Papaya Salsa

PREP: **10 MIN**

MARINATE: **2 HR**

BROIL: **16 MIN**

4 SERVINGS

4 swordfish or shark steaks, 1 inch thick (about 1 1/2 pounds)

1 tablespoon grated lime peel

1/4 cup lime juice

1/4 cup grapefruit juice

1/2 teaspoon salt

1 clove garlic, finely chopped

Papaya Salsa (below)

1 Place fish in ungreased square baking dish, 8 x 8 x 2 inches. Mix remaining ingredients except Papaya Salsa in small bowl; pour over fish. Cover and refrigerate 2 hours. Make Papaya Salsa.

2 Set oven control to broil. Spray broiler pan rack with cooking spray. Remove fish from marinade; reserve marinade. Place fish on rack in broiler pan.

3 Broil with tops about 4 inches from heat about 16 minutes, turning and brushing with marinade after 8 minutes, until fish flakes easily with fork. Discard any remaining marinade. Serve fish with salsa.

Papaya Salsa

1 large papaya, peeled, seeded and chopped (2 cups)

1/4 cup finely chopped red bell pepper

1 medium green onion, finely chopped (1 tablespoon)

1 tablespoon chopped fresh cilantro

2 to 3 tablespoons grapefruit juice

1/8 teaspoon salt

Mix all ingredients in glass or plastic bowl. Cover and refrigerate 1 hour.

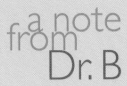

a note from Dr. B

Your doctor or pharmacist may have told you that if you are taking medicine to lower your cholesterol, you should not eat grapefruit or grapefruit juice because the grapefruit reacts with the medicine, and it may not work as well. In this recipe, you could use orange or lemon juice for a great citrus taste.

1 Serving: Calories 245 (Calories from Fat 70); Fat 8g; Saturated Fat 2g (8% of Calories from Saturated Fat); *Trans* Fat 0g; Cholesterol 90mg; Omega-3 2g; Sodium 460mg

Carbohydrate 13g (Dietary Fiber 2g); Protein 30g

% Daily Value: Vitamin A 38%; Vitamin C 76%; Calcium 4%; Iron 6%; Folic Acid 10%

Exchanges: 1 Fruit, 4 Very Lean Meat, 1 Fat

Carbohydrate Choices: 1

PREP: **15 MIN**
BAKE: **10 MIN**

Graham-Crusted Tilapia

4 SERVINGS

1 pound tilapia, cod, haddock or other medium-firm fish fillets, about 3/4 inch thick

1/2 cup graham cracker crumbs (about 8 squares)

1 teaspoon grated lemon peel

1/4 teaspoon salt

1/8 teaspoon pepper

1/4 cup milk

2 tablespoons canola or soybean oil

2 tablespoons chopped toasted pecans*

*To toast nuts, bake uncovered in ungreased shallow pan in 350° oven about 10 minutes, stirring occasionally, until golden brown. Or cook in ungreased heavy skillet over medium-low heat 5 to 7 minutes, stirring frequently until browning begins, then stirring constantly until golden brown.

1. Move oven rack to position slightly above middle of oven. Heat oven to 500°.

2. Cut fish fillets crosswise into 2-inch-wide pieces. Mix cracker crumbs, lemon peel, salt and pepper in shallow dish. Place milk in another shallow dish.

3. Dip fish into milk, then coat with cracker mixture; place in ungreased rectangular pan, 13 x 9 x 2 inches. Drizzle oil over fish; sprinkle with pecans.

4. Bake uncovered about 10 minutes or until fish flakes easily with fork.

1 Serving: Calories 235 (Calories from Fat 110); Fat 12g; Saturated Fat 2g (6% of Calories from Saturated Fat); *Trans* Fat 0g; Cholesterol 60mg; Omega-3 1g; Sodium 310mg

Carbohydrate 9g (Dietary Fiber 0g); Protein 23g

% Daily Value: Vitamin A 0%; Vitamin C 0%; Calcium 4%; Iron 2%; Folic Acid 4%

Exchanges: 1/2 Starch, 3 Lean Meat, 1/2 Fat

Carbohydrate Choices: 1/2

"I try to eat fish for at least two meals per week. I'm discovering new varieties of fish and finding new ways to prepare it so my family enjoys it. I never thought my kids would like fish!"

CINDY L.

Graham-Crusted Tilapia

Baked Fish with Italian Rice

6 SERVINGS

a note from Dr. B

The fatty fishes are the ones that contain Omega-3 and have the most benefit for your heart. They include mackerel, pompano, tuna, herring and salmon.

2 tablespoons water

1 medium onion, chopped (1/2 cup)

3 cups cooked brown or white rice

1 can (14 1/2 ounces) no-salt-added Italian-style stewed tomatoes, undrained

1 teaspoon Italian seasoning, crumbled

6 mackerel, snapper, tilapia, sturgeon or any fish fillets, 1/4 inch thick (about 1 pound)

1 1/2 teaspoons canola or soybean oil

1/2 teaspoon paprika

1 Heat oven to 400°. Heat water to boiling in 2 1/2-quart saucepan over medium-high heat. Cook onion in water, stirring occasionally, until crisp-tender. Stir in rice, tomatoes and Italian seasoning; cook until thoroughly heated.

2 Spoon rice mixture into ungreased rectangular baking dish, 13 x 9 x 2 inches. Place fish fillets on rice mixture. Brush fish with oil. Sprinkle with paprika.

3 Cover and bake 20 to 25 minutes or until fish flakes easily with fork.

1 Serving: Calories 245 (Calories from Fat 65); Fat 7g; Saturated Fat 1g (4% of Calories from Saturated Fat); *Trans* Fat 0g; Cholesterol 40mg; Omega-3 2g; Sodium 45mg

Carbohydrate 27g (Dietary Fiber 3g); Protein 18g

% Daily Value: Vitamin A 8%; Vitamin C 8%; Calcium 4%; Iron 8%; Folic Acid 8%

Exchanges: 1 1/2 Starch, 1 Vegetable, 2 Lean Meat

Carbohydrate Choices: 2

Tuna Steaks with Fruit Salsa

PREP: 15 MIN
BROIL: 10 MIN

2 SERVINGS

Fruit Salsa (below)

1 tablespoon packed brown sugar

1 tablespoon fresh lime juice

2 swordfish, tuna or halibut steaks, 3/4 inch thick (4 ounces each)

1 Make Fruit Salsa. Set oven control to broil. Spray broiler pan rack with cooking spray.

2 Mix brown sugar and lime juice in small bowl. Arrange tuna steaks on rack in broiler pan. Brush with brown sugar mixture.

3 Broil with tops 4 to 6 inches from heat 4 to 5 minutes on each side or until fish flakes easily with fork, brushing occasionally with brown sugar mixture. Serve fish with salsa.

Fruit Salsa

1 can (11 ounces) pineapple and mandarin orange segments, drained, coarsely chopped

1 tablespoon chopped red onion

2 teaspoons chopped fresh cilantro

2 teaspoons lime juice

1/8 teaspoon salt

1/2 to 1 jalapeño chili, seeded, chopped (2 to 3 teaspoons)

Mix ingredients in medium microwavable bowl. Microwave on High 1 1/2 to 2 minutes, stirring once, until thoroughly heated. Cover to keep warm.

a note from Dr. B

Tuna and swordfish also contain Omega-3 fatty acids, which have heart-protective benefits. Another way to help your heart and your body is to increase your physical activity. Exercising regularly builds healthy muscles (your heart is a muscle), joints and bones, and reduces the risk of heart disease, cancer and diabetes.

1 Serving: Calories 215 (Calories from Fat 45); Fat 5g; Saturated Fat 2g (6% of Calories from Saturated Fat); *Trans* Fat 0g; Cholesterol 60mg; Omega-3 2g; Sodium 210mg

Carbohydrate 22g (Dietary Fiber 2g); Protein 20g

% Daily Value: Vitamin A 10%; Vitamin C 28%; Calcium 4%; Iron 6%; Folic Acid 6%

Exchanges: 1 1/2 Fruit, 3 Very Lean Meat, 1/2 Fat

Carbohydrate Choices: 1 1/2

"I know that I should eat more fish, but I have a hard time finding recipes I can get excited about.
This is a great recipe because the fruit salsa gives a fresh flavor."

PAT R.

A Heart-to-Heart Talk with Women

Though you may think that cancer is a greater health threat, the fact is that nearly twice as many women in the United States die of heart disease and stroke as die from all forms of cancer, including breast cancer. Heart disease is the leading cause of death in women age 65 and older in the United States, with six times as many victims in that age group as breast cancer victims.

Several key factors increase the risk of heart disease and stroke. The more risk factors a woman has, the greater her chance of a heart attack or stroke.

Some risk factors you cannot control:

Increasing age: Risk of heart disease and stroke begins to rise—and keeps rising—with age.

Gender: More than half of total stroke deaths occur in women.

Family History: Women are more likely to develop heart disease or stroke if close blood relatives had them.

Race: African-American women have a greater risk of heart disease and stroke than do white women. Compared with whites, African-American women (and men) are more likely to die of stroke.

Previous heart attack or stroke: Women who've had a heart attack are at higher risk of having a second heart attack or stroke. Women who've had a stroke are at much higher risk of having another one or of having a heart attack.

Some risk factors, however, you *can* control:

Don't smoke: Women who smoke cigarettes or cigars have a much higher risk of death from heart disease or stroke. Second-hand smoke also increases the risk, even for nonsmokers. And women smokers who use birth control pills have a higher risk of heart attack and stroke than do the nonsmokers who use them.

Keep your cholesterol down: High levels of LDL (bad) cholesterol raise the risk of heart disease and heart attack. High levels of HDL (good) cholesterol lower the risk of heart disease. Research shows that low levels of HDL cholesterol are a stronger risk factor for women than for men. From age 55 on, women's cholesterol is often higher than men's.

Keep your blood pressure reduced: Women have an increased risk of developing high blood pressure if they are 20 pounds or more over a healthy weight for their height and build, have a family history of high blood pressure, are pregnant, take certain types of birth control pills or have reached menopause. On average, African-American women have higher blood pressure levels than do white women.

Be physically active: Inactive people are almost twice as likely to develop heart disease as people who are active. The American Heart Association (AHA) recommends we invest in at least 30 to 60 minutes of physical activity on most or all days of the week.

Control your weight: If your body carries too much fat, particularly near your waist, you're at higher risk for health problems, including high blood pressure, high cholesterol, high triglycerides, diabetes, heart disease and stroke.

Control your diabetes: Women with diabetes have from three to seven times the risk of heart disease and heart attack as nondiabetics, and they are at much greater risk for stroke. Women with diabetes often are overweight, have high blood pressure and high cholesterol, increasing their risk even more.

Other factors contributing to heart disease risk and stroke in women:

Birth control pills: Today's low-dose oral contraceptives carry a much lower risk of heart disease and stroke than did earlier versions of The Pill. The exception is in women who smoke or already have high blood pressure.

High triclycerides (total fats in the blood): A high triglyceride level often goes with high levels of total cholesterol and LDL, lower levels of HDL and an increased risk of diabetes. Research suggests that having high triglycerides may increase the risk for women more than for men.

Alcohol abuse: Excess drinking and binge drinking can contribute to obesity, high triglycerides, cancer and other diseases, raise blood pressure, cause heart failure and lead to stroke.

Your response to stress: Research hasn't yet defined the role stress plays in the development of heart disease, but we know that individuals respond differently to stressful situations. Risky behaviors such as smoking and overeating may be unhealthy responses to stress.

Take wellness to heart. After reading the risk factors, you may want to throw up your hands, and say, "What's the use?" Remember all the things you can do to improve your health and live in a heart-healthy way. Women are the greatest caregivers in the world, taking care of husbands, children and parents. Direct some of that caring toward yourself, and take these small, heart-saving steps:

1. **Eat well:** Include plenty of whole grains, fruits and vegetables and fiber in your diet to make sure you are getting the most nutrients out of the calories you take in.

2. **See your doctor and take your medication:** If you are taking medication to reduce your cholesterol or blood pressure, take it without fail. Talk to your doctor about your concerns; you deserve to get the best care possible.

3. **Exercise:** Take the time to go for a walk before work or during lunch. Try to work in some kind of exercise every day, even if it's only for a short time.

4. **Listen to your body:** Don't be afraid to call your doctor or to dial 9-1-1 if you think you are having a heart attack. If you feel your doctor does not listen to you, find a doctor who does listen—it's your right.

5. **Take time for yourself:** Spend a few minutes each day doing something you enjoy, whether it's reading, meditating, doing yoga, gardening—anything that just makes you feel good.

6. **Get plenty of rest:** Sleep is your body's way of recharging itself, of regaining energy so you can start anew. Encourage your body to fall asleep at night by slowing down before bedtime and by limiting caffeine late in the day.

7. **Express yourself:** If things are bothering you, talk to good friends or other people who care. Express your feelings, thoughts and hopes in a journal. Being able to share your feelings will help you release tensions.

Pecan-Crusted Catfish

4 SERVINGS

a note from Dr. B

Besides eating healthfully, kick up your exercising, too. The best way to increase HDL cholesterol (the good kind) is to increase the amount of exercise you get. The best choices are walking, biking, cycling, jumping rope and swimming, but any aerobic exercise will do the trick.

1/2 cup cornflake crumbs

1/4 cup finely ground pecans (1 ounce)

1/4 teaspoon paprika

1/8 teaspoon garlic powder

1/8 teaspoon ground red pepper (cayenne)

1 egg white

1 pound catfish, haddock, orange roughy, sole, flounder or other medium-firm fish fillets, about 3/4 inch thick, cut into 4 pieces

1 Heat oven to 450°. Spray jelly roll pan, 15 1/2 x 10 1/2 x 1 inch, with cooking spray. Mix cornflake crumbs, pecans, paprika, garlic powder and ground red pepper in large resealable plastic food-storage bag.

2 Beat egg white slightly with fork in shallow dish. Dip fish into egg white, then place in bag. Seal bag and shake until evenly coated. Place in pan.

3 Bake 15 to 20 minutes or until fish flakes easily with fork.

"What a terrific-tasting fish recipe— crunchy coating without deep-frying! I love serving this with brown rice and steamed or roasted vegetables."

MARILYN B.

1 Serving: Calories 225 (Calories from Fat 110); Fat 12g; Saturated Fat

2g (7% of Calories from Saturated Fat); *Trans* Fat 0g; Cholesterol 85mg; Omega-3 1g; Sodium 105mg

Carbohydrate 4g (Dietary Fiber 1g); Protein 25g

% Daily Value: Vitamin A 4%; Vitamin C 2%; Calcium 6%; Iron 16%; Folic Acid 8%

Exchanges: 3 1/2 Lean Meat, 1/2 Fat

Carbohydrate Choices: 0

Grilled Halibut with Tomato-Avocado Salsa

PREP: **20 MIN**
MARINATE: **30 MIN**
GRILL: **15 MIN**

6 SERVINGS

1 1/2 pounds halibut, tuna or swordfish steaks, 3/4 to 1 inch thick

2 tablespoons canola or soybean oil

2 tablespoons lemon or lime juice

1/4 teaspoon salt

1/4 teaspoon ground cumin

1/8 teaspoon ground red pepper (cayenne)

1 clove garlic, finely chopped

Tomato-Avocado Salsa (below)

1 If fish steaks are large, cut into 6 serving pieces. Mix remaining ingredients except Tomato-Avocado Salsa in shallow glass or plastic dish. Add fish; turn to coat with marinade. Cover and refrigerate at least 30 minutes but no longer than 2 hours.

2 Heat coals or gas grill for direct heat. Remove fish from marinade; reserve marinade. Cover and grill fish 4 to 5 inches from medium heat 10 to 15 minutes, brushing 2 or 3 times with marinade and turning once, until fish flakes easily with fork. Discard any remaining marinade.

3 While fish is grilling, make Tomato-Avocado Salsa. Serve fish with salsa.

Tomato-Avocado Salsa

3 medium tomatoes, chopped (1 1/2 cups)

1 medium avocado, pitted, peeled and coarsely chopped

1 small jalapeño chili, seeded and finely chopped

1/4 cup chopped fresh cilantro

2 teaspoons lemon or lime juice

Mix all ingredients in medium bowl.

"I stop to exercise at a fitness center on my way home from the office. It works out great, because if I went home first, I might not get there."

LORI S.

a note from Dr. B

You may have heard of the Mediterranean "diet," which includes a high consumption of fish, fruits, raw and cooked vegetables, the use of olive oil and wine in low to moderate amounts. A major study in Italy confirmed that eating a diet rich in these foods lowers the risk of heart disease.

1 Serving: Calories 205 (Calories from Fat 90); Fat 10g; Saturated Fat 1g (3% of Calories from Saturated Fat); *Trans* Fat 0g; Cholesterol 60mg; Omega-3 1g; Sodium 170mg

Carbohydrate 6g (Dietary Fiber 2g); Protein 23g

% Daily Value: Vitamin A 12%; Vitamin C 16%; Calcium 2%; Iron 4%; Folic Acid 10%

Exchanges: 1 Vegetable, 3 Lean Meat

Carbohydrate Choices: 1/2

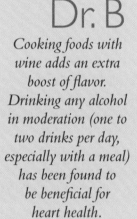

PREP: **5 MIN**
BAKE: **25 MIN**

Lemon- and Wine-Baked Halibut

4 SERVINGS

4 halibut, swordfish or tuna
fillets, about 1 inch thick
(about 1 1/2 pounds)

1/4 teaspoon salt

4 sprigs dill weed

4 slices lemon

4 black peppercorns

1/4 cup dry white wine or
chicken broth

1 Heat oven to 450°. Place fish in ungreased
rectangular baking dish, 11 x 7 x 1 1/2 inches.
Sprinkle with salt. Place dill weed sprig and lemon slice
on each. Top with peppercorns. Pour wine over fish.

2 Bake uncovered 20 to 25 minutes or until fish
flakes easily with fork.

*"Having diabetes and high cholesterol, I make a conscious
effort to get my daily balance of carbohydrates, fat and protein.*
*This recipe helps out in a big way, because it has no carbs and is high in protein and low in
cholesterol. Then I can decide what and how much carbohydrates I want to eat with it."*

LORI S.

1 Serving: Calories 145 (Calories
from Fat 20); Fat 2g; Saturated Fat 0g
(2% of Calories from Saturated Fat);
Trans Fat 0g; Cholesterol 90mg;
Omega-3 1g; Sodium 290mg

Carbohydrate 0g (Dietary Fiber 0g);
Protein 32g

% Daily Value: Vitamin A 0%;
Vitamin C 0%; Calcium 2%; Iron 2%;
Folic Acid 0%

Exchanges: 4 Very Lean Meat

Carbohydrate Choices: 0

Garlic- and Herb-Broiled Rainbow Trout

PREP: 10 MIN
BROIL: 4 MIN

4 SERVINGS

4 rainbow trout or other medium-firm fish fillets, 1/4 to 1/2 inch thick (about 1 pound)

2 tablespoons lime or lemon juice

2/3 cup soft bread crumbs (about 1 slice bread)

1 teaspoons Italian seasoning

2 teaspoons canola or soybean oil

1/2 teaspoon garlic powder

1/4 teaspoon pepper

1. Set oven control to broil. Spray broiler pan rack with cooking spray. Place fish on rack in broiler pan. Brush with lime juice. Broil with tops about 4 inches from heat 3 minutes.

2. While fish is broiling, mix remaining ingredients.

3. Spoon bread crumb mixture on top of fish. Broil about 1 minute longer or until fish flakes easily with fork.

"Garlic and Omega-3 oil in the trout make this recipe a good start for a healthy heart."

WANDA S.

a note from Dr. B

Another way to get Omega-3! Because soybean oil contains Omega-3 fatty acids, which are very good for your heart, the American Heart Association recommends substituting it frequently. Olive and canola oils, mono-unsaturated oils, are also very good choices when selecting a cooking oil.

1 Serving: Calories 175 (Calories from Fat 70); Fat 8g; Saturated Fat 2g (9% of Calories from Saturated Fat); *Trans* Fat 0g; Cholesterol 65mg; Omega-3 2g; Sodium 95mg

Carbohydrate 4g (Dietary Fiber 0g); Protein 22g

% Daily Value: Vitamin A 2%; Vitamin C 2%; Calcium 2%; Iron 6%; Folic Acid 2%

Exchanges: 3 Lean Meat

Carbohydrate Choices: 0

Grilled Sea Bass with Citrus-Olive Oil

4 SERVINGS

a note from Dr. B

Omega-3 fatty acids benefit the heart of healthy people and those at high risk of—or who have— cardiovascular disease. For this reason and because fish is also high in protein and doesn't contain the saturated fat that fatty meat products do, the American Heart Association recommends eating fish, especially fatty fish, at least two times per week.

Citrus-Olive Oil (below)

1 pound sea bass, tuna or halibut fillets, about 1 inch thick

1 tablespoon canola or soybean oil

1/4 teaspoon salt

1/8 teaspoon pepper

1 Make Citrus-Olive Oil. Refrigerate 30 minutes. Heat coals or gas grill for direct heat. Brush all surfaces of fish with oil; sprinkle with salt and pepper.

2 Cover and grill fish 4 to 5 inches from medium heat 10 to 13 minutes, turning fish after 5 minutes, until fish flakes easily with fork. Serve with Citrus-Olive Oil.

Citrus-Olive Oil

1 tablespoon finely chopped Kalamata olives

2 teaspoons chopped fresh parsley

1/4 teaspoon grated orange peel

1 tablespoon canola or soybean oil

1/2 teaspoon balsamic vinegar

Mix all ingredients in small bowl.

1 Serving: Calories 180 (Calories from Fat 90); Fat 10g; Saturated Fat 2g (5% of Calories from Saturated Fat); *Trans* Fat 0g; Cholesterol 55mg; Omega-3 1g; Sodium 230mg

Carbohydrate 0g (Dietary Fiber 0g); Protein 22g

% Daily Value: Vitamin A 2%; Vitamin C 0%; Calcium 2%; Iron 8%; Folic Acid 0%

Exchanges: 3 Lean Meat, 1/2 Fat

Carbohydrate Choices: 0

"My main meal is at noon. I eat a well-rounded low-fat, low-calorie lunch with a lot of fruit and veggies included. This recipe makes a great low-fat, low-calorie lunch, and I can add whatever vegetables I like."

WANDA S.

Grilled Sea Bass with Citrus-Olive Oil

PREP: 15 MIN

Curried Tuna Salad with Toasted Pecans

4 SERVINGS

2 cans (6 ounces each) tuna in water, drained

1/2 cup fat-free mayonnaise or salad dressing

1 1/2 teaspoons sugar

1 teaspoon curry powder

1/2 cup chopped bell pepper

1/4 cup chopped celery

1 small onion, finely chopped (1/4 cup)

1 can (8 ounces) sliced water chestnuts, drained and cut into slivers

1 can (8 ounces) pineapple tidbits, drained

4 slices whole-wheat bread, toasted and cut diagonally in half

2 medium unpeeled eating apples, sliced

2 tablespoons chopped pecans, toasted

1 Mix tuna, mayonnaise, sugar and curry powder in medium bowl. Stir in bell pepper, celery, onion, water chestnuts and pineapple.

2 Arrange 2 toast halves on each plate. Arrange apple slices around edge of plate. Place tuna mixture on center of each plate. Sprinkle pecans over tuna mixture.

1 Serving: Calories 320 (Calories from Fat 45); Fat 5g; Saturated Fat 1g (2% of Calories from Saturated Fat); *Trans* Fat 0g; Cholesterol 25mg; Omega-3 0g; Sodium 690mg

Carbohydrate 49g (Dietary Fiber 7g); Protein 26g

% Daily Value: Vitamin A 4%; Vitamin C 26%; Calcium 6%; Iron 18%; Folic Acid 8%

Exchanges: 1 Starch, 2 Fruit, 1 Vegetable, 3 Very Lean Meat

Carbohydrate Choices: 3

"Great low-calorie lunch with a lot of veggies, and the pineapple and toasted pecans make it taste great! I use the tuna in pouches, whole wheat bread with 5 grams of fiber per slice, and add a bowl of berries or peaches."

LORI S.

Shrimp Florentine Stir-Fry

PREP: 10 MIN
COOK: 7 MIN

4 SERVINGS

1 tablespoon canola or soybean oil

1 pound uncooked peeled deveined medium shrimp, thawed if frozen

4 cups lightly packed washed spinach leaves

1 can (14 ounces) baby corn nuggets, drained

1/4 cup coarsely chopped drained roasted red bell peppers (from 7-ounce jar)

1 1/2 teaspoons chopped fresh or 1/2 teaspoon dried tarragon leaves

1/2 teaspoon garlic salt

Lemon wedges

1 Heat wok or 12-inch nonstick skillet over medium-high heat. Add oil; rotate wok to coat side.

2 Add shrimp; stir-fry 2 to 3 minutes or until shrimp are pink and firm. Add spinach, corn, bell peppers, tarragon and garlic salt; stir-fry 2 to 4 minutes or until spinach is wilted. Serve with lemon wedges.

a note from the Nutritionist

Canola oil is the best choice for sautéing, stir-frying and baking. Because it is very high in monounsaturated fat, it can help lower cholesterol and triglycerides.

1 Serving: Calories 210 (Calories from Fat 45); Fat 5g; Saturated Fat 1g (3% of Calories from Saturated Fat); *Trans* Fat 0g; Cholesterol 160mg; Omega-3 1g; Sodium 540mg

Carbohydrate 20g (Dietary Fiber 3g); Protein 21g

% Daily Value: Vitamin A 74%; Vitamin C 32%; Calcium 6%; Iron 24%; Folic Acid 28%

Exchanges: 4 Vegetable, 2 Lean Meat

Carbohydrate Choices: 1

Sweet Apricot BBQ Shrimp Kabobs

4 SERVINGS

a note from the Nutritionist

Shrimp are fairly high in cholesterol, but they're low in saturated fat and total fat. You can enjoy shrimp as part of a low-fat, low-cholesterol diet—just try to watch your total cholesterol and saturated fat intake each day.

1/3 cup hickory-smoked barbecue sauce

1/3 cup apricot preserves

1/4 teaspoon crushed red pepper

4 slices turkey bacon, each cut lengthwise into 6 strips

1 can (8 ounces) whole water chestnuts, drained

1 pound uncooked peeled deveined large shrimp, thawed if frozen

2 cups hot cooked couscous, pasta or rice

1 Soak four 10-inch bamboo skewers in water for at least 30 minutes to prevent burning.

2 Set oven control to broil. Mix barbecue sauce, preserves and red pepper in small bowl; set aside.

3 Wrap strip of bacon around each water chestnut. Thread shrimp and water chestnuts alternately on each bamboo skewer, leaving space between each piece. Place on rack in broiler pan.

4 Broil kabobs with tops about 4 inches from heat 6 minutes, brushing frequently with sauce mixture. Turn kabobs; brush with sauce mixture. Broil 5 to 6 minutes longer or until shrimp are pink and firm. Discard any remaining sauce mixture. Serve kabobs with couscous.

To Grill Shrimp: Heat coals or gas grill for direct heat. Follow recipe through step 3. Grill kabobs uncovered 4 to 6 inches from medium heat 6 to 8 minutes, turning frequently and brushing several times with sauce mixture, until shrimp are pink and firm.

1 Serving: Calories 345 (Calories from Fat 35); Fat 4g; Saturated Fat 1g (3% of Calories from Saturated Fat); *Trans* Fat 0g; Cholesterol 170mg; Omega-3 0g; Sodium 600mg

Carbohydrate 54g (Dietary Fiber 3g); Protein 23g

% Daily Value: Vitamin A 6%; Vitamin C 6%; Calcium 6%; Iron 20%; Folic Acid 4%

Exchanges: 2 1/2 Starch, 1 Fruit, 2 Very Lean Meat

Carbohydrate Choices: 3 1/2

"This recipe also works great on the grill. I love grilling as a wonderful way to keep extra fat down—it's a healthy way to cook. Plus, my husband helps with the grilling."

MARGOT C.

Sweet Apricot BBQ Shrimp Kabobs

Apple-Rosemary Pork and Barley (page 124)

Take Heart with Poultry and Meat

Good news—lean cuts of meat and poultry are loaded with protein, folic acid and iron, so are good for your heart.

Spicy Chicken Drumsticks

5 SERVINGS

2 pounds chicken drumsticks

1/3 cup all-purpose flour

1/3 cup yellow whole-grain cornmeal

1/2 teaspoon ground cumin

1/2 teaspoon chili powder

1/4 teaspoon salt

1/3 cup buttermilk

1/4 teaspoon red pepper sauce

Cooking spray

1 Heat oven to 400°. Spray rectangular pan, 13 x 9 x 2 inches, with cooking spray. Remove skin and fat from chicken.

2 Mix flour, cornmeal, cumin, chili powder and salt in heavy-duty resealable plastic food-storage bag. Mix buttermilk and pepper sauce in medium bowl. Dip chicken into buttermilk mixture, then place in bag. Seal bag and shake until evenly coated. Place chicken in pan; spray chicken lightly with cooking spray.

3 Bake uncovered 40 to 45 minutes or until juice of chicken is no longer pink when centers of thickest pieces are cut.

"All the women in my family have died of heart attacks, so I make certain to keep the fat I eat as low as possible. I remove the skin from chicken and cut off all visible fat."

NANCI D.

1 Serving: Calories 185 (Calories from Fat 35); Fat 4g; Saturated Fat 1g (6% of Calories from Saturated Fat); *Trans* Fat 0g; Cholesterol 85mg; Omega-3 0g; Sodium 200mg

Carbohydrate 14g (Dietary Fiber 1g); Protein 23g

% Daily Value: Vitamin A 4%; Vitamin C 0%; Calcium 4%; Iron 14%; Folic Acid 8%

Exchanges: 1 Starch, 3 Very Lean Meat

Carbohydrate Choices: 1

Glazed Chicken over Couscous Pilaf

PREP: 10 MIN
COOK: 2 MIN
STAND: 5 MIN
BROIL: 10 MIN

2 SERVINGS

Couscous Pilaf (below)

2 tablespoons orange juice

1 tablespoon apricot preserves or honey

1/2 teaspoon spicy brown mustard

2 boneless skinless chicken breast halves

1 Make Couscous Pilaf. Set oven control to broil. Mix orange juice, preserves and mustard in small bowl. Pour half of mixture (about 2 tablespoons) into another small dish; reserve for topping.

2 Place chicken on rack in broiler pan; brush with about half of remaining orange juice glaze.

3 Broil with tops about 4 inches from heat 8 to 10 minutes, turning and brushing with glaze after 5 minutes, until juice of chicken is no longer pink when centers of thickest pieces are cut. Discard any remaining glaze.

4 Stir pilaf lightly with fork; divide evenly onto plates. Top with chicken; drizzle with reserved orange juice mixture.

Couscous Pilaf

1/2 cup frozen sweet peas

3/4 cup water

1/8 teaspoon ground ginger

1/2 cup uncooked couscous

Place peas, water and ginger in 1-quart saucepan. Heat to boiling over high heat; reduce heat to medium–low. Cover and simmer 2 minutes. Remove from heat; stir in couscous. Cover; let stand 5 minutes.

"I'm such a chicken fan, and this is definitely a balanced meal, delicious and easy."

MARILYN B.

1 Serving: Calories 360 (Calories from Fat 35); Fat 4g; Saturated Fat 1g (3% of Calories from Saturated Fat); *Trans* Fat 0g; Cholesterol 75mg; Omega-3 0g; Sodium 260mg

Carbohydrate 47g (Dietary Fiber 4g); Protein 34g

% Daily Value: Vitamin A 4%; Vitamin C 8%; Calcium 4%; Iron 10%; Folic Acid 8%

Exchanges: 2 Starch, 1 Fruit, 4 Very Lean Meat

Carbohydrate Choices: 3

Plum-Glazed Turkey Tenderloins

6 SERVINGS

a note from Dr. B

To keep stress from building up, plan your day and week so that you can control the amount of rushing around. Try to get a good night's sleep, and sneak in a few quiet moments of relaxation or meditation every day. In other words, enjoy life!

1 cup plum jam or any fruit jam

1/4 cup dry sherry or chicken broth

2 tablespoons olive or canola oil

1 medium onion, finely chopped (1/2 cup)

2 teaspoons chopped fresh or 1/2 teaspoon dried rosemary leaves, crumbled

1 1/2 teaspoons garlic salt

1/4 teaspoon pepper

1 1/2 pounds turkey breast tenderloins (about 3 tenderloins)

1 Mix all ingredients except turkey in medium bowl. Place turkey in shallow glass or plastic dish or heavy-duty resealable plastic food-storage bag. Pour half of the plum mixture over turkey; turn turkey to coat. Reserve remaining half of plum mixture. Cover dish or seal bag and refrigerate 30 minutes, turning once.

2 If using charcoal grill, place drip pan directly under grilling area, and arrange coals around edge of firebox. Heat coals or gas grill for indirect heat.

3 Remove turkey from marinade; reserve marinade for basting. Cover and grill turkey over drip pan or over unheated side of gas grill and 4 to 6 inches from medium-high heat 25 to 30 minutes, turning and brushing with reserved basting marinade occasionally, until juice of turkey is no longer pink when centers of thickest pieces are cut. Discard any remaining basting marinade.

4 Heat reserved plum mixture. Serve with sliced turkey.

1 Serving: Calories 290 (Calories from Fat 45); Fat 5g; Saturated Fat 1g (3% of Calories from Saturated Fat); *Trans* Fat 0g; Cholesterol 75mg; Omega-3 0g; Sodium 270mg

Carbohydrate 34g (Dietary Fiber 1g); Protein 27g

% Daily Value: Vitamin A 0%; Vitamin C 4%; Calcium 2%; Iron 8%; Folic Acid 6%

Exchanges: 2 Fruit, 4 Very Lean Meat, 1/2 Fat

Carbohydrate Choices: 2

"Cutting fat when I'm entertaining is a real challenge. This recipe is a perfect choice for company, with grilled vegetables and steamed rice. Not only is it very heart healthy, cleanup is a breeze. It even allows us time to walk or jog around the block after dinner for a little light exercise!"

CINDY L.

PREP: 10 MIN
COOK: 12 MIN

Dijon Chicken Smothered in Mushrooms

a note from Dr. B

If you are watching your salt intake, opt for low-sodium chicken broth and leave out the salt. For a meal that's sure to satisfy, serve this saucy chicken dish with a small baked potato, cooked green beans and 1/2 cup cut-up fresh fruit and you'll have a heart-healthy meal.

4 SERVINGS

4 boneless skinless chicken breast halves (about 1 pound) or 1-pound pork tenderloin

1/4 cup all-purpose flour

1/2 teaspoon salt

1/4 teaspoon pepper

2 tablespoons olive or canola oil

1/2 cup roasted garlic-seasoned chicken broth (from 14-ounce can)

1 1/2 tablespoons Dijon mustard

1 jar (4 1/2 ounces) sliced mushrooms, drained

Chopped fresh thyme, if desired

1 If using pork, cut into 1-inch-thick slices. Place chicken (or pork) between 2 sheets of plastic wrap or waxed paper. Flatten chicken to 1/4-inch thickness with meat mallet or rolling pin. Mix flour, salt and pepper in shallow dish.

2 Heat oil in 12-inch nonstick skillet over medium-high heat. Coat both sides of chicken with flour mixture. Cook chicken in hot oil 6 to 8 minutes, turning once, until chicken is no longer pink in center (pork is no longer pink and meat thermometer inserted in center reads 160°). Remove chicken to serving plate; cover to keep warm.

3 Stir broth into skillet. Heat to boiling over medium-high heat. Stir in mustard and mushrooms. Cook 2 to 3 minutes, stirring frequently, until slightly thickened. Spoon sauce over chicken. Sprinkle with thyme.

"Heart disease runs in my family, so watching my carbohydrates and triglycerides is the only way to go. This recipe is a great low-fat choice to keep them in check."

KEN B.

1 Serving: Calories 230 (Calories from Fat 90); Fat 10g; Saturated Fat 2g (7% of Calories from Saturated Fat); *Trans* Fat 0g; Cholesterol 70mg; Omega-3 0g; Sodium 760mg

Carbohydrate 8g (Dietary Fiber 1g); Protein 27g

% Daily Value: Vitamin A 0%; Vitamin C 0%; Calcium 2%; Iron 8%; Folic Acid 4%

Exchanges: 1/2 Starch, 3 1/2 Lean Meat

Carbohydrate Choices: 1/2

Dijon Chicken Smothered in Mushrooms

PREP: **5 MIN**

COOK: **23 MIN**

Honey-Mustard Chicken and Carrots

4 SERVINGS

a note from Dr. B

Adding fruits or vegetables when you cook makes it easier and more tasty to get your "five a day." One of the best things you can do for your heart and overall health is to increase the servings of fruits and vegetables you eat every day.

2 teaspoons canola or soybean oil

4 boneless skinless chicken breast halves

1/2 cup apple juice

2 cups frozen baby-cut carrots

2 tablespoons sweet honey mustard

3 tablespoons coarsely chopped honey-roasted peanuts

1 Heat oil in 10-inch nonstick skillet over medium-high heat. Cook chicken in hot oil 5 to 8 minutes or until chicken is browned on both sides.

2 Add apple juice; reduce heat to medium. Cover and cook 5 minutes. Add carrots; cover and cook 5 to 10 minutes or until juice of chicken is no longer pink when centers of thickest pieces are cut and carrots are crisp-tender.

3 Remove chicken and carrots from skillet with slotted spoon; cover to keep warm. Stir mustard into liquid in skillet. Spoon mustard sauce over chicken and carrots. Sprinkle with peanuts.

"My husband likes the crunch of the honey-roasted peanuts.

They disguise the fact he is eating something good for him."

PAT R.

1 Serving: Calories 280 (Calories from Fat 90); Fat 10g; Saturated Fat 2g (6% of Calories from Saturated Fat); *Trans* Fat 0g; Cholesterol 70mg; Omega-3 0g; Sodium 160mg

Carbohydrate 19g (Dietary Fiber 3g); Protein 29g

% Daily Value: Vitamin A 100%; Vitamin C 0%; Calcium 4%; Iron 8%; Folic Acid 4%

Exchanges: 1 Starch, 1 Vegetable, 3 Lean Meat

Carbohydrate Choices: 1

Potato-Topped Turkey and Green Bean Bake

PREP: 15 MIN
BAKE: 25 MIN
STAND 5 MIN

8 SERVINGS

1 pound lean ground turkey

1 medium onion, chopped (1/2 cup)

1/2 teaspoon garlic powder

3/4 to 1 teaspoon dried thyme leaves

2/3 cup fat-free (skim) milk

2 packages (9 ounces each) frozen French-style green beans, thawed, drained

1 can (10 3/4 ounces) condensed 98% fat-free cream of mushroom soup

1 can (8 ounces) sliced water chestnuts, drained

1 jar (4 1/2 ounces) sliced mushrooms, drained

1 bag (16 ounces) frozen seasoned potato nuggets

1 Heat oven to 450°. Spray rectangular baking dish, 13 x 9 x 2 inches, with cooking spray.

2 Spray 10-inch nonstick skillet with cooking spray. Cook turkey, onion, garlic powder and thyme in skillet over medium–high heat until turkey is no longer pink. Stir in milk, green beans, soup, water chestnuts and mushrooms. Heat to boiling. Pour turkey mixture into baking dish. Top with potato nuggets.

3 Bake 20 to 25 minutes or until hot and bubbly. Let stand 5 minutes before serving.

a note from the Nutritionist

Become a food label reader to make sure you are getting the most nutrition and the least fat and calories as well as keeping portion sizes right for you. Every food package gives you important information about the nutrients and number of servings it contains.

"I now work flex hours, so I can get home in time to fit in exercise. This gives me time with my kids,
dinner and evening activities without sacrificing my exercise."

CINDY L.

1 Serving: Calories 270 (Calories from Fat 100); Fat 11g; Saturated Fat 4g (16% of Calories from Saturated Fat); *Trans* Fat 0g; Cholesterol 40mg; Omega-3 0g; Sodium 840mg

Carbohydrate 31g (Dietary Fiber 5g); Protein 17g

% Daily Value: Vitamin A 8%; Vitamin C 6%; Calcium 10%; Iron 12%; Folic Acid 8%

Exchanges: 2 Starch, 1 1/2 Lean Meat, 1/2 Fat

Carbohydrate Choices: 2

Turkey–Wild Rice Soup

10 SERVINGS

1 tablespoon butter

2 tablespoons canola or soybean oil

1/2 cup all-purpose flour

2 cups water

2 cups cut-up cooked turkey, chicken or ham

2 cans (14 ounces each) chicken broth

1 jar (4 1/2 ounces) sliced mushrooms, drained

2 tablespoons instant chopped onion

1 package (6 ounces) original-flavor long-grain and wild rice mix

2 cups original soy milk or fat-free (skim) milk

1/4 cup slivered almonds, toasted*

To toast nuts, bake uncovered in ungreased shallow pan in 350° oven about 10 minutes, stirring occasionally, until golden brown. Or cook in ungreased heavy skillet over medium-low heat 5 to 7 minutes, stirring frequently until browning begins, then stirring constantly until golden brown.

1 Melt butter in 5-quart Dutch oven over medium heat. Stir in oil and flour with wire whisk until well blended. Stir in water, turkey, broth, mushrooms, onion, rice and rice seasoning packet.

2 Heat to boiling over high heat, stirring occasionally. Reduce heat to medium-low. Cover and simmer about 25 minutes or until rice is tender.

3 Stir in soy milk; heat just to boiling. Remove from heat. Sprinkle each serving with almonds.

a note from Dr. B

Soy milk is a great alternative to regular milk because it gives you many of the same nutrients, and studies show that soy protein, when eaten in the context of a low-fat, low-cholesterol diet, can help reduce the risk of heart disease.

1 Serving: Calories 190 (Calories from Fat 80); Fat 9g; Saturated Fat 2g (9% of Calories from Saturated Fat); Trans Fat 0g; Cholesterol 25mg; Omega-3 0g; Sodium 480mg

Carbohydrate 14g (Dietary Fiber 1g); Protein 13g

% Daily Value: Vitamin A 2%; Vitamin C 0%; Calcium 8%; Iron 8%; Folic Acid 6%

Exchanges: 1 Starch, 1 1/2 Medium-Fat Meat

Carbohydrate Choices: 1

"I eat a broth-based soup every single day, even weekends, because it fills me up and I can eat a lot. This turkey soup, being low-fat and low in calories and carbs, is great!"

NANCY D.

Summer Harvest Chicken-Potato Salad

PREP: 15 MIN

COOK: 17 MIN

4 SERVINGS

4 medium red potatoes (1 pound), cut into 3/4-inch cubes

1/2 pound fresh green beans, trimmed, cut into 1-inch pieces (about 2 cups)

1/2 cup fat-free plain yogurt

1/3 cup fat-free ranch dressing

1 tablespoon prepared horseradish

1/4 teaspoon salt

Dash of pepper

2 cups cut-up cooked chicken breast

2/3 cup thinly sliced celery

Torn salad greens, if desired

1 Heat 6 cups lightly salted water to boiling in 2-quart saucepan. Add potatoes; return to boiling. Reduce heat; simmer 5 minutes. Add green beans; cook uncovered 8 to 12 minutes longer or until potatoes and beans are crisp-tender.

2 Meanwhile, mix yogurt, dressing, horseradish, salt and pepper in small bowl; set aside.

3 Drain potatoes and green beans; rinse with cold water to cool. Mix potatoes, green beans, chicken and celery in large serving bowl. Pour yogurt mixture over salad; toss gently to coat. Line plates with greens; spoon salad onto greens.

a note from the Nutritionist

Not only is this a great-tasting, low-fat comfort food, it is also an excellent source of fiber from the potatoes, green beans and celery. When these foods are eaten together, the fiber adds up!

"Given my family history of heart disease, we all strive to eat right and exercise. This great potato salad is good for get-togethers and we like the fact that we don't have to give up our family traditions."

KEVIN W.

1 Serving: Calories 275 (Calories from Fat 25); Fat 3g; Saturated Fat 1g (3% of Calories from Saturated Fat); *Trans* Fat 0g; Cholesterol 60mg; Omega-3 0g; Sodium 460mg

Carbohydrate 38g (Dietary Fiber 5g); Protein 26g

% Daily Value: Vitamin A 6%; Vitamin C 16%; Calcium 12%; Iron 20%; Folic Acid 8%

Exchanges: 2 Starch, 2 Vegetable, 2 Very Lean Meat

Carbohydrate Choices: 2 1/2

Border Chicken and Bean Soup

6 SERVINGS

3/4 pound boneless skinless chicken thighs or breast halves

3 cups fat-free reduced-sodium chicken broth

1 can (15 to 16 ounces) navy beans, rinsed and drained

1 can (14 1/2 ounces) no-salt-added diced tomatoes, undrained

1 envelope (1 1/4 ounces) taco seasoning mix

1 1/2 teaspoons sugar

1 Cut chicken into 1/2-inch pieces. Spray 4-quart Dutch oven with cooking spray; heat over medium–high heat. Cook chicken in Dutch oven about 3 minutes, stirring frequently, until brown.

2 Stir in remaining ingredients. Heat to boiling; reduce heat to low. Simmer uncovered about 15 minutes or until chicken is no longer pink in center.

a note from Dr. B

Don't underestimate the value of a good friend. If things are bothering you, talk to a friend or others who care. Express your thoughts and feelings in a journal. Being able to share your feelings will help you release tensions.

"I always buy the no-salt, low-sodium, low-fat or reduced-fat version of a food if it's available."

NANCY D.

1 Serving: Calories 225 (Calories from Fat 55); Fat 6g; Saturated Fat 2g (6% of Calories from Saturated Fat); *Trans* Fat 0g; Cholesterol 35mg; Omega-3 0g; Sodium 790mg

Carbohydrate 27g (Dietary Fiber 6g); Protein 22g

% Daily Value: Vitamin A 14%; Vitamin C 10%; Calcium 10%; Iron 20%; Folic Acid 28%

Exchanges: 2 Starch, 2 Very Lean Meat

Carbohydrate Choices: 2

Glazed Beef Tenderloin with Herbed New Potatoes

PREP: 15 MIN
MARINATE: 1 HR
GRILL: 13 MIN

4 SERVINGS

1/3 cup steak sauce

1 1/2 tablespoons packed brown sugar

4 beef tenderloin steaks, about 1 inch thick (1 pound)

8 small new potatoes (1 pound), cut lengthwise in half

2 tablespoons water

1 teaspoon chopped fresh or 1/4 teaspoon dried rosemary leaves, crumbled

1 teaspoon chopped fresh or 1/4 teaspoon dried thyme leaves

1/4 teaspoon paprika

1/2 teaspoon salt

1/4 teaspoon pepper

1 Mix steak sauce and brown sugar in shallow dish; reserve 2 tablespoons. Add beef to remaining sauce (about 1/4 cup); turn to coat. Cover and refrigerate, turning beef 2 or 3 times, at least 1 hour but no longer than 24 hours.

2 Spray grill rack with cooking spray. Heat coals or gas grill for direct heat.

3 Place potatoes and water in 2-quart microwavable casserole. Cover and microwave on High 3 to 5 minutes or until potatoes are just tender. Place potatoes on sheet of heavy-duty aluminum foil. Spray potatoes with cooking spray; sprinkle with rosemary, thyme and paprika. Wrap securely in foil.

4 Grill beef and potatoes uncovered 4 to 6 inches from medium heat about 13 minutes for medium doneness, turning beef and potatoes after 6 minutes and brushing reserved sauce frequently over beef. Sprinkle salt and pepper over potatoes.

To Broil: Marinate beef and microwave potatoes as directed. Spray potatoes with cooking spray; sprinkle with rosemary, thyme and paprika, but do not wrap in foil. Set oven control to broil. Place beef and potatoes on rack in broiler pan. Broil with tops 4 to 6 inches from heat about 15 minutes for medium doneness, turning beef and potatoes after 6 minutes and brushing reserved sauce frequently over beef.

"Great low-cal recipe for beef on the grill! I go to my local farmers' market to use the first-of-the-season new potatoes."

LORI S.

a note from Dr. B

Take a look: The nutrients in this recipe clearly show that you don't have to give up red meat to be heart-healthy. Along with protein, beef contains iron, folic acid and other nutrients important for heart health.

1 Serving: Calories 290 (Calories from Fat 70); Fat 8g; Saturated Fat 3g (9% of Calories from Saturated Fat); *Trans* Fat 0g; Cholesterol 65mg; Omega-3 0g; Sodium 660mg

Carbohydrate 28g (Dietary Fiber 3g); Protein 27g

% Daily Value: Vitamin A 6%; Vitamin C 14%; Calcium 4%; Iron 24%; Folic Acid 4%

Exchanges: 2 Starch, 3 Very Lean Meat, 1/2 Fat

Carbohydrate Choices: 2

Hearty Beef and Vegetables

4 SERVINGS

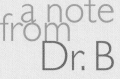

a note from **Dr. B**

This recipe is a super source of both vitamin B-12, which is important for all body cells, and iron, a mineral that's vital for oxygen transfer in the blood.

1 pound beef top sirloin steak, about 3/4 inch thick

1 bag (16 ounces) frozen stew vegetables, thawed and drained

1 cup frozen cut green beans, thawed and drained

1/2 cup water

1 tablespoon Worcestershire sauce

1/4 package (2-ounce size) onion soup mix (1/2 envelope)

3 tablespoons chopped fresh parsley

1 Trim fat from beef; cut beef into 1/2-inch pieces. Spray 4-quart Dutch oven with cooking spray; heat over medium-high heat. Cook beef in Dutch oven 2 minutes, stirring constantly.

2 Stir in stew vegetables, green beans, water, Worcestershire sauce and soup mix (dry). Heat to boiling; reduce heat to low. Cover and simmer 12 to 14 minutes, stirring occasionally, just until potatoes are tender. Remove from heat; stir in parsley.

1 Serving: Calories 230 (Calories from Fat 35); Fat 4g; Saturated Fat 1g (5% of Calories from Saturated Fat); *Trans* Fat 0g; Cholesterol 60mg; Omega-3 0g; Sodium 1360mg

Carbohydrate 24g (Dietary Fiber 4g); Protein 25g

% Daily Value: Vitamin A 100%; Vitamin C 14%; Calcium 8%; Iron 18%; Folic Acid 14%

Exchanges: 1 1/2 Starch, 3 Very Lean Meat

Carbohydrate Choices: 1 1/2

Flank Steak Sandwiches

PREP: 10 MIN
MARINATE: 4 HR
GRILL: 12 MIN

8 SERVINGS

2 beef flank steaks (1 pound each)

1/4 cup honey

2 tablespoons soy sauce

1 tablespoon grated gingerroot

1 can or bottle (12 ounces) regular or nonalcoholic beer

8 pita breads (6 inches in diameter), cut in half to form pockets

2 medium tomatoes, sliced

1 large grilled sliced onion

1 Trim fat from beef. Make cuts about 1/2 inch apart and 1/8 inch deep in diamond pattern on both sides of beef. Place in shallow glass dish. Mix honey, soy sauce, gingerroot and beer in small bowl; pour over beef. Cover and refrigerate, turning occasionally, at least 4 hours but no longer than 24 hours.

2 Brush grill rack with canola or soybean oil. Heat coals or gas grill for direct heat. Remove beef from marinade; reserve marinade. Cover and grill beef 6 inches from medium heat about 12 minutes for medium doneness, turning after 6 minutes and brushing frequently with marinade. Discard any remaining marinade.

3 Cut beef diagonally into thin slices. Serve beef in pita bread halves with tomato and onion.

"With my husband being the 'king of sandwiches,' this is good for us. The steak is a lean cut with hardly any fat."

CATHY P.

a note from Dr. B

Lunching on an oversized deli sandwich can cost you anywhere from 600 to 800 calories. Instead, bring a healthy lunch from home. Pack sandwiches that feature lean meats or cheeses for a midday protein punch. Also include raw vegetable sticks and fresh fruit for fiber and nutrients.

1 Sandwich: Calories 360 (Calories from Fat 80); Fat 9g; Saturated Fat 3g (8% of Calories from Saturated Fat); *Trans* Fat 0g; Cholesterol 65mg; Omega-3 0g; Sodium 510mg

Carbohydrate 40g (Dietary Fiber 2g); Protein 30g

% Daily Value: Vitamin A 6%; Vitamin C 6%; Calcium 6%; Iron 20%; Folic Acid 16%

Exchanges: 2 1/2 Starch, 3 Lean Meat

Carbohydrate Choices: 2 1/2

Broiled Dijon Burgers

6 SERVINGS

1/4 cup fat-free cholesterol-free egg product or 2 egg whites

2 tablespoons fat-free (skim) milk

2 teaspoons Dijon mustard or horseradish sauce

1/4 teaspoon salt

1/8 teaspoon pepper

1 cup soft bread crumbs (about 2 slices bread)

1 small onion, finely chopped (1/4 cup)

1 pound extra-lean ground beef

6 whole-grain hamburger buns, split and toasted

1 Set oven control to broil. Spray broiler pan rack with cooking spray.

2 Mix egg product, milk, mustard, salt and pepper in medium bowl. Stir in bread crumbs and onion. Stir in beef. Shape mixture into 6 patties, each about 1/2 inch thick. Place patties on rack in broiler pan.

3 Broil with tops of patties about 5 inches from heat 6 minutes. Turn; broil until meat thermometer inserted in center reads 160°, about 4 to 6 minutes longer. Serve patties in buns.

"I love hamburgers and still eat them, but I buy the leanest beef available. These burgers are great, because I like to use high-flavor ingredients like mustard or horseradish for an extra kick!"

NANCI D.

1 Sandwich: Calories 250 (Calories from Fat 55); Fat 6g; Saturated Fat 2g (7% of Calories from Saturated Fat); *Trans* Fat 0g; Cholesterol 45mg; Omega-3 0g; Sodium 470mg

Carbohydrate 26g (Dietary Fiber 3g); Protein 23g

% Daily Value: Vitamin A 2%; Vitamin C 0%; Calcium 6%; Iron 18%; Folic Acid 10%

Exchanges: 2 Starch, 2 1/2 Very Lean Meat

Carbohydrate Choices: 1 1/2

Pizza Casserole

6 SERVINGS

8 ounces uncooked wheel-shaped macaroni (about 3 1/2 cups)

1/2 pound bulk turkey Italian sausage

2 3/4 cups meatless tomato pasta sauce

1/4 cup sliced ripe olives

1 can (4 ounces) mushroom pieces and stems, drained

1 cup shredded fat-free or part-skim mozzarella cheese (4 ounces)

1 Heat oven to 350°. Cook macaroni as directed on package; drain. Cook sausage in skillet, stirring frequently, until no longer pink; drain.

2 Mix macaroni, sausage, pasta sauce, olives and mushrooms in 2 1/2-quart casserole.

3 Cover and bake about 30 minutes or until hot. Sprinkle with cheese. Let stand 5 minutes or until cheese is melted.

"When using any ground meat, I rinse it off in hot water after cooking to remove even more fat. I have found that the fewer ingredients in a dish, the less added fat it contains."

NANCY D.

a note from Dr. B

Here's a real all-family staple recipe. Studies confirm that a low-fat diet rich in milk, milk products, fruits and vegetables (pasta sauce counts as a vegetable!) may help reduce the risk of high blood pressure and other factors for heart disease.

1 Serving: Calories 400 (Calories from Fat 115); Fat 13g; Saturated Fat 4g (9% of Calories from Saturated Fat); *Trans* Fat 0g; Cholesterol 30mg; Omega-3 0g; Sodium 1040mg

Carbohydrate 53g (Dietary Fiber 4g); Protein 18g

% Daily Value: Vitamin A 18%; Vitamin C 14%; Calcium 18%; Iron 16%; Folic Acid 24%

Exchanges: 3 Starch, 1 Vegetable, 1 Medium-Fat Meat, 1 Fat

Carbohydrate Choices: 3 1/2

PREP: 15 MIN
GRILL: 40 MIN
STAND: 10 MIN

Grilled Garlic-Sage Pork Roast

6 SERVINGS

8 cloves garlic, finely chopped

3 tablespoons chopped fresh sage leaves

1/2 teaspoon salt

1/4 teaspoon pepper

2 tablespoons olive or canola oil

1 1/2-pound boneless center-cut pork loin roast

1 Brush grill rack with canola or soybean oil. Heat coals or gas grill for direct heat. Mix garlic, sage, salt, pepper and oil in small bowl; rub over pork.

2 Cover and grill pork 4 to 5 inches from medium heat 35 to 40 minutes, turning occasionally, until meat thermometer inserted into center of pork reads 155°. Remove from heat; cover with aluminum foil and let stand 10 minutes until thermometer reads 160°. Cut pork across grain into thin slices.

To bake in oven, heat oven to 400°; place pork in ungreased rectangular pan, 13 x 9 x 2 inches. Bake 50 to 60 minutes or until meat thermometer inserted into center of pork reads 155°. Remove from oven; cover with aluminum foil and let stand 10 minutes until thermometer reads 160°.

"My family gets tired of chicken and fish, so I cook more lean pork now. I usually cook extra and use the leftovers for a low-fat, vegetable-heavy stir-fry the next day."

NANCI D.

I Serving: Calories 220 (Calories from Fat 115); Fat 13g; Saturated Fat 4g (15% of Calories from Saturated Fat); Trans Fat 0g; Cholesterol 75mg; Omega-3 0g; Sodium 180mg

Carbohydrate 0g (Dietary Fiber 0g); Protein 26g

% Daily Value: Vitamin A 0%; Vitamin C 0%; Calcium 0%; Iron 4%; Folic Acid 2%

Exchanges: 4 Lean Meat

Carbohydrate Choices: 0

Barbecued Pork Tenderloin

6 SERVINGS

2 pork tenderloins
(about 3/4 pound each)

1/4 teaspoon seasoned salt

1/3 cup barbecue sauce

1/4 cup teriyaki baste and glaze
(from 12-ounce bottle)

2 tablespoons finely chopped onion

2 tablespoons finely chopped
chipotle chili in adobo sauce
(from 7-ounce can)

1 Heat coals or gas grill for direct heat. Sprinkle pork with seasoned salt. Mix remaining ingredients in small bowl. Brush pork with barbecue sauce mixture.

2 Cover and grill pork 4 to 6 inches from medium-low heat 18 to 22 minutes, turning several times and basting generously with remaining sauce mixture, until pork has slight blush of pink in center and meat thermometer inserted in center reads 160°. Discard any remaining sauce mixture.

a note from the Nutritionist

Add veggies to this meal equation by grilling corn on the cob along with the pork and serving sliced fresh tomatoes sprinkled with cilantro.
For a great sandwich, slice the pork and serve it in toasted whole-grain buns with shredded lettuce and sliced tomato.

1 Serving: Calories 165 (Calories from Fat 35); Fat 4g; Saturated Fat 2g (8% of Calories from Saturated Fat); *Trans* Fat 0g; Cholesterol 70mg; Omega-3 0g; Sodium 640mg

Carbohydrate 6g (Dietary Fiber 0g); Protein 26g

% Daily Value: Vitamin A 0%; Vitamin C 0%; Calcium 0%; Iron 8%; Folic Acid 2%

Exchanges: 1/2 Starch, 3 1/2 Very Lean Meat

Carbohydrate Choices: 1/2

Harvest Skillet Supper

4 SERVINGS

2 teaspoons canola or soybean oil

3/4-pound pork tenderloin, cut into 1/4-inch slices

3/4 cup apple juice

2 tablespoons Dijon mustard

2 teaspoons cornstarch

2 teaspoons packed brown sugar

Dash of salt

Dash of pepper

2 medium sweet potatoes, peeled, cut into 1/4-inch slices (2 cups) or 2 cups sliced carrots

1 1/4 cups water

1 cup uncooked instant brown rice

1/2 cup coarsely chopped green bell pepper

1 apple, cut into 16 wedges

1 Heat oil in 10-inch nonstick skillet over medium–high heat. Cook pork in hot oil 2 to 3 minutes, turning once, until brown on both sides. Remove pork from skillet; cover to keep warm. Drain drippings from skillet.

2 Mix apple juice, mustard, cornstarch, brown sugar, salt and pepper in small bowl. Add to skillet with sweet potatoes; reduce heat. Cover and cook 10 to 15 minutes, stirring occasionally, until sweet potatoes are crisp–tender.

3 While sweet potatoes are cooking, heat water to boiling in medium saucepan; stir in rice. Reduce heat to low; cover and simmer 10 minutes.

4 Stir bell pepper, apple and pork into sweet potato mixture. Cover and cook 5 minutes longer, stirring occasionally, until bell pepper is crisp-tender and pork is no longer pink in center. Serve over rice; garnish with chopped fresh parsley if desired.

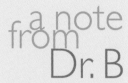

a note from Dr. B

You may have heard of the DASH Diet (see page 23). Key findings from it showed that when people ate more fruits and vegetables, more low-fat dairy products and less saturated fat than a typical American diet, their blood pressures dropped significantly. More good news: If salt was also reduced, their blood pressure dropped even more.

1 Serving: Calories 380 (Calories from Fat 65); Fat 7g; Saturated Fat 2g (4% of Calories from Saturated Fat); *Trans* Fat 0g; Cholesterol 55mg; Omega-3 0g; Sodium 300mg

Carbohydrate 55g (Dietary Fiber 5g); Protein 24g

% Daily Value: Vitamin A 100%; Vitamin C 22%; Calcium 4%; Iron 12%; Folic Acid 6%

Exchanges: 2 1/2 Starch, 1 Fruit, 2 1/2 Lean Meat

Carbohydrate Choices: 3 1/2

"Knowing that weight is also a heart concern,
I look at main dishes and keep them under 400 to 500
calories, which is a good thing for my whole family. I am trying to include
the kids in our choices, so they learn about healthy eating, too."

NANCY D.

Apple-Rosemary Pork and Barley

4 SERVINGS

1 1/2 cups apple juice

3/4 cup uncooked quick-cooking barley

2 tablespoons chopped fresh or 2 teaspoons dried rosemary leaves, crushed

3/4-pound pork tenderloin

2 teaspoons canola or soybean oil

1 medium onion, chopped (1/2 cup)

1 clove garlic, finely chopped

1/4 cup apple jelly

1 large unpeeled red cooking apple, sliced (1 1/2 cups)

1 Heat apple juice to boiling in 2-quart saucepan. Stir in barley and 1 tablespoon of the rosemary; reduce heat to low. Cover and simmer 10 to 12 minutes until liquid is absorbed and barley is tender.

2 While barley is cooking, cut pork into 1/4-inch slices.

3 Heat oil in 10-inch nonstick skillet over medium-high heat. Cook pork, onion, garlic and remaining 1 tablespoon rosemary in hot oil about 5 minutes, stirring frequently, until pork is no longer pink in center. Stir in apple jelly and apple slices; cook until hot. Serve over barley.

1 Serving: Calories 400 (Calories from Fat 55); Fat 6g; Saturated Fat 1g (3% of Calories from Saturated Fat); *Trans* Fat 0g; Cholesterol 55mg; Omega-3 0g; Sodium 50mg

Carbohydrate 63g (Dietary Fiber 8g); Protein 23g

% Daily Value: Vitamin A 2%; Vitamin C 6%; Calcium 2%; Iron 14%; Folic Acid 6%

Exchanges: 2 Starch, 2 Fruit, 2 1/2 Very Lean Meat, 1 Fat

Carbohydrate Choices: 4

Parmesan Breaded Pork Chops

4 SERVINGS

4 butterflied boneless pork loin chops, about 1/2 inch thick (about 1 pound)

1/3 cup Italian-style dry bread crumbs

2 tablespoons grated Parmesan cheese

1/4 cup fat-free cholesterol-free egg product or 2 egg whites

1 small green bell pepper, chopped (1/2 cup)

1 can (14 1/2 ounces) chunky tomatoes with olive oil, garlic and spices, undrained

1 can (8 ounces) tomato sauce

1 Trim fat from pork. Mix bread crumbs and cheese in shallow dish. Pour egg product into another shallow dish. Dip pork into egg product, then coat with crumb mixture.

2 Spray 12-inch nonstick skillet with cooking spray; heat over medium heat. Cook pork in skillet about 5 minutes, turning once, until brown on both sides.

3 Stir in remaining ingredients. Heat to boiling; reduce heat. Cover and simmer 10 to 12 minutes, stirring occasionally, until pork is no longer pink in center.

"I am always thinking of ways to be more physical. I park farther away, garden more and go for a short walk at noon."

LORI S.

a note from Dr. B

See your doctor for an evaluation before you begin exercising. Your doctor may ask you to do a treadmill or cardiac stress test to determine how vigorously you can work out.

1 Serving: Calories 290 (Calories from Fat 90); Fat 10g; Saturated Fat 4g (12% of Calories from Saturated Fat); *Trans* Fat 0g; Cholesterol 70mg; Omega-3 0g; Sodium 860mg

Carbohydrate 20g (Dietary Fiber 2g); Protein 30g

% Daily Value: Vitamin A 16%; Vitamin C 30%; Calcium 10%; Iron 14%; Folic Acid 10%

Exchanges: 1 Starch, 1 Vegetable, 3 1/2 Lean Meat

Carbohydrate Choices: 1

Pork Chops in Country Onion Gravy

4 SERVINGS

4 boneless pork loin chops (about 1 pound)

2 cups chopped onions

1 cup beef broth

1/8 teaspoon pepper

1/3 cup fat-free (skim) milk

2 tablespoons all-purpose flour

1. Generously spray 12-inch nonstick skillet with cooking spray; heat over medium-high heat. Cook pork chops in skillet about 6 minutes, turning once, until brown on both sides. Remove pork from skillet; cover to keep warm.

2. Reduce heat to medium. Add onions to skillet; cook 3 minutes. Stir in broth and pepper. Return pork to skillet; spoon onion mixture over pork. Cover tightly and simmer 12 minutes or until pork is no longer pink and meat thermometer inserted in center reads 160°.

3. Mix milk and flour in small bowl. Add to skillet; cook 2 to 3 minutes, stirring constantly, until thickened.

1 Serving: Calories 235 (Calories from Fat 80); Fat 9g; Saturated Fat 3g (12% of Calories from Saturated Fat); *Trans* Fat 0g; Cholesterol 70mg; Omega-3 0g; Sodium 310mg

Carbohydrate 11g (Dietary Fiber 2g); Protein 27g

% Daily Value: Vitamin A 2%; Vitamin C 4%; Calcium 4%; Iron 6%; Folic Acid 8%

Exchanges: 1/2 Starch, 1 Vegetable, 3 Lean Meat

Carbohydrate Choices: 1

"Pork is one of my favorites, but I've never thought of it as a 'healthy' option. This tasty recipe changed my mind."

MARILYN B.

PREP: 10 MIN
COOK: 20 MIN

Spanish Lamb and Couscous

4 SERVINGS

4 lamb sirloin chops, 1/2 inch thick (about 2 pounds)

1 medium green bell pepper, chopped (1 cup)

1/4 cup chili sauce

1 can (14 1/2 ounces) diced tomatoes, undrained

1/2 teaspoon ground cumin

1/2 teaspoon dried marjoram leaves

1/4 teaspoon garlic powder

1/4 teaspoon salt

1/4 cup pitted ripe olives, cut in half

2 tablespoons chopped fresh parsley

2 cups hot cooked couscous

1 Spray 12-inch nonstick skillet with cooking spray; heat over medium heat. Cook lamb in skillet, turning once, until brown on both sides.

2 Stir in bell pepper, chili sauce, tomatoes, cumin, marjoram, garlic powder and salt; reduce heat to medium-low. Cover and simmer about 10 minutes or until lamb is light pink in center.

3 Stir in olives; sprinkle with parsley. Serve with couscous.

1 Serving: Calories 320 (Calories from Fat 80); Fat 9g; Saturated Fat 3g (8% of Calories from Saturated Fat); *Trans* Fat 0g; Cholesterol 70mg; Omega-3 0g; Sodium 640mg

Carbohydrate 33g (Dietary Fiber 4g); Protein 27g

% Daily Value: Vitamin A 16%; Vitamin C 38%; Calcium 6%; Iron 20%; Folic Acid 10%

Exchanges: 2 Starch, 1 Vegetable, 3 Very Lean Meat, 1/2 Fat

Carbohydrate Choices: 2

"Exercise is one of the best things I can do for my heart, and for me, I try to keep it moderate. Any exercise is good, but I like walking and do it faithfully every day."

SHERRY L.

Making Heart-Healthy Choices in Restaurants

Many restaurants now use special menu symbols to indicate dishes made with lower fat—if the symbols aren't included on the menu, follow these guidelines:

Choose whole-grain breads and rolls; avoid croissants and other butter-rich breads.

Select foods prepared by baking, broiling, steaming or stir-frying rather than frying. If you're not sure how your food will be prepared, ask.

Choose vegetable, bean, or tomato-based soups over creamed soups.

Share large portions or ask for a carry-out box and save the remainder for another meal.

Ask for reduced-calorie or reduced-fat salad dressings, condiments, sauces and seasonings on the side. Instead of mayo, use mustard.

Chicken breast or turkey make the best sandwich choices; hold the mayo and cheese. Avoid sandwiches with high-fat meats like bologna, pastrami, corned beef, meatballs, sausage or meat loaf.

For dessert, choose fruit sorbet, low-fat frozen yogurt or ice cream, or a slice of angel food cake.

Some ethnic foods are naturally healthful, but some are not; start with these wise choices:

1. **Chinese** menus include many steamed and stir-fried chicken and seafood dishes containing many vegetables. Look for entrees that are steamed, and ask for sauce on the side.

   Choose steamed rice over fried rice; be sure the food is prepared without MSG (monosodium glutamate); and, because of its high sodium content, use soy sauce sparingly. Fortune cookies are low in calories, so share your fortunes while munching away.

2. **Mexican, Caribbean and other Latin-American** cuisines are based on beans, rice and corn. As long as the dishes are prepared with less fat, they are healthful choices.

   For starters, black bean soup, gazpacho or spicy seafood broth are great. Fajitas, soft tacos or burritos made with vegetables, grilled chicken fish or seafood are good, too. Bananas, melons or pineapple make refreshing and healthy desserts.

3. **Italian** food includes plenty of healthful options. Begin with minestrone or other broth-based vegetable soups. Order pasta topped with seafood, such as clams or mussels, in a tomato or vegetable sauce. Good main dish choices include chicken, shrimp or veal in a tomato or mushroom sauce. Italian ice is a virtually fat-free dessert.

4. **French** restaurants usually offer fish, shellfish, chicken and lean meats that have been broiled, grilled or poached, then seasoned with fresh herbs and wine-based sauces. French bread is lean, crusty and delicious. Try sorbet for dessert.

5. **Japanese** food is quite lean, so you can enjoy it often. Start with broth-based miso or a hearty broth soup with noodles. Teriyaki-seasoned fish or chicken, grilled vegetables, sushi—a rice and fish combination is good; stay away from battered and fried tempuras.

In **fast-food restaurants**, there are a surprising number of good options. Some of the best:

For **breakfast:** Order a plain English muffin, bagel or a breakfast burrito.

For **lunch or dinner:** Choose salads, chili without cheese, a regular hamburger without cheese, potato cakes, marinated grilled chicken, grilled chicken sandwich, roast beef sandwich, soft chicken tacos, baked potato or one slice of pizza. To avoid saturated and trans fats, stay away from the fries, curly fries and onion rings.

For **dessert:** Try a vanilla reduced-fat ice-cream cone, cinnamon twists, a small sundae or a small cookie. Drink water, skim milk or diet beverages instead of super-sized sodas or juice. Finally, don't be a victim of portion distortion. If you super-size any food item, the calories and fat grams skyrocket.

Halibut-Asparagus Stir-Fry (page 150)

Easy Dinners in 25 Minutes

Just because you're in a rush doesn't mean you have to eat extra calories and fat; the key is finding super-easy, good-to-your-heart recipes, like these.

Loaded Potatoes

4 SERVINGS

a note from **Dr. B**

With the time you save preparing this easy recipe, do something you enjoy today. Talk to friends, read, meditate, do yoga or gardening, anything that makes you feel good. The reward will be that you feel more relaxed, and that in turn will be passed on to those you interact with.

4 medium unpeeled red potatoes

1 package (8 ounces) sliced fresh mushrooms (3 cups)

3/4 cup chopped fully cooked ham

8 medium green onions, sliced (1/2 cup)

1/8 teaspoon ground red pepper (cayenne)

1/2 cup reduced-fat sour cream

1/2 cup shredded reduced-fat sharp Cheddar cheese (2 ounces)

1 Pierce potatoes with fork. Arrange potatoes about 1 inch apart in circle on microwavable paper towel in microwave oven. Microwave uncovered on High 8 to 10 minutes or until tender. (Or bake potatoes in 375° oven 1 to 1 1/2 hours.) Let potatoes stand until cool enough to handle.

2 While potatoes are cooking, spray 4-quart Dutch oven with cooking spray; heat over medium-high heat. Cook mushrooms in Dutch oven 1 minute, stirring frequently; reduce heat to medium. Cover and cook 3 minutes; remove from heat. Stir in ham, green onions and red pepper. Cover and let stand 4 minutes.

3 Split baked potatoes lengthwise in half; fluff with fork. Spread 1 tablespoon of the sour cream over each potato half. Top with ham mixture and cheese.

1 Serving: Calories 225 (Calories from Fat 55); Fat 6g; Saturated Fat 3g (10% of Calories from Saturated Fat); *Trans* Fat 0g; Cholesterol 25mg; Omega-3 0g; Sodium 560mg

Carbohydrate 34g (Dietary Fiber 5g); Protein 16g

% Daily Value: Vitamin A 10%; Vitamin C 20%; Calcium 20%; Iron 20%; Folic Acid 8%

Exchanges: 2 Starch, 1 Vegetable, 1 Very Lean Meat

Carbohydrate Choices: 2

"I really try to say good things to people. A ready smile and a kind word go a long way. It makes me feel good, and people may notice and change their ways, too."

SHERRY L.

Asian Steak Salad

6 SERVINGS

1 pound cut-up beef for stir-fry

1 package (3 ounces) Oriental-flavor ramen noodle soup mix

1/2 cup Asian marinade and dressing

1 bag (10 ounces) romaine and leaf lettuce mix

1 cup fresh snow (Chinese) pea pods

1/2 cup matchstick-cut carrots (from 10-ounce bag)

1 can (11 ounces) mandarin orange segments, drained

1 Spray 12-inch nonstick skillet with cooking spray; heat over medium-high heat. Place beef in skillet; sprinkle with 1 teaspoon seasoning mix from soup mix. (Discard remaining seasoning mix.) Cook beef 4 to 5 minutes, stirring occasionally, until brown. Stir in 1 tablespoon of the dressing.

2 Break block of noodles from soup mix into small pieces. Mix noodles, lettuce, pea pods, carrots and orange segments in large bowl. Add remaining dressing; toss until well coated. Divide mixture among individual serving plates. Top with beef strips.

"This will impress your family and won't add to their waistlines."

WANDA S.

a note from Dr. B

What color is your diet? Even the colors of fruits and vegetables tell us that they are good for us, so choose colorful ones! Fruits and veggies contain antioxidants, which may help prevent cholesterol from damaging arteries by preventing LDL (bad) cholesterol from "sticking to" your arteries.

1 Serving: Calories 185 (Calories from Fat 25); Fat 3g; Saturated Fat 1g (5% of Calories from Saturated Fat); *Trans* Fat 0g; Cholesterol 40mg; Omega-3 0g; Sodium 570mg

Carbohydrate 22g (Dietary Fiber 3g); Protein 18g

% Daily Value: Vitamin A 74%; Vitamin C 48%; Calcium 4%; Iron 16%; Folic Acid 26%

Exchanges: 1 Starch, 1 Vegetable, 2 Very Lean Meat

Carbohydrate Choices: 1 1/2

Southwestern Chicken BLT Salad

6 SERVINGS

Salsa-Bacon Dressing (below)

1 bag (10 ounces) romaine and leaf lettuce mix

2 packages (6 ounces each) refrigerated cooked Southwest-flavor chicken breast strips

4 roma (plum) tomatoes, coarsely chopped

1/2 cup chopped cooked bacon

1/2 cup croutons

1 Make Salsa-Bacon Dressing; set aside.

2 Mix remaining ingredients in large bowl. Add dressing; toss until coated.

Salsa-Bacon Dressing

1/2 cup chunky-style salsa

1/2 cup nonfat ranch dressing

1 tablespoon chopped fresh parsley

Mix all ingredients in small bowl.

1 Serving: Calories 190 (Calories from Fat 44); Fat 6g; Saturated Fat 2g (9% calories from Saturated Fat); *Trans* Fat 0g; Cholesterol 55mg; Omega-3 0g; Sodium 580mg

Carbohydrate 13g (Dietary Fiber 2g); Protein 21g

% Daily Value: Vitamin A 38%; Vitamin C 14%; Calcium 4%; Iron 10%; Folic Acid 20%

Exchanges: 1/2 Starch, 1 Vegetable, 3 Very Lean Meat, 1/2 Fat

Carbohydrate Choices: 1

"This is a quick-prep, on-the-go salad I easily make at home and take with me—
and it helps me stay on my heart-healthy routine."
KEVIN W.

Southwestern Chicken BLT Salad

Fajita Salad

4 SERVINGS

3/4 pound boneless lean beef
sirloin steak

1 tablespoon canola or soybean oil

2 medium bell peppers, cut into strips

1 small onion, thinly sliced

4 cups bite-size pieces salad greens

1/3 cup fat-free Italian dressing

1/4 cup fat-free plain yogurt

1 Cut beef across grain into bite-size strips. Heat oil in 10-inch nonstick skillet over medium-high heat. Cook beef in oil about 3 minutes, stirring occasionally, until brown. Remove beef from skillet.

2 Cook bell peppers and onion in skillet about 3 minutes, stirring occasionally, until bell peppers are crisp-tender. Stir in beef.

3 Place salad greens on serving platter. Top with beef mixture. Mix dressing and yogurt in small bowl; drizzle over salad.

a note from Dr. B

Even if you are on medication to reduce your cholesterol or blood pressure, eating a low-fat, high-nutrient diet is still wise. In anything, moderation is the best-played game. This recipe is a great choice because the fat and cholesterol are very low and it's a good source of fiber.

1 Serving: Calories 175 (Calories from Fat 55); Fat 6g; Saturated Fat 1g (6% of Calories from Saturated Fat); *Trans* Fat 0g; Cholesterol 45mg; Omega-3 0g; Sodium 330mg

Carbohydrate 10g (Dietary Fiber 3g); Protein 20g

% Daily Value: Vitamin A 40%; Vitamin C 52%; Calcium 6%; Iron 14%; Folic Acid 24%

Exchanges: 2 Vegetable, 2 Lean Meat

Carbohydrate Choices: 1/2

Grilled Barbecued Beef and Bean Burgers

5 SERVINGS

1/2 pound extra-lean ground beef

1 can (15 to 16 ounces) great northern beans, rinsed and drained

1/4 cup finely crushed saltine crackers (about 7 squares)

2 tablespoons barbecue sauce

1/4 teaspoon pepper

1 egg

5 teaspoons barbecue sauce

5 whole-grain hamburger buns, split

Leaf lettuce, sliced tomatoes and sliced onions, if desired

1 Brush grill rack with canola or soybean oil. Heat coals or gas grill for direct heat.

2 Mix beef, beans, cracker crumbs, 2 tablespoons barbecue sauce, the pepper and egg in large bowl. Shape mixture into 5 patties, about 1/2 inch thick.

3 Cover and grill patties 4 to 6 inches from medium heat 5 minutes. Turn patties; spread each patty with 1 teaspoon barbecue sauce. Grill until meat thermometer inserted in center of patties reads 160°, about 6 to 8 minutes longer.

4 Fill buns with lettuce, patties, tomatoes and onions.

1 Serving: Calories 315 (Calories from Fat 65); Fat 7g; Saturated Fat 2g (6% of Calories from Saturated Fat); *Trans* Fat 1g; Cholesterol 70mg; Omega-3 0g; Sodium 420mg

Carbohydrate 48g (Dietary Fiber 9g); Protein 24g

% Daily Value: Vitamin A 2%; Vitamin C 0%; Calcium 12%; Iron 32%; Folic Acid 24%

Exchanges: 3 Starch, 2 Very Lean Meat

Carbohydrate Choices: 3

"I love hamburgers and am glad I can still eat them. These burgers, combined with the beans, give me a lot of fiber! I top them with my favorites: grilled onions, lettuce and tomato. I might even melt a piece of fat-free American cheese on top for extra flavor!"

LORI S.

Garbanzo Bean Sandwiches

8 SERVINGS

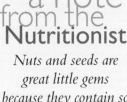

a note from the Nutritionist

Nuts and seeds are great little gems because they contain so many nutrients, but adding them in moderation is best because they are high in fat. Fortunately, a little goes a long way in terms of flavor, and if nuts and seeds are lightly toasted, they become flavor giants!

1 can (15 to 16 ounces) garbanzo beans, rinsed and drained

1/2 cup water

2 tablespoons chopped fresh parsley

2 tablespoons chopped walnuts

1 tablespoon finely chopped onion

1 clove garlic, finely chopped

1/2 medium cucumber, sliced

4 whole-wheat pita breads (6 inches in diameter)

Lettuce leaves

1 medium tomato, seeded and chopped (3/4 cup)

1/2 cup cucumber ranch dressing

1 Place beans, water, parsley, walnuts, onion and garlic in food processor or blender. Cover and process until smooth.

2 Cut cucumber slices into fourths. Cut each pita bread in half to form 2 pockets; line with lettuce leaves. Spoon 2 tablespoons bean mixture into each pita half. Add tomato, cucumber and dressing.

1 Serving: Calories 225 (Calories from Fat 90); Fat 10g; Saturated Fat 1g (4% of Calories from Saturated Fat); *Trans* Fat 0g; Cholesterol 5mg; Omega-3 1g; Sodium 370mg

Carbohydrate 32g (Dietary Fiber 7g); Protein 9g

% Daily Value: Vitamin A 8%; Vitamin C 6%; Calcium 6%; Iron 14%; Folic Acid 30%

Exchanges: 2 Starch, 1/2 Lean Meat, 1 Fat

Carbohydrate Choices: 2

"Twice a week, I take an exercise class, and I also go dancing once or twice a week.
That burns off calories and keeps me in shape—it is also a lot of fun."

WANDA S.

Chunky Vegetable Chowder

PREP: 10 MIN
COOK: 10 MIN

6 SERVINGS

1 tablespoon butter

1 medium green bell pepper, coarsely chopped (1 cup)

1 medium red bell pepper, coarsely chopped (1 cup)

8 medium green onions, sliced (1/2 cup)

3 cups water

3/4 pound new potatoes, cut into 1-inch pieces (2 1/2 cups)

1 tablespoon chopped fresh or 1 teaspoon dried thyme leaves

1/2 teaspoon salt

1 cup nonfat half-and-half

1/8 teaspoon pepper

2 cans (15 ounces each) cream-style corn

1 Melt butter in 4-quart Dutch oven over medium heat. Cook bell peppers and green onions in butter 3 minutes, stirring occasionally.

2 Stir in water, potatoes, thyme and salt. Heat to boiling; reduce heat to low. Cover and simmer about 10 minutes or until potatoes are tender.

3 Stir in remaining ingredients; cook about 1 minute or until hot (do not boil).

a note from the Nutritionist

Make a meatless meal one or two nights a week. If you are making the switch to meatless eating, you may want to cut your ingredients, as in this hearty chowder, into larger pieces, which makes them seem more filling and plentiful.

"I look for recipes with lots of antioxidants, like the green and red peppers, that are good for your heart. From reading labels and recipes, I've learned that I'll get a good portion of my daily veggies from this chowder."

CATHY P.

1 Serving: Calories 260 (Calories from Fat 90); Fat 10g; Saturated Fat 3g (11% of Calories from Saturated Fat); *Trans* Fat 2g; Cholesterol 10mg; Omega-3 0g; Sodium 650mg

Carbohydrate 41g (Dietary Fiber 5g); Protein 7g

% Daily Value: Vitamin A 40%; Vitamin C 56%; Calcium 10%; Iron 10%; Folic Acid 14%

Exchanges: 2 1/2 Starch, 1 Vegetable, 1 Fat

Carbohydrate Choices: 3

Vegetarian Virtues

Nutrition Components

Being a vegetarian can be a healthful way to eat if you plan carefully, get your essential nutrients and eat a wide variety of foods—all of which are easy to do.

Nutritious components of a good vegetarian diet include:

Plant proteins, which alone *can* provide enough of the essential and nonessential amino acids (the building blocks of protein), as long as the sources of protein are varied.

Soy protein has been shown to be equal to animal protein. It can be your sole protein source, if you choose.

Whole grains, legumes, vegetables, seeds and nuts all contain both essential and nonessential amino acids, so you no longer need to combine these foods within a given meal to create a "complete" protein.

Dried beans, spinach, enriched products, brewer's yeast and dried fruits are good plant sources of **iron**.

Your body can best use the iron these foods provide if you eat them with foods that are good sources of **vitamin C** such as oranges, tomatoes, strawberries or bell peppers.

Vitamin B-12 can be the most challenging vitamin for vegetarians to get, since it is found naturally only in animal sources. Fortified cereals, fortified soy beverages, brewer's yeast and other fortified foods, as well as food supplements, contain B-12.

Calcium and Vitamin D—Studies show that vegetarians absorb and retain more calcium from foods than do non-vegetarians. Spinach, kale, broccoli, dairy products, some legumes and soybeans are good plant sources of calcium.

Zinc is needed for growth and development; good plant sources include grains, nuts and legumes.

Nutrition Guidelines

Punch up your choices by following five simple guidelines:

Choose whole or unrefined grains or use fortified or enriched cereal products.

Eat a wide variety of fruits and vegetables, including foods that are good sources of vitamins A and C. (See "The Value of Vegetables and Fruits for Your Heart," page 197.)

Select fat-free (skim) milk and other dairy products.

Limit your use of eggs, or buy eggs that are lower in cholesterol. Cholesterol intake should be no more than 300 milligrams of cholesterol per day.

Minimize your intake of sweets and higher-fat foods; they are low in nutrients and high in calories.

Bean and Barley Soup

PREP: 10 MIN
COOK: 13 MIN

5 SERVINGS

1 tablespoon canola or soybean oil

2 small onions, sliced

2 cloves garlic, chopped

1 teaspoon ground cumin

1/2 cup uncooked quick-cooking barley

1 can (15 to 16 ounces) garbanzo beans, undrained

1 can (15 ounces) black beans, rinsed and drained

1 can (14 1/2 ounces) stewed tomatoes, undrained

1 package (10 ounces) frozen lima beans*

3 cups water

2 tablespoons chopped fresh cilantro or parsley

*1 can (15 to 16 ounces) lima beans, rinsed and drained, can be substituted for the frozen lima beans.

1 Heat oil in 4-quart Dutch oven over medium heat. Cook onions, garlic and cumin in oil about 3 minutes, stirring occasionally, until onions are crisp-tender.

2 Stir in remaining ingredients except cilantro. Heat to boiling; reduce heat to low. Cover and simmer about 10 minutes or until lima beans are tender. Stir in cilantro.

a note from Dr. B

This tasty, quick soup contains many good-for-you ingredients, including barley, beans and tomatoes. These provide high fiber, heart-friendly folic acid and lots of iron that is good for the iron in your blood, and all with a reasonable amount of fat, extremely important for your overall health.

1 Serving: Calories 390 (Calories from Fat 55); Fat 6g; Saturated Fat 1g (1% of Calories from Saturated Fat); *Trans* Fat 0g; Cholesterol 0mg; Omega-3 0g; Sodium 940mg

Carbohydrate 81g (Dietary Fiber 20g); Protein 22g

% Daily Value: Vitamin A 8%; Vitamin C 18%; Calcium 14%; Iron 34%; Folic Acid 74%

Exchanges: 5 Starch, 1 Vegetable

Carbohydrate Choices: 5 1/2

"I've made it a point to drink a lot more water. I always have some at my desk and take a water bottle with me when I am on the go. I also try to get more liquids in the foods I eat, like this yummy soup."

SHERRY L.

Broccoli-Cheese Soup

6 SERVINGS (1 CUP EACH)

a note from Dr. B

Soy protein, in the context of a low-fat, low-cholesterol diet, can help reduce the risk of heart disease. Research suggests that when about 25 grams of soy protein is eaten daily from soy foods, blood cholesterol levels tend to drop. This yummy soup is a great start, containing about one-third of the 25 daily grams in one serving.

1 tablespoon canola or soybean oil

1 medium onion, chopped (1/2 cup)

1 tablespoon all-purpose flour

1 teaspoon salt

3 cups soy milk or fat-free (skim) milk

2 teaspoons cornstarch

1 1/2 cups shredded reduced-fat sharp Cheddar cheese (6 ounces)

3 cups bite-size fresh or frozen (thawed) broccoli flowerets

1 cup low-fat popped popcorn, if desired

1 Heat oil in 3-quart saucepan over medium heat. Stir in onion, flour and salt. Cook 2 to 3 minutes, stirring constantly, until onion is soft.

2 Stir soy milk and cornstarch in small bowl with wire whisk until smooth. Gradually stir into onion mixture. Cook 5 to 6 minutes, stirring frequently, until thick and bubbly.

3 Stir in cheese. Cook about 3 minutes, stirring frequently, until cheese is melted. Stir in broccoli. Cook about 1 minute or until hot, stirring occasionally. If desired, top this creamy cheese soup with popcorn

1 Serving: Calories 140 (Calories from Fat 45); Fat 5g; Saturated Fat 1g (10% of Calories from Saturated Fat); *Trans* Fat 0g; Cholesterol 5mg; Omega-3 0g; Sodium 730mg

Carbohydrate 14g (Dietary Fiber 2g); Protein 10g

% Daily Value: Vitamin A 20%; Vitamin C 34%; Calcium 32%; Iron 4%; Folic Acid 10%

Exchanges: 1/2 Milk, 1 Vegetable, 1/2 High-Fat Meat, 1/2 Fat

Carbohydrate Choices: 1

"At every meal, I consciously choose heart-healthy foods— plenty of fruits and vegetables, lean meats, skim milk and water.

This recipe helps because it has so many great ingredients in it."

SHERRY L.

Springtime Pasta and Sausage

PREP: 10 MIN
COOK: 15 MIN

6 SERVINGS

8 ounces uncooked regular or whole-wheat spaghetti

12 ounces Italian turkey sausage links, thinly sliced

1/2 teaspoon fennel seed

2 cloves garlic, minced

1 package (9 ounces) frozen sugar snap peas in a pouch, thawed

2 cups sliced fresh mushrooms (about 5 ounces)

1/3 cup chicken broth

5 roma (plum) tomatoes, chopped

4 medium green onions, cut into 1-inch pieces

1/3 cup chopped fresh parsley

1 Cook spaghetti as directed on package in 4-quart Dutch oven or saucepan; drain and return to Dutch oven.

2 Meanwhile, cook sausage, fennel and garlic in 10-inch nonstick skillet over medium heat, stirring frequently, until sausage is no longer pink in center; drain. Remove sausage from skillet.

3 Place sugar snap peas, mushrooms and broth in skillet. Heat to boiling; reduce heat to medium-low. Simmer uncovered 3 to 4 minutes, stirring frequently. Stir in tomatoes and green onions; cook over medium heat, stirring frequently, about 2 minutes. Add sausage and parsley; cook 1 minute longer or until hot.

4 Add sausage mixture to spaghetti in Dutch oven; toss gently to mix.

a note from Dr. B

Becoming a food label reader and really keeping track of what you eat can make a difference. There are now many tasty lower-fat products. Instead of buying regular smoked sausage with 17 grams of fat per serving, you can get smoked turkey sausage with 3 grams of fat per serving.

"I grew up eating sausage and still love it, but since I'm watching my cholesterol, it's not a good choice for me. This recipe made with a healthier turkey sausage satisfies my craving without the saturated fat."

CINDY L.

1 Serving: Calories 290 (Calories from Fat 70); Fat 8g; Saturated Fat 2g (6% of Calories from Saturated Fat); *Trans* Fat 0g; Cholesterol 35mg; Omega-3 0g; Sodium 430mg

Carbohydrate 38g (Dietary Fiber 4g); Protein 17g

% Daily Value: Vitamin A 16%; Vitamin C 28%; Calcium 4%; Iron 20%; Folic Acid 28%

Exchanges: 2 Starch, 1 Vegetable, 1 1/2 Medium-Fat Meat

Carbohydrate Choices: 2 1/2

Barbecued Chicken Pizza

6 SERVINGS

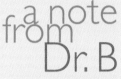

a note from Dr. B

When picking your pizza crust, think thin. The thick crust variety is much higher in fat, calories and carbohydrates per serving than the thin kind.

2 cups shredded cooked chicken breast

1/3 cup barbecue sauce

1 package (10 ounces) ready-to-serve thin Italian pizza crust (12 inches in diameter)

3 roma (plum) tomatoes, sliced

1 cup shredded reduced-fat Monterey Jack cheese (4 ounces)

Fresh cilantro leaves

1 Heat oven to 450°. Mix chicken and barbecue sauce in small bowl. Place pizza crust on ungreased cookie sheet; spread chicken mixture over crust. Arrange tomatoes over chicken; sprinkle with cheese.

2 Bake 10 minutes or until cheese is melted and crust is browned. Sprinkle with cilantro.

1 Serving: Calories 285 (Calories from Fat 80); Fat 9g; Saturated Fat 4g (11% of Calories from Saturated Fat); *Trans* Fat 0g; Cholesterol 50mg; Omega-3 0g; Sodium 560mg

Carbohydrate 29g (Dietary Fiber 1g); Protein 22g

% Daily Value: Vitamin A 8%; Vitamin C 4%; Calcium 14%; Iron 12%; Folic Acid 16%

Exchanges: 2 Starch, 2 Lean Meat

Carbohydrate Choices: 2

PREP: 10 MIN

BAKE: 10 MIN

Rush-Hour Tuna Melts

4 SERVINGS (2 SANDWICHES EACH)

a note from Dr. B

It's never too early to include kids in heart-healthy eating, so they learn good habits from day one. Ask them to help plan and prepare dinner to get them interested in foods and what they eat. In this easy recipe, they can mix the tuna and mayonnaise and make their own sandwiches. (You may need to help them use the oven, though.)

1 can (6 ounces) solid white tuna in water, drained and flaked

3/4 cup chopped celery

2 tablespoons finely chopped onion

1/2 teaspoon grated lemon peel, if desired

1/3 cup fat-free mayonnaise or salad dressing

4 whole wheat English muffins, split and lightly toasted

8 slices tomato

1 cup shredded reduced-fat Cheddar or Monterey Jack cheese (4 ounces)

1 Heat oven to 350°. Mix tuna, celery, onion, lemon peel and mayonnaise in medium bowl.

2 Spread about 3 tablespoons tuna mixture on each English muffin half. Top each with tomato slice; sprinkle with cheese. Place on ungreased cookie sheet.

3 Bake 8 to 10 minutes or until cheese is melted and sandwiches are thoroughly heated.

1 Serving: Calories 265 (Calories from Fat 35); Fat 4g; Saturated Fat 2g (6% of Calories from Saturated Fat); *Trans* Fat 0g; Cholesterol 20mg; Omega-3 0g; Sodium 895mg

Carbohydrate 33g (Dietary Fiber 5g); Protein 24g

% Daily Value: Vitamin A 12%; Vitamin C 8%; Calcium 38%; Iron 14%; Folic Acid 12%

Exchanges: 2 Starch, 2 1/2 Very Lean Meat, 1/2 Fat

Carbohydrate Choices: 2

"I am not afraid to alter recipes when possible—
I use reduced-fat cheese, no-fat cheese, turkey sausage, turkey pepperoni,
chicken for beef. Once I started doing that, I felt more confident trying it in other recipes."

NANCY D.

Snap Pea Frittata

PREP: **5 MIN**

COOK: **10 MIN**

BROIL: **2 MIN**

6 SERVINGS

1 tablespoon olive or canola oil

1/2 cup sliced onion

1 teaspoon dried tarragon leaves

1 package (9 ounces) frozen sugar snap peas in a pouch, thawed

1 cup shredded lettuce

6 eggs

1/2 teaspoon salt

1/4 teaspoon pepper

2 tablespoons grated Parmesan cheese

1 Set oven control to broil. Heat oil in 10-inch ovenproof skillet over medium heat. Cook onion in oil 2 minutes, stirring frequently. Stir in tarragon and sugar snap peas; cook uncovered 3 minutes, stirring frequently, until peas are tender. Stir in lettuce.

2 Beat eggs with salt and pepper in medium bowl with wire whisk. Pour over vegetables in skillet. Cook 8 to 10 minutes or until eggs just begin to set.

3 Sprinkle with cheese. Broil 5 inches from heat 1 to 2 minutes or until frittata is golden brown and puffs up.

"In this wonderful change-from-the-ordinary dish, the vegetables are right in the main dish and there's no way I can get out of eating them. After trying to eat more vegetables, I discovered that I like them!"

PAT R.

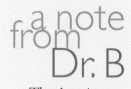

The American Heart Association recommends that cholesterol intake be no more than 300 milligrams a day. If you are watching your cholesterol, you might try using egg product substitutes instead of eggs or using the Omega-3 eggs with less cholesterol that are available in some markets.

1 Serving: Calories 125 (Calories from Fat 70); Fat 8g; Saturated Fat 2g (17% of Calories from Saturated Fat); *Trans* Fat 0g; Cholesterol 215mg; Omega-3 0g; Sodium 300mg

Carbohydrate 4g (Dietary Fiber 1g); Protein 9g

% Daily Value: Vitamin A 8%; Vitamin C 16%; Calcium 6%; Iron 8%; Folic Acid 10%

Exchanges: 1 Vegetable, 1 Medium-Fat Meat

Carbohydrate Choices: 0

PREP: 10 MIN
COOK: 10 MIN

Halibut-Asparagus Stir-Fry

4 SERVINGS

1 pound halibut, swordfish or tuna fillets, cut into 1-inch pieces

1 medium onion, thinly sliced

1 teaspoon finely chopped gingerroot

3 cloves garlic, finely chopped

1 package (9 ounces) frozen asparagus cuts in a pouch, thawed and drained

1 package (8 ounces) sliced fresh mushrooms (3 cups)

1 medium tomato, cut into thin wedges

2 tablespoons reduced-sodium soy sauce

1 tablespoon lemon juice

1 Spray 10-inch nonstick skillet with cooking spray; heat over medium-high heat. Stir-fry fish, onion, gingerroot, garlic and asparagus in skillet 2 to 3 minutes or until fish almost flakes with fork.

2 Carefully stir in remaining ingredients. Cook 5 to 7 minutes or until thoroughly heated and fish flakes easily with fork. Serve with additional soy sauce if desired.

"This is a great way to eat more fish. I love stir-fry, but I've always used chicken or beef and never thought of using fish."

MARILYN B.

1 Serving: Calories 165 (Calories from Fat 20); Fat 2g; Saturated Fat 0g (2% of Calories from Saturated Fat); *Trans* Fat 0g; Cholesterol 60mg; Omega-3 0g; Sodium 370mg

Carbohydrate 11g (Dietary Fiber 3g); Protein 26g

% Daily Value: Vitamin A 16%; Vitamin C 20%; Calcium 4%; Iron 8%; Folic Acid 28%

Exchanges: 2 Vegetable, 3 Very Lean Meat

Carbohydrate Choices: 1

Grilled Salmon with Hazelnut Butter

PREP: 10 MIN
GRILL: 10 MIN

4 SERVINGS

Hazelnut Butter (below)

1 pound salmon, trout or other medium-firm fish fillets

1/2 teaspoon salt

1/8 teaspoon pepper

1 Brush grill rack with canola or soybean oil. Heat coals or gas grill for direct heat. Make Hazelnut Butter; set aside.

2 If fish fillets are large, cut into 4 serving pieces. Sprinkle both sides of fish with salt and pepper.

3 Cover and grill fish 4 to 6 inches from medium heat 4 minutes. Turn; spread about 1 tablespoon hazelnut butter over each fillet. Cover and grill 4 to 6 minutes longer or until fish flakes easily with fork.

a note from the Nutritionist

Nuts contain a type of good-for-you fat. Any type of nut— almond, pecan, walnut or cashew—can be substituted for the hazelnuts. Nuts can become rancid quickly, so it's best to store them in the freezer and taste them before using in your recipes.

Hazelnut Butter

2 tablespoons finely chopped hazelnuts

1 tablespoon chopped fresh parsley

2 tablespoons butter, softened

1 teaspoon lemon juice

Spread nuts in shallow microwavable bowl or pie plate. Microwave uncovered on High 30 seconds to 1 minute, stirring once or twice, until light brown; cool. Mix hazelnuts and remaining ingredients in small bowl.

1 **Serving:** Calories 230 (Calories from Fat 125); Fat 14g; Saturated Fat 6g (22% of Calories from Saturated Fat); *Trans* Fat 0g; Cholesterol 90mg; Omega-3 0g; Sodium 400mg

Carbohydrate 1g (Dietary Fiber 0g); Protein 25g

% **Daily Value:** Vitamin A 8%; Vitamin C 2%; Calcium 2%; Iron 4%; Folic Acid 10%

Exchanges: 3 1/2 Lean Meat, 1 Fat

Carbohydrate Choices: 0

"I've increased the amount of fish in my diet, and this is one of my favorites. Not only is fish good for prevention of heart disease, but my arthritis has improved since I'm eating good Omega-3 oils."

TIMOTHY C.

Three-Grain Medley (page 169)

Great Grains, Beans and Legumes

Look to these great grain, bean and legume recipes to solve the puzzle of how to serve appealing meals that are also good for you.

PREP: 10 MIN
COOK: 55 MIN

Confetti Wild Rice

6 SERVINGS

a note from Dr. B

If your overall amount of saturated fat is low, it's okay to use a small amount of butter, as in this recipe where a little butter adds a great amount of flavor. If you prefer to use oil, canola, olive or soybean oil is recommended.

1 tablespoon butter

1 1/2 cups sliced fresh mushrooms (4 ounces)

1/2 cup uncooked wild rice

2 medium green onions, thinly sliced (2 tablespoons)

1 1/4 cups water

1/2 teaspoon salt

1/4 teaspoon pepper

1 package (10 ounces) frozen chopped broccoli, thawed and drained

1 tablespoon lemon juice

1 Melt butter in 10-inch nonstick skillet over medium heat. Cook mushrooms, wild rice and green onions in butter about 3 minutes, stirring occasionally, until onions are tender.

2 Stir in water, salt and pepper. Heat to boiling, stirring occasionally; reduce heat to medium-low. Cover and simmer 40 to 50 minutes or until rice is tender; drain if necessary.

3 Stir in broccoli and lemon juice. Cook uncovered about 2 minutes, stirring occasionally, until thoroughly heated.

"When reading labels, I usually read just the percentage of fat;
it is much quicker than searching for everything on the label.
I don't buy or eat anything in the double digits in total fat.
Usually just under 5 percent per serving, preferably under 3 percent."

NANCY D.

1 Serving: Calories 85 (Calories from Fat 20); Fat 2g; Saturated Fat 1g (13% of Calories from Saturated Fat); *Trans* Fat 0g; Cholesterol 5mg; Omega-3 0g; Sodium 220mg

Carbohydrate 15g (Dietary Fiber 3g); Protein 4g

% Daily Value: Vitamin A 16%; Vitamin C 14%; Calcium 2%; Iron 4%; Folic Acid 10%

Exchanges: 1 Starch

Carbohydrate Choices: 1

Mexican Rice and Bean Bake

PREP: 10 MIN
COOK: 10 MIN
BAKE: 35 MIN
STAND: 5 MIN

6 SERVINGS

1 1/4 cups water

1 cup uncooked instant brown rice

1 1/2 cups picante sauce

1 cup shredded reduced-fat Cheddar cheese (4 ounces)

1/4 cup fat-free cholesterol-free egg product or 1 egg

1 can (15 to 16 ounces) pinto beans, drained

1/4 teaspoon chili powder

1. Heat water to boiling in 1-quart saucepan. Stir in rice; reduce heat to low. Cover and simmer 10 minutes. Meanwhile, heat oven to 350°. Spray square baking dish, 8 x 8 x 2 inches, with cooking spray.

2. Mix rice, 1/2 cup of the picante sauce, 1/2 cup of the cheese and the egg product in medium bowl; press in bottom of baking dish.

3. Mix beans and remaining 1 cup picante sauce in small bowl; spoon over rice mixture. Sprinkle with remaining 1/2 cup cheese and the chili powder.

4. Bake uncovered 30 to 35 minutes or until cheese is melted and bubbly. Let stand 5 minutes before serving.

a note from Dr. B

To lose 1 pound a week, you need to create a 500-calorie daily deficit. Well-balanced plans recommend eating 250 fewer calories each day and burning an additional 250 calories through exercise. The best equation for losing weight and keeping it off equals a healthy diet plus exercise, rather than focusing too much on one or the other.

"If I eat a good lunch, like this rice and bean bake, I can keep going for a few hours before getting hungry. I keep carrots, an apple or other fruit at work to munch on if I'm hungry in the afternoon."

WANDA S.

1 Serving: Calories 195 (Calories from Fat 20); Fat 2g; Saturated Fat 1g (4% of Calories from Saturated Fat); *Trans* Fat 0g; Cholesterol 5mg; Omega-3 0g; Sodium 620mg

Carbohydrate 38g (Dietary Fiber 8g); Protein 14g

% Daily Value: Vitamin A 14%; Vitamin C 8%; Calcium 20%; Iron 16%; Folic Acid 36%

Exchanges: 2 Starch, 1 Vegetable

Carbohydrate Choices: 2 1/2

PREP: **10 MIN**

COOK: **20 MIN**

Onion and Mushroom Quinoa

4 SERVINGS

I teaspoon canola or soybean oil

I cup uncooked quinoa

I small onion, cut into fourths and sliced

I medium carrot, shredded (2/3 cup)

I small green bell pepper, chopped (1/2 cup)

I cup sliced fresh mushrooms (about 2 1/2 ounces)

I teaspoon chopped fresh or 1/4 teaspoon dried thyme leaves

1/4 teaspoon salt

I can (14 ounces) fat-free vegetable broth

1 Heat oil in 2-quart saucepan over medium heat. Cook quinoa and onion in oil 4 to 5 minutes, stirring occasionally, until light brown.

2 Stir in remaining ingredients. Heat to boiling; reduce heat to low. Cover and simmer about 15 minutes or until liquid is absorbed. Fluff with fork.

"Since learning about my high cholesterol, I have been working whole grains into my eating choices. I've found this quinoa is a 'super grain' with a lot of protein and no cholesterol."

KEVIN W.

I Serving: Calories 205 (Calories from Fat 35); Fat 4g; Saturated Fat 0g (2% of Calories from Saturated Fat); *Trans* Fat 0g; Cholesterol 0mg; Omega-3 0g; Sodium 600mg

Carbohydrate 35g (Dietary Fiber 4g); Protein 7g

% Daily Value: Vitamin A 52%; Vitamin C 16%; Calcium 4%; Iron 24%; Folic Acid 8%

Exchanges: 2 Starch, I Vegetable, 1/2 Fat

Carbohydrate Choices: 2

Quinoa-Almond Salad

PREP: 10 MIN
COOK: 17 MIN
STAND: 5 MIN
COOL: 15 MIN

6 SERVINGS

1 cup uncooked quinoa, rinsed

2 cups water

1/2 teaspoon salt

Balsamic Vinaigrette (below)

1/2 cup coarsely shredded carrot (about 1 small)

1/4 cup sliced almonds, toasted*

1/4 cup dried cherries or cranberries

*To toast nuts, bake uncovered in ungreased shallow pan in 350° oven about 10 minutes, stirring occasionally, until golden brown. Or cook in ungreased heavy skillet over medium-low heat 5 to 7 minutes, stirring frequently until browning begins, then stirring constantly until golden brown.

1 Heat quinoa, water and salt to boiling in 2-quart saucepan, stirring once or twice; reduce heat to low. Cover and simmer 12 to 15 minutes or until tender.

2 Remove saucepan from heat; let stand 5 minutes. Fluff quinoa with fork; cool 15 minutes. Meanwhile, make Balsamic Vinaigrette.

3 Mix vinaigrette, quinoa and remaining ingredients in large bowl. Serve warm, or cover and refrigerate about 4 hours or until chilled.

a note from the Nutritionist

Adding toasted nuts to grains, such as quinoa, really brings out the flavor. Quinoa is higher in unsaturated (good) fats and lower in carbohydrates than most grains and is considered a complete protein, so there are many reasons to include it in a heart-healthy diet.

Balsamic Vinaigrette

2 tablespoons chopped fresh parsley

2 tablespoons canola or soybean oil

2 tablespoons balsamic vinegar

1/2 teaspoon salt

Dash of pepper

Shake all ingredients in tightly covered container.

"The addition of almonds and other nuts to my diet helps lower cholesterol, and this colorful salad is a great way to add them."

WANDA S.

1 Serving: Calories 205 (Calories from Fat 80); Fat 9g; Saturated Fat 1g (3% of Calories from Saturated Fat); Trans Fat 0g; Cholesterol 0mg; Omega-3 0g; Sodium 400mg

Carbohydrate 26g (Dietary Fiber 3g); Protein 5g

% Daily Value: Vitamin A 32%; Vitamin C 2%; Calcium 4%; Iron 16%; Folic Acid 4%

Exchanges: 2 Starch, 1 Fat

Carbohydrate Choices: 2

PREP: 10 MIN

COOK: 15 MIN

Orzo Parmesan

4 SERVINGS

a note from the Nutritionist

Italian for "barley," orzo is really a tiny, rice-shaped pasta. Add variety to your meals by substituting this small, complex-carbohydrate-rich pasta for rice in pilafs, salads, soups and casseroles.

1 can (14 ounces) fat-free chicken broth

1/2 cup water

1/4 teaspoon salt

1 1/3 cups uncooked orzo or rosamarina pasta (about 9 ounces)

8 medium green onions, sliced (1/2 cup)

2 cloves garlic, finely chopped

1/4 cup grated Parmesan cheese

1 tablespoon chopped fresh or 1 teaspoon dried basil leaves

1/8 teaspoon freshly ground pepper

1 Heat broth, water and salt to boiling in 2-quart saucepan. Stir in pasta, green onions and garlic.

2 Heat to boiling; reduce heat. Cover and simmer about 12 minutes, stirring occasionally, until most of the liquid is absorbed. Stir in remaining ingredients.

1 Serving: Calories 215 (Calories from Fat 25); Fat 3g; Saturated Fat 1g (6% of Calories from Saturated Fat); *Trans* Fat 0g; Cholesterol 5mg; Omega-3 0g; Sodium 720mg

Carbohydrate 36g (Dietary Fiber 2g); Protein 11g

% Daily Value: Vitamin A 6%; Vitamin C 4%; Calcium 12%; Iron 12%; Folic Acid 28%

Exchanges: 2 1/2 Starch, 1/2 Very Lean Meat

Carbohydrate Choices: 2 1/2

Curried Lentil and Barley Casserole

PREP: 10 MIN
COOK: 45 MIN

4 SERVINGS

1/4 cup dried lentils, sorted and rinsed

2 cups fat-free vegetable or chicken broth

1 teaspoon curry powder

3 cloves garlic, finely chopped

3/4 cup uncooked quick-cooking barley

1 bag (1 pound) frozen corn, green peas and carrots (or other combination)

1 cup crumbled feta cheese (2 ounces)

1 Heat lentils, broth, curry powder and garlic to boiling in 3-quart saucepan; reduce heat. Cover and simmer 30 minutes, stirring occasionally.

2 Stir in barley and frozen vegetables. Heat to boiling; reduce heat. Cover and simmer 10 to 15 minutes, stirring occasionally, until lentils and barley are tender and liquid is absorbed. Sprinkle with cheese.

"This is an excellent choice for a cool fall day. Lentils and barley give me a great supply of fiber and the curry adds a little flavor zing! Great with a tossed salad and warm roll."

LORI S.

a note from Dr. B

Scientists are discovering that the process of aging is in many cases somewhat reversible. Recent statistics show that a sedentary life, leads to obesity, a weakened heart muscle, lack of energy and a sluggish metabolism. Exercise is a major component of the health package, so get moving today and stay moving!

1 Serving: Calories 290 (Calories from Fat 65); Fat 7g; Saturated Fat 4g (12% of Calories from Saturated Fat); *Trans* Fat 0g; Cholesterol 25mg; Omega-3 0g; Sodium 880mg

Carbohydrate 56g (Dietary Fiber 13g); Protein 14g

% Daily Value: Vitamin A 100%; Vitamin C 6%; Calcium 18%; Iron 18%; Folic Acid 30%

Exchanges: 3 Starch, 1 Other Carbohydrates

Carbohydrate Choices: 4

Getting to the Heart of the Matter with Whole Grains

The American Heart Association (AHA) recommends that you get most of your carbohydrates from complex carbohydrates—found in vegetables, fruits and grains—rather than from simple carbohydrates found in refined sugars. Complex-carbohydrate foods are usually low in calories, saturated fat and cholesterol. The AHA also recommends that we consume 25 to 30 grams of fiber every day.

WHICH FOODS ARE SOURCES OF COMPLEX CARBOHYDRATES?

Starches—flour, bread, rice, corn, oats, barley, potatoes, legumes, fruits and vegetables

Insoluble Fiber—whole-wheat breads and cereals, wheat bran, apples, beets, Brussels sprouts, cabbage, carrots, cauliflower and turnips

Soluble Fiber—oat bran, oats, legumes, citrus fruits, strawberries, apples, rice bran, barley and psyllium seed

HOW MUCH OF THESE FOODS SHOULD I EAT EVERY DAY?

At least 6 servings of grains and cereals

At least 5 servings of fruits and vegetables

WHICH FOODS ARE SOURCES OF SIMPLE CARBOHYDRATES?

Table sugar, brown sugar, honey, corn syrup, sugar alcohols and any other simple sugars

THE WHOLE PACKAGE

Whole-grain foods are excellent sources of heart-healthy soluble fiber; because they include all parts of the grain, they include all the grain's nutrients, too. Foods made with refined grains lack the nutritious bran and germ components—even if the grains are enriched later, only some of these nutrients are restored. Choosing the "whole food" gives you the whole package of health benefits.

WHOLE-GRAIN BOOSTERS

Make sure that at least half of the grain-based foods you eat come from whole-grain sources. Here are some easy places to start:

Eat whole-grain hot or cold cereals, like oatmeal, oat bran or farina. (Skip granola as it is often high in fat.)

Instead of breads made with refined flours, eat whole wheat, rye or multi-grain breads. Enjoy bagels, English muffins, pita bread and corn tortillas.

Choose brown rice over white rice, hulled barley over pearled barley.

Choose whole wheat pasta over plain pasta.

Substitute whole wheat flour for half the white flour called for when baking breads, bran or fruit muffins, pancakes, biscuits or waffles.

Experiment with less-common whole grains like whole-grain barley, bulgur, kasha and quinoa. (For delicious recipes, see pages 156–157.)

Boost your fiber amount by:

Eating a variety of fresh fruits and vegetables, including the skins and seeds.

Snacking on fiber-rich foods like air-popped popcorn, nuts and soy nuts, raisins or other dried fruits.

Eating high-fiber cereal with fruit for breakfast, a whole-grain-bread sandwich with veggies for lunch and vegetable soup with whole-grain crackers for dinner.

Add fiber cereals, such as Fiber One, or bran when making muffins, cookies and snack mixes.

Top salads and soups with flaxseed, popcorn, wheat germ or high-fiber cereal. Top pancakes, waffles or toast with fruit sauces with seeds, such as strawberries, raspberries or kiwifruit.

Add beans to chilis, soups, stews, casseroles, tortillas, tacos and other ethnic dishes.

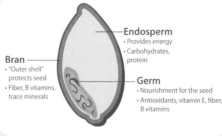

Endosperm
· Provides energy
· Carbohydrates, protein

Bran
· "Outer shell" protects seed
· Fiber, B vitamins, trace minerals

Germ
· Nourishment for the seed
· Antioxidants, vitamin E, fiber, B vitamins

Barley, Corn and Lima Bean Sauté

PREP: **10 MIN**
COOK: **20 MIN**
STAND: **5 MIN**

4 SERVINGS

1 1/3 cups water

2/3 cup uncooked quick-cooking barley

1 tablespoon butter

1 large onion, chopped (1 cup)

1 clove garlic, finely chopped

2 tablespoons chopped fresh or 2 teaspoons dried thyme leaves

1/2 teaspoon salt

1 bag (1 pound) frozen whole kernel corn, thawed and drained

1 package (10 ounces) frozen lima beans, thawed and drained

1 Heat water to boiling in 1 1/2-quart saucepan. Stir in barley; reduce heat to low. Cover and simmer 10 to 12 minutes or until tender. Let stand covered 5 minutes.

2 Melt butter in 10-inch skillet over medium-high heat. Cook onion and garlic in butter about 2 minutes, stirring occasionally, until onion is crisp-tender.

3 Stir in barley and remaining ingredients. Cook about 5 minutes, stirring occasionally, until thoroughly heated.

a note from Dr. B

Attitude is everything! Telling yourself that you have to exercise in order to lose weight takes the fun out of your workout. Instead, focus on positive outcomes: the extra energy you'll get from working out and the well-toned body you'll have—plus the healthy heart!

1 Serving: Calories 335 (Calories from Fat 35); Fat 4g; Saturated Fat 2g (5% of Calories from Saturated Fat); *Trans* Fat 0g; Cholesterol 10mg; Omega-3 0g; Sodium 360mg

Carbohydrate 77g (Dietary Fiber 15g); Protein 13g

% Daily Value: Vitamin A 12%; Vitamin C 12%; Calcium 4%; Iron 14%; Folic Acid 16%

Exchanges: 4 Starch, 1 Other Carbohydrates

Carbohydrate Choices: 5

PREP: 10 MIN
STAND: 10 MIN
BAKE: 10 MIN

White Bean and Spinach Pizza

8 SERVINGS

1/2 cup sun-dried tomato halves (not oil-packed)

1 can (15 to 16 ounces) great northern or navy beans, rinsed and drained

2 medium cloves garlic, finely chopped

1 package (10 ounces) ready-to-serve thin Italian pizza crust (12 inches in diameter)

1/4 teaspoon dried oregano leaves

1 cup firmly packed washed fresh spinach leaves (from 10-ounce bag), shredded

1/2 cup shredded reduced-fat Colby-Monterey Jack cheese (2 ounces)

1 Heat oven to 425°. Pour enough boiling water over dried tomatoes to cover; let stand 10 minutes. Drain. Cut into thin strips; set aside.

2 Place beans and garlic in food processor. Cover and process until smooth. Spread beans over pizza crust. Sprinkle with oregano, tomatoes, spinach and cheese. Place on ungreased cookie sheet.

3 Bake about 10 minutes or until cheese is melted.

"This recipe allows Dave and me to eat pizza and enjoy it. It has lots of good vitamins, is high in fiber and has no cholesterol. Just the right pizza for a healthy heart."

CATHY P.

1 Serving: Calories 180 (Calories from Fat 25); Fat 3g; Saturated Fat 1g (3% of Calories from Saturated Fat); *Trans* Fat 0g; Cholesterol 0mg; Omega-3 0g; Sodium 310mg

Carbohydrate 33g (Dietary Fiber 5g); Protein 10g

% Daily Value: Vitamin A 10%; Vitamin C 2%; Calcium 10%; Iron 20%; Folic Acid 24%

Exchanges: 2 Starch, 1/2 Fat

Carbohydrate Choices: 2

Tabbouleh with Garbanzo Beans

PREP: 15 MIN
STAND: 1 HR

a note from the Nutritionist

Seeking new adventures and eating experiences can be key for heart-healthy eating. Other countries give us many foods that are low in fat and high in fiber, complex carbohydrates, vitamins and minerals. Tabbouleh, a favorite from the Middle East, features bulgur wheat kernels that have been steamed, dried and crushed.

1 Serving: Calories 300 (Calories from Fat 65); Fat 7g; Saturated Fat 1g (3% of Calories from Saturated Fat); *Trans* Fat 0g; Cholesterol 0mg; Omega-3 0g; Sodium 330mg

Carbohydrate 60g (Dietary Fiber 16g); Protein 15g

% Daily Value: Vitamin A 44%; Vitamin C 60%; Calcium 12%; Iron 31%; Folic Acid 64%

Exchanges: 3 Starch, 3 Vegetable

Carbohydrate Choices: 4

4 SERVINGS

1 1/2 cups boiling water

3/4 cup uncooked bulgur

Lemon-Garlic Dressing (below)

3 medium tomatoes, chopped (about 2 1/4 cups)

8 medium green onions, sliced (1/2 cup)

1 medium green bell pepper, chopped (1 cup)

1 cup chopped cucumber

3/4 cup chopped fresh parsley

3 tablespoons chopped fresh or 1 tablespoon dried mint leaves, crumbled

1 can (15 to 16 ounces) garbanzo beans, drained

1. Pour boiling water over bulgur in medium bowl; let stand 1 hour. Meanwhile, make Lemon-Garlic Dressing.

2. Drain any remaining water from bulgur. Mix bulgur and remaining ingredients in large bowl; toss with dressing.

"For my sweet tooth, I keep sugarless candy on hand and have one of them once in a while in the afternoon. I like to try different foods, so this is a great recipe for me; it is very refreshing and has lots of vegetables, which I like."

WANDA S

Lemon-Garlic Dressing

1/4 cup lemon juice

1 tablespoon canola or soybean oil

1/4 teaspoon salt

1/4 teaspoon pepper

3 cloves garlic, finely chopped

Shake all ingredients in tightly covered container.

Roasted Sweet Pepper Pasta Salad with Herbs and Feta

6 SERVINGS

2 large red or yellow bell peppers, cut into 1-inch pieces

1 medium red onion, cut into wedges (about 2 cups)

Cooking spray

3 cups uncooked penne pasta (10 ounces)

1 cup sliced 70%-less-fat turkey pepperoni (about 3 ounces), cut in half

2 ounces feta cheese, crumbled (1/2 cup)

1/2 cup fat-free Italian dressing

2 tablespoons chopped fresh basil leaves

1 tablespoon chopped fresh mint leaves

1 Heat oven to 450°. Spray rectangular pan, 13 x 9 x 2 inches, with cooking spray. Place bell peppers and onion in single layer in pan. Spray vegetables with cooking spray. Bake uncovered 15 to 20 minutes or until vegetables are lightly browned and tender.

2 Meanwhile, cook and drain pasta as directed on package. Rinse with cold water; drain.

3 Toss bell peppers, onion, pasta and remaining ingredients in large bowl. Serve immediately, or refrigerate 1 to 2 hours.

1 Serving: Calories 270 (Calories from Fat 45); Fat 5g; Saturated Fat 2g (7% of Calories from Saturated Fat); *Trans* Fat 0g; Cholesterol 20mg; Omega-3 0g; Sodium 640mg

Carbohydrate 44g (Dietary Fiber 3g); Protein 12g

% Daily Value: Vitamin A 68%; Vitamin C 88%; Calcium 6%; Iron 14%; Folic Acid 30%

Exchanges: 2 1/2 Starch, 1 Vegetable, 1 Lean Meat

Carbohydrate Choices: 3

"Having high blood pressure, I am sure to take my medicine every day and consistently monitor it.
I also see my doctor very faithfully."

LORI S.

Gorgonzola Linguine with Toasted Walnuts

PREP: 10 MIN
COOK: 15 MIN

6 SERVINGS

4 ounces uncooked linguine

1 tablespoon butter

1 clove garlic, crushed

1 tablespoon all-purpose flour

1 cup evaporated skimmed milk

1/4 cup dry white wine or
chicken broth

1/4 teaspoon salt

1/2 cup crumbled Gorgonzola cheese
(2 ounces)

3 tablespoons walnuts, toasted
and finely chopped*

*To toast nuts, bake uncovered in ungreased
shallow pan in 350° oven about 10 minutes,
stirring occasionally, until golden brown. Or cook
in ungreased heavy skillet over medium-low
heat 5 to 7 minutes, stirring frequently until
browning begins, then stirring constantly
until golden brown.

1 Cook and drain linguine as directed on package.

2 Meanwhile, melt butter in 2-quart saucepan over medium heat. Cook garlic in butter, stirring occasionally, until garlic is golden brown. Stir in flour until smooth and bubbly. Stir in milk, wine and salt. Cook, stirring constantly, until mixture begins to thicken.

3 Reduce heat to medium-low. Stir cheese into sauce; cook, stirring frequently, until cheese is melted. Toss linguine and sauce in large bowl. Sprinkle with walnuts.

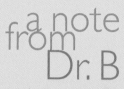

a note from Dr. B

Rethink your drink. Drinking a glass of skim (fat-free) milk with your dinner adds calcium, an important mineral for proper muscle and nerve function (your heart is a muscle). Or drink a glass of cold water, your body's favorite fluid.

"If my family wants butter on something,
I take my portion out first. I use lots of seasonings,
like butter sprinkles, to help lower my cholesterol."

NANCI D.

1 Serving: Calories 185 (Calories from Fat 65); Fat 7g; Saturated Fat 3g (16% of Calories from Saturated Fat); *Trans* Fat 0g; Cholesterol 15mg; Omega-3 0g; Sodium 200mg

Carbohydrate 22g (Dietary Fiber 1g); Protein 8g

% Daily Value: Vitamin A 6%; Vitamin C 0%; Calcium 18%; Iron 8%; Folic Acid 12%

Exchanges: 1 1/2 Starch, 1/2 High-Fat Meat, 1/2 Fat

Carbohydrate Choices: 1 1/2

Nutty Pasta

4 SERVINGS

Think color! Red pepper, papaya and tomato all contain folic acid. Folic acid protects the heart by lowering the body's levels of homocysteine, produced when the body breaks down proteins. High levels of homocysteine give you a higher risk of coronary artery disease, and folic acid may be one reason diets rich in fruits and vegetables are heart-healthy.

4 ounces uncooked vermicelli	1. Cook and drain vermicelli as directed on package. Rinse with cold water; drain.
1 medium red bell pepper, cut into 2 x 1/4-inch strips	
1 small papaya, peeled, seeded and chopped (about 1 cup)	2. Toss vermicelli and remaining ingredients except peanuts in large bowl. Sprinkle with peanuts.
1 medium tomato, chopped (about 3/4 cup)	
2 tablespoons chopped fresh cilantro	
1 tablespoon peanut, canola or soybean oil	
1/2 teaspoon salt	
1/2 teaspoon ground cardamom	
1/4 cup cocktail peanuts, chopped	

"If it has pasta in it, I know my husband will eat it.
He thinks of pasta as a satisfying and filling dinner,
and this one is very tasty and colorful."

PAT R.

1 Serving: Calories 230 (Calories from Fat 65); Fat 7g; Saturated Fat 1g (4% of Calories from Saturated Fat); *Trans* Fat 0g; Cholesterol 0mg; Omega-3 0g; Sodium 390mg

Carbohydrate 36g (Dietary Fiber 5g); Protein 6g

% Daily Value: Vitamin A 56%; Vitamin C 100%; Calcium 2%; Iron 8%; Folic Acid 28%

Exchanges: 1 1/2 Starch, 1/2 Fruit, 1 Vegetable, 1 Fat

Carbohydrate Choices: 2 1/2

Three-Grain Medley

PREP: 10 MIN
COOK: 6 HR

6 SERVINGS

2/3 cup uncooked wheat berries

1/2 cup uncooked hulled or pearl barley

1/2 cup uncooked wild rice

1/4 cup chopped fresh parsley

1/4 cup butter, melted, or canola or soybean oil

2 teaspoons finely shredded lemon peel

6 medium green onions, thinly sliced (6 tablespoons)

2 cloves garlic, finely chopped

2 cans (14 ounces each) vegetable broth

1 jar (2 ounces) diced pimientos, undrained

1 Mix all ingredients in 3 1/2- to 6-quart slow cooker.

2 Cover and cook on Low heat setting 4 to 6 hours or until liquid is absorbed. Stir before serving.

Variation: Use this scrumptious grain filling to stuff bell pepper shells. Steam cleaned bell pepper halves (any color that you are in the mood for) just until tender so that they still hold their shape. Spoon the hot cooked grain mixture into the halves, and sprinkle with shredded Parmesan cheese.

a note from the Nutritionist

Canola oil is recommended for its heart-healthy benefits when you are sautéing or baking. Because this recipe is so low in fat and because the butter imparts a wonderful flavor to the grains, butter is listed first in the ingredient in this recipe. If you prefer to use canola oil, that also works very well in this tasty side dish.

"I now cook a wider variety of foods that are heart-healthy.
My family is not only getting used to more unusual foods,
they like trying them. We usually have at least one meatless dinner a week."

NANCI D.

1 Serving: Calories 195 (Calories from Fat 70); Fat 8g; Saturated Fat 5g (22% of Calories from Saturated Fat); *Trans* Fat 0g; Cholesterol 20mg; Omega-3 0g; Sodium 1030mg

Carbohydrate 28g (Dietary Fiber 4g); Protein 4g

% Daily Value: Vitamin A 24%; Vitamin C 12%; Calcium 2%; Iron 6%; Folic Acid 8%

Exchanges: 2 Starch, 1 Fat

Carbohydrate Choices: 2

PREP: 10 MIN
COOK: 1 HR
CHILL: 2 HR

Wheat Berry Salad

a note from Dr. B

Being a vegetarian can be a very heart-healthy way to eat if you plan carefully, eat a wide variety of foods and get enough calories to meet your energy needs. We know now that plant proteins alone can provide enough of the protein we need daily, as long as the sources of protein are varied.

4 SERVINGS

2 1/2 cups water

1 cup uncooked wheat berries

1 1/2 cups fresh broccoli flowerets

1/2 cup sliced green onions (8 medium)

1 medium carrot, chopped (about 1/2 cup)

1 can (15 to 16 ounces) garbanzo beans, rinsed and drained

Vinaigrette Dressing (below)

1 Heat water and wheat berries to boiling in 2-quart saucepan, stirring occasionally; reduce heat to low. Cover and simmer 50 to 60 minutes or until wheat berries are tender but still chewy; drain if needed.

2 Toss wheat berries and remaining ingredients in large bowl. Cover and refrigerate 1 to 2 hours to blend flavors.

Vinaigrette Dressing

1/4 cup balsamic or cider vinegar

1 tablespoon chopped fresh or 1 teaspoon dried basil leaves

2 tablespoons canola or soybean oil

1/4 teaspoon paprika

1/8 teaspoon salt

1 clove garlic, crushed

Mix all ingredients in small bowl.

1 Serving: Calories 255 (Calories from Fat 90); Fat 10g; Saturated Fat 1g (3% of Calories from Saturated Fat); *Trans* Fat 0g; Cholesterol 0mg; Omega-3 0g; Sodium 240mg

Carbohydrate 45g (Dietary Fiber 17g); Protein 13g

% Daily Value: Vitamin A 68%; Vitamin C 66%; Calcium 10%; Iron 30%; Folic Acid 60%

Exchanges: 2 1/2 Starch, 1 Vegetable, 1/2 Lean Meat

Carbohydrate Choices: 3

Spicy Pear and Bulgur Salad

PREP: 15 MIN
STAND: 1 HR
COOL: 15 MIN
CHILL: 2 HR

6 SERVINGS

2 cups boiling water

2/3 cup uncooked bulgur

2 medium pears, peeled and coarsely chopped (about 2 cups)

1/2 cup raisins

1/4 cup orange juice

2 tablespoons packed brown sugar

1 teaspoon ground cinnamon

1 Pour boiling water over bulgur in medium bowl; let stand 1 hour. Drain any remaining water from bulgur; cool 15 minutes.

2 Mix bulgur, pears and raisins in large bowl.

3 Shake orange juice, brown sugar and cinnamon in tightly covered container. Pour over bulgur mixture; toss to mix. Cover and refrigerate 1 to 2 hours to blend flavors.

a note from Dr. B

Besides strengthening your heart and lungs, exercise has many other benefits: It increases HDL (healthy) cholesterol, lowers blood pressure, strengthens and tones muscles, increases energy and boosts productivity, reduces anxiety and depression, improves posture and strengthens bones.

1 Serving: Calories 140 (Calories from Fat 10); Fat 1g; Saturated Fat 0g (0% of Calories from Saturated Fat); *Trans* Fat 0g; Cholesterol 0mg; Omega-3 0g; Sodium 5mg

Carbohydrate 35g (Dietary Fiber 5g); Protein 2g

% Daily Value: Vitamin A 0%; Vitamin C 10%; Calcium 2%; Iron 6%; Folic Acid 2%

Exchanges: 1 Starch, 1 Fruit

Carbohydrate Choices: 2

Kasha and Beef Supper

4 SERVINGS

2 cups beef broth

1 cup uncooked kasha (roasted buckwheat groats)

1/2 pound extra-lean ground beef

1 medium stalk celery, sliced (1/2 cup)

4 medium green onions, sliced (1/4 cup)

1 can (14 1/2 ounces) diced tomatoes with crushed red pepper and basil, undrained

1/4 teaspoon pepper

1 Heat broth to boiling in 2-quart saucepan. Stir in kasha; reduce heat to medium. Cover and cook about 7 minutes or until tender; drain if needed.

2 Meanwhile, cook beef, celery and green onions in 10-inch nonstick skillet over medium heat 8 to 10 minutes, stirring frequently, until beef is thoroughly cooked; drain.

3 Stir tomatoes and pepper into beef mixture. Heat to boiling; reduce heat. Cover and simmer 5 minutes. Stir in kasha; cook until thoroughly heated.

"I always keep fruit around, an apple in my purse, an orange on my desk. That way, if I am hungry, I am sure to eat something good for me. My kids like this dinner; they are up for trying something new."

NANCI D.

1 Serving: Calories 235 (Calories from Fat 45); Fat 5g; Saturated Fat 2g (7% of Calories from Saturated Fat); *Trans* Fat 0g; Cholesterol 30mg; Omega-3 0g; Sodium 840mg

Carbohydrate 29g (Dietary Fiber 4g); Protein 18g

% Daily Value: Vitamin A 8%; Vitamin C 12%; Calcium 6%; Iron 14%; Folic Acid 10%

Exchanges: 2 Starch, 2 Very Lean Meat

Carbohydrate Choices: 2

PREP: 15 MIN
COOK: 20 MIN

Polenta with Italian Vegetables

6 SERVINGS

a note from Dr. B

Anytime you start mixing grains, fruits and vegetables in one dish, the result is the same: You get high fiber, high vitamins and minerals, low calories, low saturated fat, low cholesterol—and great flavor. Now that's heart-healthy eating at its finest.

1 cup whole-grain yellow cornmeal

3/4 cup cold water

2 1/2 cups boiling water

1/2 teaspoon salt

2/3 cup shredded Swiss cheese

2 teaspoons canola or soybean oil

4 medium zucchini or yellow summer squash, sliced (about 4 cups)

1 medium red bell pepper, chopped (1 cup)

1 small onion, chopped (1/4 cup)

1 clove garlic, finely chopped

1/4 cup chopped fresh or 1 tablespoon dried basil leaves

1 can (about 14 ounces) artichoke hearts, drained

1 Beat cornmeal and cold water in 2-quart saucepan with wire whisk. Stir in boiling water and salt. Cook over medium-high heat, stirring constantly, until mixture thickens and boils; reduce heat. Cover and simmer 10 minutes, stirring occasionally. Stir in cheese until smooth; keep polenta warm.

2 Heat oil in 10-inch nonstick skillet over medium-high heat. Cook zucchini, bell pepper, onion and garlic in oil about 5 minutes, stirring occasionally, until vegetables are crisp-tender. Stir in basil and artichoke hearts. Serve vegetable mixture over polenta.

1 Serving: Calories 185 (Calories from Fat 55); Fat 6g; Saturated Fat 2g (11% of Calories from Saturated Fat); *Trans* Fat 0g; Cholesterol 10mg; Omega-3 0g; Sodium 430mg

Carbohydrate 31g (Dietary Fiber 7g); Protein 9g

% Daily Value: Vitamin A 48%; Vitamin C 46%; Calcium 16%; Iron 14%; Folic Acid 24%

Exchanges: 1 Starch, 3 Vegetable, 1 Fat

Carbohydrate Choices: 2

"Cornmeal has such a great flavor, so polenta with lots of good-for-me veggies is a great way to get more vegetables into my daily eating!"
MARILYN B.

Oriental Stir-Fry with Millet

6 SERVINGS

2 1/4 cups chicken broth

1 cup uncooked millet

2 bags (1 pound each) frozen broccoli, red pepper, onions and mushrooms, thawed

1 1/3 cups apple juice

1/4 cup reduced-sodium soy sauce

2 tablespoons cornstarch

1/2 teaspoon ground ginger

2 cups cut-up cooked chicken or turkey

1 Heat broth to boiling in 1 1/2-quart saucepan. Stir in millet; reduce heat to low. Cover and simmer 20 minutes.

2 Meanwhile, spray 12-inch nonstick skillet with cooking spray; heat over medium-high heat. Add vegetables; stir-fry 2 minutes. Stir in 1/3 cup of the apple juice; reduce heat to medium. Cover and cook about 3 minutes or until vegetables are crisp-tender.

3 While vegetables are cooking, mix remaining 1 cup apple juice, the soy sauce, cornstarch and ginger in small bowl until smooth.

4 Gradually stir apple juice mixture into vegetable mixture. Heat to boiling, stirring constantly. Boil and stir 1 minute. Stir in chicken; cook until thoroughly heated. Toss with cooked millet.

*"I keep sugarless
flavored ice pops in the freezer
for a frozen treat after a meal."*

NANCY D.

1 Serving: Calories 295 (Calories from Fat 55); Fat 6g; Saturated Fat 1g (4% of Calories from Saturated Fat); *Trans* Fat 0g; Cholesterol 40mg; Omega-3 0g; Sodium 790mg

Carbohydrate 44g (Dietary Fiber 6g); Protein 22g

% Daily Value: Vitamin A 56%; Vitamin C 74%; Calcium 4%; Iron 16%; Folic Acid 18%

Exchanges: 2 Starch, 3 Vegetable, 1 1/2 Lean Meat

Carbohydrate Choices: 3

California Black Bean Burgers

PREP: 15 MIN
COOK: 15 MIN

5 SERVINGS

1 can (15 ounces) black beans with cumin and chili spices, undrained

1 can (4 1/2 ounces) chopped green chiles, undrained

1 cup unseasoned dry bread crumbs

1 egg, beaten

1/4 cup yellow cornmeal

2 tablespoons canola or soybean oil

5 whole wheat hamburger buns, split and toasted

1 tablespoon reduced-fat mayonnaise or salad dressing

1 1/4 cups shredded lettuce

3 tablespoons chunky-style salsa

1 Place beans in food processor or blender. Cover and process until slightly mashed; remove from food processor. Mix beans, chiles, bread crumbs and egg in medium bowl. Shape mixture into 5 patties, about 1/2 inch thick. Coat each patty with cornmeal.

2 Heat oil in 10-inch skillet over medium heat. Cook patties in oil 10 to 15 minutes, turning once, until crisp and thoroughly cooked on both sides.

3 Spread bottom halves of buns with mayonnaise. Top with lettuce, patties, salsa and top halves of buns.

a note from Dr. B

The black beans provide a hefty amount of iron, so good for your heart and blood vessels. Your body can use the iron that foods provide if you eat them along with a good source of vitamin C, such as oranges, tomatoes, bell peppers, strawberries and kiwifruit.

1 Serving: Calories 390 (Calories from Fat 100); Fat 11g; Saturated Fat 2g (4% of Calories from Saturated Fat); *Trans* Fat 0g; Cholesterol 45mg; Omega-3 0g; Sodium 1240mg

Carbohydrate 66g (Dietary Fiber 10g); Protein 17g

% Daily Value: Vitamin A 8%; Vitamin C 4%; Calcium 16%; Iron 32%; Folic Acid 48%

Exchanges: 4 Starch, 1 Vegetable, 1 Fat

Carbohydrate Choices: 4 1/2

PREP: 15 MIN
COOK: **25 MIN**
STAND: 10 MIN

Five-Spice Tofu Stir-Fry

4 SERVINGS

1 1/4 cups water

1 cup uncooked instant brown rice

1/4 cup stir-fry sauce

2 tablespoons orange juice

1 tablespoon honey

3/4 teaspoon five-spice powder

1 package (14 ounces) firm tofu, cut into 3/4-inch cubes

1 small red onion, cut into thin wedges

1 bag (1 pound) frozen baby bean and carrot blend

1/4 cup water

1 Heat 1 1/4 cups water to boiling in 1-quart saucepan. Stir in rice; reduce heat to low. Cover and simmer 10 minutes.

2 Meanwhile, mix stir-fry sauce, orange juice, honey and five-spice powder in medium bowl. Press tofu between paper towels to absorb excess moisture. Stir tofu into sauce mixture; let stand 10 minutes to marinate.

3 Spray 12-inch nonstick skillet with cooking spray; heat over medium heat. Remove tofu from sauce mixture; reserve sauce mixture. Cook tofu in skillet 3 to 4 minutes, stirring occasionally, just until light golden brown. Remove tofu from skillet.

4 Cook onion in skillet 2 minutes, stirring constantly. Add frozen vegetables and 1/4 cup water. Heat to boiling; reduce heat to medium. Cover and cook 6 to 8 minutes, stirring occasionally, until vegetables are crisp-tender.

5 Stir in reserved sauce mixture and tofu. Cook 2 to 3 minutes, stirring occasionally, until mixture is slightly thickened and hot. Serve over rice.

1 Serving: Calories 260 (Calories from Fat 65); Fat 7g; Saturated Fat 0g (3% of Calories from Saturated Fat); *Trans* Fat 0g; Cholesterol 0mg; Omega-3 0g; Sodium 580mg

Carbohydrate 43g (Dietary Fiber 6g); Protein 12g

% Daily Value: Vitamin A 100%; Vitamin C 6%; Calcium 22%; Iron 18%; Folic Acid 24%

Exchanges: 2 Starch, 2 Vegetable, 1 Fat

Carbohydrate Choices: 3

Harvest Salad

PREP: **15 MIN**
COOK: **12 MIN**
STAND: **5 MIN**
COOL: **30 MIN**

6 SERVINGS

1 1/3 cups water

2/3 cup uncooked
quick-cooking barley

2 cups frozen whole kernel
corn, thawed

1/2 cup dried cranberries

1/4 cup thinly sliced green onions
(4 medium)

1 medium unpeeled apple, chopped
(about 1 cup)

1 small carrot, coarsely shredded
(about 1/3 cup)

2 tablespoons canola or soybean oil

2 tablespoons honey

1 tablespoon lemon juice

1 Heat water to boiling in 1 1/2-quart saucepan.
Stir in barley; reduce heat to low. Cover and simmer
10 to 12 minutes or until tender. Let stand covered
5 minutes. Uncover; cool 30 minutes.

2 Mix barley, corn, cranberries, green onions, apple
and carrot in large bowl.

3 Shake oil, honey and lemon juice in tightly covered
container. Pour over barley mixture; toss to mix.

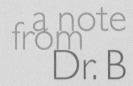

a note
from
Dr. B

*Quick-cooking barley
contains all the
nutrients of pearled
barley in a quick-
cooking form. This
whole grain contains
complex carbohydrates
and—when mixed
with fruits and
vegetables—makes
a delicious high-fiber,
great-for-your-heart
choice.*

*"Can a salad get any
healthier than this one?
I can't believe it tastes so good."*
WANDA S.

1 Serving: Calories 360 (Calories
from Fat 55); Fat 6g; Saturated Fat 1g
(1% of Calories from Saturated Fat);
Trans Fat 0g; Cholesterol 0mg;
Omega-3 0g; Sodium 15mg

Carbohydrate 81g (Dietary
Fiber 13g); Protein 8g

% Daily Value: Vitamin A 34%;
Vitamin C 12%; Calcium 2%;
Iron 12%; Folic Acid 10%

Exchanges: 3 Starch, 1 Fruit,
1 Other Carbohydrates

Carbohydrate Choices: 5 1/2

Asian Chicken Salad with Peanut-Soy Dressing (page 187)

Simple Salads and Vegetables

It's not news that fruits and vegetables are heart-healthy. Here Betty Crocker adds the great new flavors and familiar favorites you've been looking for.

Easy Fresh-Fruit Salad

6 SERVINGS

1 medium pineapple (2 pounds), peeled and cut into 1-inch chunks (3 cups)

1 pint (2 cups) fresh strawberries, sliced

1 pint (2 cups) fresh blueberries

2 cups seedless green grapes

1 bunch leaf lettuce

1/2 cup raspberry vinaigrette dressing

3/4 to 1 cup crumbled feta cheese (3 to 4 ounces)

1 | Mix pineapple, strawberries, blueberries and grapes in large bowl.

2 | Line individual serving plates with lettuce; spoon salad onto lettuce. Drizzle with dressing; sprinkle with cheese.

a note from Dr. B

Try to view having a healthy heart and circulatory system as an opportunity to prepare and eat the best possible foods to maintain your body. The whole family can reap the rewards of eating well. Who knows, someday they may even thank you for showing them how to begin healthy eating habits.

1 Serving: Calories 170 (Calories from Fat 35); Fat 4g; Saturated Fat 2g (12% of Calories from Saturated Fat); *Trans* Fat 0g; Cholesterol 15mg; Omega-3 0g; Sodium 400mg

Carbohydrate 34g (Dietary Fiber 4g); Protein 4g

% Daily Value: Vitamin A 14%; Vitamin C 100%; Calcium 10%; Iron 6%; Folic Acid 16%

Exchanges: 2 Fruit, 1/2 High-Fat Meat

Carbohydrate Choices: 2

"This is a very refreshing salad and a wonderful late summer choice, when fruit is fresh and juicy. The calories and fat are very reasonable, and it helps me get in my daily fruit servings."

LORI S.

Easy Fresh-Fruit Salad

Mediterranean Vegetable Salad

6 SERVINGS

1/3 cup tarragon or white wine vinegar

2 tablespoons canola or soybean oil

2 tablespoons chopped fresh or
2 teaspoons dried oregano leaves

1/2 teaspoon sugar

1/2 teaspoon salt

1/2 teaspoon ground mustard

1/2 teaspoon pepper

2 cloves garlic, finely chopped

3 large tomatoes, sliced

2 large yellow bell peppers,
sliced into thin rings

6 ounces washed fresh spinach leaves
(from 10-ounce bag), stems removed
(about 1 cup)

1/2 cup crumbled feta cheese
(2 ounces)

Kalamata olives, if desired

1 Mix vinegar, oil, oregano, sugar, salt, mustard, pepper and garlic in small bowl. Place tomatoes and bell peppers in glass or plastic container. Pour vinegar mixture over vegetables. Cover and refrigerate at least 1 hour to blend flavors.

2 Line serving platter with spinach. Drain vegetables; place on spinach. Sprinkle with cheese; garnish with olives.

a note from Dr. B

Research shows that spinach and other leafy green vegetables are high in antioxidants. Spinach is an excellent source of the antioxidant lutein, vitamin C, and the vitamin folic acid—all beneficial nutrients for your health.

1 Serving: Calories 120 (Calories from Fat 65); Fat 7g; Saturated Fat 2g (14% of Calories from Saturated Fat); *Trans* Fat 0g; Cholesterol 10mg; Omega-3 0g; Sodium 330mg

Carbohydrate 11g (Dietary Fiber 2g); Protein 4g

% Daily Value: Vitamin A 70%; Vitamin C 100%; Calcium 8%; Iron 8%; Folic Acid 22%

Exchanges: 2 Vegetable, 1 1/2 Fat

Carbohydrate Choices: 1

"My family has such a strong history of heart disease, and we are always sharing healthy recipes. This is a great one with extra veggies. Studies have shown that eating veggies helps prevent heart disease."

CATHY P.

Nutty Greens with Ranch Dressing

PREP: 5 MIN

8 SERVINGS

1/2 package (12-ounce size) soft silken tofu

1 envelope (1 ounce) ranch dressing mix*

1/2 cup soy milk

1 bag (12 ounces) salad greens with red cabbage and shredded carrots (8 cups)

2/3 cup roasted soy nuts

1/2 cup shredded reduced-fat Cheddar or blue cheese (2 ounces)

Use the ranch dressing mix that calls for milk and mayonnaise (not buttermilk and mayonnaise).

1 Place tofu, dressing mix and soy milk in blender or food processor. Cover and blend on high speed until smooth and creamy.

2 Toss salad greens with tofu mixture in large serving bowl. Sprinkle with soy nuts and cheese.

a note from the Nutritionist

Bursting with fresh, good-for-you greens, this sensational salad makes it easy to get your "five (or more) a day" as it is high in vitamin A, vitamin C, calcium and folic acid. Plus you're getting the heart-protective benefits of soy protein from the tofu, soy milk and soy.

1 Serving: Calories 85 (Calories from Fat 25); Fat 3g; Saturated Fat 1g (8% of Calories from Saturated Fat); *Trans* Fat 0g; Cholesterol 0mg; Omega-3 0g; Sodium 360mg

Carbohydrate 7g (Dietary Fiber 2g); Protein 8g

% Daily Value: Vitamin A 36%; Vitamin C 14%; Calcium 10%; Iron 6%; Folic Acid 20%

Exchanges: 1 Vegetable, 1 Lean Meat

Carbohydrate Choices: 1/2

Corn and Black Bean Salad

6 SERVINGS

I can (15 ounces) black beans, rinsed and drained

I can (about 8 ounces) whole kernel corn, drained

I can (4 1/2 ounces) chopped green chiles, drained

1/2 cup medium chunky-style salsa

1/4 cup chopped onion

2 tablespoons chopped fresh cilantro

Mix all ingredients in medium bowl. Cover and refrigerate until chilled, at least 2 hours but no longer than 24 hours.

I Serving: Calories 135 (Calories from Fat 10); Fat 1g; Saturated Fat 0g (1% of Calories from Saturated Fat); *Trans* Fat 0g; Cholesterol 0mg; Omega-3 0g; Sodium 800mg

Carbohydrate 29g (Dietary Fiber 6g); Protein 8g

% Daily Value: Vitamin A 8%; Vitamin C 16%; Calcium 6%; Iron 14%; Folic Acid 30%

Exchanges: 2 Starch

Carbohydrate Choices: 2

Asian Chicken Salad with Peanut-Soy Dressing

6 Servings

Peanut-Soy Dressing (below)

6 cups coleslaw mix
(from 16-ounce bag)

3 cups washed fresh spinach leaves
(from 10-ounce bag)

3 cups cut-up cooked chicken

1 medium bell pepper, cut into
bite-size strips

1 can (8 ounces) bamboo shoots,
rinsed and drained

Make Peanut-Soy Dressing. Toss remaining ingredients in large bowl; drizzle with dressing.

Peanut-Soy Dressing

3 tablespoons reduced-sodium
soy sauce

3 tablespoons cider vinegar

2 tablespoons honey

1 tablespoon creamy peanut butter

1/2 teaspoon crushed red pepper

1/2 teaspoon grated gingerroot

Beat all ingredients in small bowl with wire whisk until blended.

a note from Dr. B

It's never too late to reap the benefits of exercise. In a study at Tufts University, researchers introduced strength-training to nursing home residents. At the beginning of the study, most were so frail they needed help getting out of a chair. Within two months, they had doubled their strength, and two of the residents even threw away their canes.

1 Serving: Calories 210 (Calories from Fat 65); Fat 7g; Saturated Fat 2g (8% of Calories from Saturated Fat); *Trans* Fat 0g; Cholesterol 60mg; Omega-3 0g; Sodium 360mg

Carbohydrate 14g (Dietary Fiber 3g); Protein 23g

% Daily Value: Vitamin A 30%; Vitamin C 74%; Calcium 6%; Iron 12%; Folic Acid 18%

Exchanges: 3 Vegetable, 2 1/2 Lean Meat

Carbohydrate Choices: 1

Italian Tuna Toss

6 SERVINGS

1 medium cucumber, sliced
(1 1/2 cups)

2 cans (6 ounces each) tuna in
water, drained

1 bag (16 ounces) fresh
cauliflower florets

1 bag (10 ounces) mixed
salad greens

1 jar (2 ounces) sliced pimientos,
drained (1/4 cup)

1/3 cup Italian dressing

1/4 cup bacon flavor bits or chips

1 Toss all ingredients except dressing and bacon bits
in large bowl.

2 Pour dressing over salad and sprinkle with bacon
bits; toss to mix.

a note from Dr. B

Take a break and go for a walk to help clear your body, mind and spirit. Instead of eating lunch at your desk every day, make it a goal to get up, stretch, go for a walk and return to your desk refreshed and ready for the afternoon.

"I love the flavor of bacon, and the bacon flavor chips are a great low-fat way to still get that flavor in my food."

NANCI D.

1 Serving: Calories 170 (Calories from Fat 65); Fat 7g; Saturated Fat 1g (4% of Calories from Saturated Fat); *Trans* Fat 0g; Cholesterol 20mg; Omega-3 0g; Sodium 400mg

Carbohydrate 8g (Dietary Fiber 3g); Protein 19g

% Daily Value: Vitamin A 32%; Vitamin C 74%; Calcium 6%; Iron 12%; Folic Acid 30%

Exchanges: 2 Vegetable, 2 Lean Meat

Carbohydrate Choices: 1/2

PREP: 10 MIN

Tuscan Panzanella Salad

6 SERVINGS

1 bag (10 ounces) romaine and leaf lettuce mix

1 can (19 ounces) cannellini beans, rinsed and drained

2 cups large reduced-fat or fat-free croutons

1 cup sweet grape tomatoes

1/2 cup thinly sliced red onion

1/3 cup pitted Kalamata olives, cut in half

1/3 cup balsamic vinaigrette

1 Toss all ingredients except vinaigrette in large bowl.

2 Pour vinaigrette over salad; toss to coat.

a note from the Nutritionist

Grape tomatoes are small and very sweet. If they're not available, you can use cherry tomatoes instead and just cut them in half. Or try yellow pear tomatoes if they are available at your market. Make sure to eat a variety of veggies and fruits to ensure that your body benefits from many nutrients.

1 Serving: Calories 215 (Calories from Fat 65); Fat 7g; Saturated Fat 1g (3% of Calories from Saturated Fat); *Trans* Fat 0g; Cholesterol 0mg; Omega-3 0g; Sodium 270mg

Carbohydrate 35g (Dietary Fiber 8g); Protein 11g

% Daily Value: Vitamin A 30%; Vitamin C 26%; Calcium 12%; Iron 26%; Folic Acid 38%

Exchanges: 2 Starch, 1 Vegetable, 1 1/2 Lean Meat

Carbohydrate Choices: 2

Caribbean Crabmeat Pasta Salad

PREP: 25 MIN
CHILL: 1 HR

6 SERVINGS

3 cups uncooked rotelle pasta
(8 ounces)

Honey-Lime Dressing (below)

1 package (8 ounces) refrigerated
flake-style imitation crabmeat

1 medium red bell pepper, cut into thin
bite-size strips

1 medium mango, peeled, seeded and
cubed (about 1 cup)

1/2 to 1 jalapeño chili, seeded and
finely chopped

2 tablespoons chopped fresh cilantro

1 Cook and drain pasta as directed on package. Rinse with cold water; drain.

2 Meanwhile, make Honey-Lime Dressing.

3 Gently toss pasta and remaining ingredients in large bowl. Pour dressing over salad; toss gently to coat. Cover and refrigerate at least 1 hour to blend flavors.

a note from the Nutritionist

Large, thin and crisp wafer-like crackers are low in calories and a great accompaniment to this flavorful salad. Look for them near the deli cheese case, gourmet foods aisle or snacks section of your supermarket.

Honey-Lime Dressing

1 teaspoon grated lime peel

3 tablespoons lime juice

2 tablespoons canola or soybean oil

1 tablespoon honey

1/2 teaspoon ground cumin

1/2 teaspoon ground ginger

1/4 teaspoon salt

Mix all ingredients in small bowl until well blended.

"Refreshing, yummy and light tasting."

PAT R.

1 Serving: Calories 270 (Calories from Fat 55); Fat 6g; Saturated Fat 1g (2% of Calories from Saturated Fat); *Trans* Fat 0g; Cholesterol 10mg; Omega-3 0g; Sodium 430mg

Carbohydrate 43g (Dietary Fiber 3g); Protein 11g

% Daily Value: Vitamin A 28%; Vitamin C 82%; Calcium 2%; Iron 10%; Folic Acid 22%

Exchanges: 2 Starch, 1 Fruit, 1 Very Lean Meat, 1/2 Fat

Carbohydrate Choices: 3

PREP: **20 MIN**

COOK: **5 MIN**

Gyro Salad

6 SERVINGS

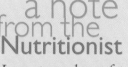
a note
from the
Nutritionist

*Learn to use lower-fat
meats and dressings in
your favorite recipes.
For example, beef
sirloin, a very lean cut
of meat, is used here
instead of the lamb
typically used in gyros.
And yogurt, instead
of sour cream or
mayonnaise, makes a
fantastic dressing that
adds a refreshing and
tangy touch. Warm pita
bread, cut into wedges,
is the perfect choice to
serve with this salad.*

1 Serving: Calories 185 (Calories
from Fat 65); Fat 7g; Saturated Fat 2g
(13% of Calories from Saturated
Fat); *Trans* Fat 0g; Cholesterol 50mg;
Omega-3 0g; Sodium 280mg

Carbohydrate 10g (Dietary
Fiber 2g); Protein 20g

% Daily Value: Vitamin A 54%;
Vitamin C 36%; Calcium 12%;
Iron 16%; Folic Acid 30%

Exchanges: 2 Vegetable, 2 Lean
Meat, 1/2 Fat

Carbohydrate Choices: 1/2

Yogurt Dressing (below)

1-pound boneless beef sirloin steak,
1 to 1 1/2 inches thick

1 tablespoon canola or soybean oil

1 1/4 teaspoons Greek seasoning

8 cups torn mixed salad greens

1 medium cucumber, thinly sliced
(1 1/2 cups)

1 small red onion, thinly sliced and
separated into rings

1 large tomato, chopped (1 cup)

1 Make Yogurt Dressing; set aside.

2 Cut beef across grain into 4 x 1/4-inch strips. Heat
oil in 12-inch nonstick skillet over medium-high
heat. Add beef to skillet; sprinkle with Greek seasoning.
Cook about 5 minutes, stirring frequently, until beef is
brown. Drain if necessary.

3 Arrange salad greens on serving platter or
individual serving plates. Top with cucumber,
onion, tomato and beef. Serve with dressing.

Yogurt Dressing

1/2 cup plain fat-free yogurt

1/2 cup reduced-fat sour cream

1/4 cup fat-free (skim) milk

1 teaspoon Greek seasoning

Mix all ingredients in small bowl with wire whisk
until creamy.

PREP: 15 MIN
COOK: 10 MIN
COOL: 15 MIN
CHILL: 3 HRS

Tropical Fruit, Rice and Tuna Salad

4 SERVINGS

1 cup water

3/4 cup uncooked instant brown rice

1/2 cup vanilla low-fat yogurt

1 can (8 ounces) pineapple tidbits in juice, drained and 1 teaspoon juice reserved

2 kiwifruit, peeled and sliced

1 medium mango, peeled, seeded and chopped (about 1 cup)

1 can (6 ounces) white tuna in water, drained and flaked

1 tablespoon coconut, toasted*

*To toast coconut, bake uncovered in ungreased shallow pan in 350° oven 5 to 7 minutes, stirring occasionally, until golden brown. Or cook in ungreased heavy skillet over medium-low heat 6 to 14 minutes, stirring frequently until browning begins, then stirring constantly until golden brown.

1 Heat water to boiling in 1-quart saucepan. Stir in rice; reduce heat to low. Cover and simmer 10 minutes. Uncover; cool 15 minutes. Refrigerate at least 1 hour or until cold.

2 Mix rice, yogurt and reserved pineapple juice in medium bowl. Cover and refrigerate 1 to 2 hours to blend flavors.

3 Cut kiwifruit slices into fourths. Gently stir kiwifruit, pineapple, mango and tuna into rice mixture. Sprinkle with coconut.

1 Serving: Calories 260 (Calories from Fat 20); Fat 2g; Saturated Fat 1g (3% of Calories from Saturated Fat); *Trans* Fat 0g; Cholesterol 15mg; Omega-3 0g; Sodium 170mg

Carbohydrate 47g (Dietary Fiber 4g); Protein 15g

% Daily Value: Vitamin A 10%; Vitamin C 94%; Calcium 8%; Iron 8%; Folic Acid 8%

Exchanges: 2 Starch, 1 Fruit, 1 1/2 Very Lean Meat

Carbohydrate Choices: 3

"I've never thought of adding fruit to tuna, so this combination is unique to me. This is a complete meal with lots of flavor—and it's healthy!"

MARILYN B.

Fresh Spinach, Orange and Red Onion Salad

PREP: 15 MIN
BROIL: 5 MIN

8 SERVINGS

8 cups torn washed fresh spinach leaves (from 10-ounce bag), stems removed

4 medium seedless oranges

Orange juice

1/3 cup honey

3 tablespoons raspberry vinegar

2 tablespoons canola or soybean oil

1/2 teaspoon salt

1 medium red onion, cut into 1/4-inch-thick slices

1 Arrange spinach on serving platter or individual serving plates.

2 Peel off eight 2 1/2 x 2-inch strips of orange peel with vegetable peeler, being careful to remove only orange part. Cut strips lengthwise into thin slivers.

3 Cut remaining peel and white pith from oranges with sharp knife. Remove segments of orange by cutting between membranes, catching juice in small bowl; set orange segments aside. Squeeze membranes of oranges into bowl to remove all of juice; if necessary, add orange juice to make 1/2 cup. Beat in honey, vinegar, oil and salt with wire whisk.

4 Place onion slices in single layer on ungreased cookie sheet; brush with orange juice mixture. Broil 2 to 3 inches from heat 4 to 5 minutes or just until edges begin to darken.

5 Arrange orange segments on spinach. Separate onion slices into rings; scatter over oranges. Drizzle with remaining orange juice mixture; garnish with strips of orange peel.

a note from Dr. B

This recipe is quite low in sodium. If you are salt-sensitive, have high blood pressure or blood pressure runs in your family, it's a good idea to keep your sodium low. Avoid foods high in salt, like chips and pickles, and reduce or leave out the salt in recipes. See "Instead of Salt, Sprinkle On:" (page 23).

1 Serving: Calories 135 (Calories from Fat 35); Fat 4g; Saturated Fat 0g (2% of Calories from Saturated Fat); *Trans* Fat 0g; Cholesterol 0mg; Omega-3 0g; Sodium 170mg

Carbohydrate 23g (Dietary Fiber 3g); Protein 2g

% Daily Value: Vitamin A 58%; Vitamin C 40%; Calcium 6%; Iron 6%; Folic Acid 20%

Exchanges: 1 Fruit, 1 Vegetable, 1 Fat

Carbohydrate Choices: 1 1/2

"I am choosing salads for lunch as a way to keep my goal of better eating for my health and heart. Luckily, spinach has been one of my favorites since childhood, so I've found this recipe brings back some fond memories."

KEVIN W.

Triple-Cabbage Slaw

4 SERVINGS

2 cups thinly sliced Chinese (napa) cabbage

1 1/2 cups shredded green cabbage

1/2 cup shredded red cabbage

1 tablespoon chopped fresh chives

3 tablespoons orange marmalade

2 tablespoons rice vinegar

1 teaspoon grated gingerroot

1 Mix cabbages and chives in large glass or plastic bowl.

2 Mix marmalade, vinegar and gingerroot in small bowl until blended. Add to cabbage mixture; toss lightly to mix.

a note from Dr. B

Fat-free and low in calories, cabbage is a cruciferous vegetable that contains nitrogen compounds that have heart-protective benefits. Other cruciferous veggies include broccoli, cauliflower, kale, collard greens, mustard greens and Brussels sprouts.

"I consider vegetables and fruits 'free' food, and I eat as much of them as I want."

NANCI D.

1 Serving: Calories 50 (Calories from Fat 0); Fat 0g; Saturated Fat 0g (0% of Calories from Saturated Fat); *Trans* Fat 0g; Cholesterol 0mg; Omega-3 0g; Sodium 35mg

Carbohydrate 13g (Dietary Fiber 1g); Protein 1g

% Daily Value: Vitamin A 24%; Vitamin C 54%; Calcium 6%; Iron 4%; Folic Acid 10%

Exchanges: 1/2 Fruit, 1 Vegetable

Carbohydrate Choices: 1

The Value of Vegetables and Fruits for Your Heart

Increasing the amount of fruits and vegetables you eat has many benefits, and evidence now suggests that eating a veggie-and-fruit-rich diet can lower your risk of heart disease. Fruits and vegetables are rich in folic acids, which reduce blood levels of homocysteine, a substance which may be a risk factor for heart disease. Veggies and fruits are also rich in potassium, a mineral which may help control blood pressure and prevent irregular heart rhythms.

For best results, aim for five to nine servings of veggies and fruits a day. Try these sure-fire tips to increase your intake of heart-healthy fruits and vegetables:

Snack on cut-up carrots, celery, cucumbers, radishes, bell peppers and cherry tomatoes. Wash a big batch at the beginning of the week to have on hand, or buy packages of baby carrots, edamame (soy beans in their pods) or other ready-to-eat vegetables.

Prepare a smoothie incorporating chopped fresh fruit, ice and a little fat-free plain yogurt. Or try frozen fruit (without sugar) and leave out the ice.

Eat your cereal with fruit for an energizing breakfast or snack.

Start meals with a vegetable-based soup such as minestrone or tomato soup, or with a green salad.

Sprinkle fresh berries or sliced citrus fruit onto your salad.

Use salsa as a dip for vegetables and as a topping for baked potatoes or burgers.

Load your sandwiches with sliced tomatoes, lettuce, onions, roasted peppers or other vegetables.

Stir frozen chopped spinach, onion-pepper blends, green beans, shredded carrots or zucchini into soups, stews and casseroles. When you make lasagna, layer them in with your other ingredients.

Toss pasta with cooked chopped vegetables (or their frozen equivalents) before topping with sauce.

Eat fresh fruit or water-packed canned fruit for dessert.

COLOR THEM HEALTHY

Eat a colorful abundance of fruits and vegetables each day; the pigments that give produce its beautiful colors are the phytonutrients that can help prevent diseases. There is a whole palate of reasons to eat "a rainbow a day":

Red: tomatoes, watermelon, and pink grapefruit are colored by lycopene, a heart-healthy antioxidant. Cooking makes the lycopene more available to the body, so enjoy your tomato sauce, tomato soup and ketchup!

Orange: carrots, cantaloupes, mangoes, winter squash and sweet potatoes help protect the body's cells against oxidative damage and may help prevent heart disease and cancer.

Red and purple: grapes, blueberries, blackberries, strawberries and red cabbage contain anthocyanins, which have antioxidant properties.

Yellow and green: spinach, collards, turnip greens, corn, green peas and honeydew melon contain lutein and zeaxanthin, both of which may help prevent macular degeneration, a disease of the eye.

Green: broccoli, cabbage and kale contain sulforaphane and indoles, substances which may help fight certain cancers.

Wilted Spinach Vinaigrette

6 SERVINGS

1 tablespoon canola or soybean oil

2 cloves garlic, minced

1 package (10 ounces) washed fresh spinach leaves, stems removed

1/3 cup raisins

1/4 cup sunflower nuts or pine nuts

2 teaspoons sugar

2 tablespoons white wine vinegar

1 Heat oil in 4-quart nonstick Dutch oven over medium heat. Cook garlic in oil 1 minute, stirring constantly.

2 Add spinach and raisins; cook about 1 minute, stirring constantly, or just until spinach is barely wilted. Remove from heat; stir in sunflower nuts, sugar and vinegar. Serve immediately.

a note from Dr. B

The information you don't know can have a major impact on your health. Cardiovascular disease is the No. 1 killer of women in the United States. Each year, more than eleven times as many women die of heart attacks and strokes as die from breast cancer. If your life keeps you very busy, set aside time to take charge of your health.

1 Serving: Calories 105 (Calories from Fat 45); Fat 5g; Saturated Fat 0g (5% of Calories from Saturated Fat); *Trans* Fat 0g; Cholesterol 0mg; Omega-3 0g; Sodium 80mg

Carbohydrate 12g (Dietary Fiber 2g); Protein 3g

% Daily Value: Vitamin A 88%; Vitamin C 10%; Calcium 6%; Iron 10%; Folic Acid 26%

Exchanges: 2 Vegetable, 1 Fat

Carbohydrate Choices: 1

Dilled Corn with Popped Amaranth

PREP: 10 MIN

5 SERVINGS

2 tablespoons uncooked amaranth

1 package (1 pound) frozen whole kernel corn

1 tablespoon butter

1 tablespoon chopped fresh or 1 teaspoon dried dill weed

1 | Heat heavy skillet over medium-high heat until very hot. Heat 1 tablespoon of the amaranth in skillet 30 to 45 seconds, stirring constantly with wooden spoon, until most of the seeds pop. Remove from skillet. Repeat with remaining 1 tablespoon amaranth.

2 | Cook and drain corn as directed on package. Stir in butter and dill weed; sprinkle with amaranth.

"I eat a lot of vegetables and am always looking for new ways to eat them and to serve them. This is a great recipe, and we love corn."

WANDA S.

a note from the Nutritionist

Amaranth is a grain that is very high in protein. It has a slightly sweet flavor, and when popped, it can be used in salads and vegetables. Popping it, as done in this recipe, is really very easy to do. Look for amaranth among the other whole grains in the natural-foods section of your grocery store or co-op.

1 Serving: Calories 125 (Calories from Fat 25); Fat 3g; Saturated Fat 2g (13% of Calories from Saturated Fat); *Trans* Fat 0g; Cholesterol 5mg; Omega-3 0g; Sodium 20mg

Carbohydrate 21g (Dietary Fiber 3g); Protein 3g

% Daily Value: Vitamin A 4%; Vitamin C 2%; Calcium 0%; Iron 4%; Folic Acid 6%

Exchanges: 1 Starch, 1/2 Other Carbohydrates, 1/2 Fat

Carbohydrate Choices: 1 1/2

Caramelized Onion and Sweet Potato Skillet

4 SERVINGS

1 teaspoon canola or soybean oil

3 medium sweet potatoes (about 1 pound), peeled and sliced (about 3 1/2 cups)

1/4 large sweet onion (Bermuda, Maui, Spanish or Walla Walla), sliced

2 tablespoons packed brown sugar

1/2 teaspoon jerk seasoning (dry)

1 tablespoon chopped fresh parsley

1 Heat oil in 10-inch skillet over medium heat. Cook sweet potatoes and onion in oil about 5 minutes, stirring occasionally, until light brown; reduce heat to low. Cover and cook 10 to 12 minutes, stirring occasionally, until potatoes are tender.

2 Stir in brown sugar and jerk seasoning. Cook uncovered about 3 minutes, stirring occasionally, until glazed. Sprinkle with parsley.

"What a great, easy side dish to serve with pork. I love Walla Walla onions; I think of them as being so good for me."

LORI S.

1 Serving: Calories 115 (Calories from Fat 10); Fat 1g; Saturated Fat 0g (1% of Calories from Saturated Fat); *Trans* Fat 0g; Cholesterol 0mg; Omega-3 0g; Sodium 10mg

Carbohydrate 28g (Dietary Fiber 3g); Protein 2g

% Daily Value: Vitamin A 100%; Vitamin C 18%; Calcium 2%; Iron 2%; Folic Acid 6%

Exchanges: 1/2 Starch, 1 Fruit, 1 Vegetable

Carbohydrate Choices: 2

Caramelized Onion and Sweet Potato Skillet

Sweet Potato Wedges

4 SERVINGS

4 medium sweet potatoes
(1 1/2 pounds), peeled and cut
lengthwise into 1/2-inch wedges

2 tablespoons canola or soybean oil

1/2 teaspoon salt

1/4 teaspoon pepper

1 Heat oven to 450°. Brush jelly roll pan, 15 1/2 x 10 1/2 x 1 inch, with canola or soybean oil.

2 Toss potatoes with 2 tablespoons oil in large bowl. Sprinkle with salt and pepper. Spread potatoes in single layer in pan.

3 Bake uncovered 25 to 30 minutes, turning occasionally, until potatoes are golden brown and tender when pierced with fork.

a note from the Nutritionist

These oven-fried sweet potato wedges are loaded with vitamin A and good amounts of potassium and calcium. August to October is the best time to buy sweet potatoes because they are at their peak and are the most moist.

1 Serving: Calories 175 (Calories from Fat 65); Fat 7g; Saturated Fat 1g (3% of Calories from Saturated Fat); *Trans* Fat 0g; Cholesterol 0mg; Omega-3 0g; Sodium 310mg

Carbohydrate 26g (Dietary Fiber 3g); Protein 2g

% Daily Value: Vitamin A 100%; Vitamin C 22%; Calcium 2%; Iron 2%; Folic Acid 6%

Exchanges: 1 Starch, 1 Other Carbohydrates, 1 Fat

Carbohydrate Choices: 2

"These are so easy to make, have none of the negatives of frying and are so much better for you than regular potatoes!"

KEN B.

Swiss Potato Patties

8 SERVINGS

4 medium potatoes (1 1/3 pounds)

1 cup shredded reduced-fat Swiss cheese (4 ounces)

1/4 teaspoon salt

1/4 teaspoon pepper

1 tablespoon butter

1 Heat 1 inch water (salted if desired) to boiling in 3-quart saucepan. Add potatoes. Cover and heat to boiling; reduce heat. Simmer 30 to 35 minutes or until tender; drain.

2 Peel and shred potatoes. Mix potatoes, cheese, salt and pepper in large bowl.

3 Melt butter in 10-inch skillet over medium-high heat. Scoop half of potato mixture by 1/3 cupfuls into skillet; flatten to 1/2-inch thickness. Cook about 8 minutes, turning once, until golden brown. Repeat with remaining potato mixture.

a note from Dr. B

Pair these potato patties with broccoli and fresh tomato slices for a great meatless meal. Enjoying meatless meals can help reduce the fat, calories and cholesterol in your diet. Other benefits of going meatless include possibly reducing your risk of heart disease, diabetes and cancer.

1 Serving: Calories 110 (Calories from Fat 45); Fat 5g; Saturated Fat 3g (25% of Calories from Saturated Fat); *Trans* Fat 0g; Cholesterol 15mg; Omega-3 0g; Sodium 120mg

Carbohydrate 11g (Dietary Fiber 1g); Protein 5g

% Daily Value: Vitamin A 4%; Vitamin C 4%; Calcium 10%; Iron 0%; Folic Acid 0%

Exchanges: 1 Starch, 1/2 Fat

Carbohydrate Choices: 1

French Country-Style Peas

4 SERVINGS

2 teaspoons canola or soybean oil

1/2 cup diced onion (1 medium)

1 cup sliced fresh mushrooms (about 2 1/2 ounces)

1 package (10 ounces) frozen peas and pearl onions

1/2 teaspoon salt

1/4 teaspoon white pepper

1 cup shredded romaine or Bibb lettuce

1 tablespoon minced fresh or 1 teaspoon dried tarragon or mint leaves, crushed

1 Heat oil in 10-inch nonstick skillet over medium heat. Cook onion in oil 1 minute, stirring occasionally. Stir in mushrooms and frozen vegetables; cook 3 minutes, stirring frequently. Stir in salt and pepper.

2 Stir in lettuce; cook 1 minute, stirring constantly, until lettuce is wilted. Sprinkle with tarragon.

a note from Dr. B

Getting a massage can benefit your fitness program. Massage loosens up kinks in your muscles, relieves stress and helps you relax. Scheduling periodic massages is also a good way to reward yourself for all of those short-term fitness goals you're reaching!

1 Serving: Calories 80 (Calories from Fat 25); Fat 3g; Saturated Fat 0g (3% of Calories from Saturated Fat); *Trans* Fat 0g; Cholesterol 0mg; Omega-3 0g; Sodium 330mg

Carbohydrate 10g (Dietary Fiber 3g); Protein 3g

% Daily Value: Vitamin A 10%; Vitamin C 8%; Calcium 2%; Iron 6%; Folic Acid 12%

Exchanges: 2 Vegetable, 1/2 Fat

Carbohydrate Choices: 1

Glazed Baby Carrots and Cranberries with Pecans

PREP: **5 MIN**
COOK: **6 MIN**

4 SERVINGS

1 package (10 ounces) frozen glazed sliced carrots in a pouch

3 tablespoons dried cranberries

2 tablespoons chopped pecans or walnuts

Cook carrots as directed on package. Stir in cranberries and pecans.

a note from Dr. B

Combine exercise with good deeds by offering to run errands for those who can't get out. Walk to the supermarket to pick up their groceries, or pick up their packages at the post office. Helping to maintain a neighbor's yard or shoveling snow are other ways to burn calories while lending a hand.

1 Serving: Calories 110 (Calories from Fat 45); Fat 5g; Saturated Fat 1g (6% of Calories from Saturated Fat); *Trans* Fat 0g; Cholesterol 0mg; Omega-3 0g; Sodium 230mg

Carbohydrate 15g (Dietary Fiber 3g); Protein 1g

% Daily Value: Vitamin A 100%; Vitamin C 2%; Calcium 2%; Iron 2%; Folic Acid 2%

Exchanges: 1/2 Other Carbohydrates, 1 Vegetable, 1 Fat

Carbohydrate Choices: 1

Crème Caramel (page 208)

Treat Your Heart to Dessert

Everyone loves a sweet treat once in a while. These heart-smart recipes will appeal to your heart and your taste buds.

PREP: **30 MIN**
BAKE: **1 HR**
CHILL: **3 HR**

Crème Caramel

8 SERVINGS

1 cup sugar

1 3/4 cups fat-free (skim) milk

1 cup fat-free cholesterol-free egg product or 8 egg whites

1/4 teaspoon salt

1 teaspoon vanilla

2 cups raspberries, blackberries, blueberries or sliced strawberries

1 Heat oven to 325°. Heat 1/2 cup of the sugar in medium nonstick skillet over medium heat 7 to 10 minutes, stirring frequently with wooden spoon, until sugar is melted and a light caramel color (mixture will be very hot and could melt a plastic spoon). Immediately pour sugar mixture into round pan, 8 x 1 1/2 inches; tilt pan to coat bottom. Place on wire rack to cool.

2 Mix remaining 1/2 cup sugar, milk, egg product, salt and vanilla in large bowl. Pour mixture over sugar mixture in pan. Place in rectangular pan, 13 x 9 x 2 inches. Pour very hot water into rectangular pan to within 1/2 inch of top of round pan.

3 Bake 50 to 60 minutes or until knife inserted in center comes out clean. Remove round pan from pan of water. Cover; refrigerate until thoroughly chilled, about 3 hours or overnight. To unmold, run knife around edge of custard to loosen; invert onto serving platter. Top with fruit.

a note from Dr. B

This restaurant-favorite dessert is made a great low-fat way with no cholesterol. It's also a great choice because it contains fruit, so good for your heart. Fruits and vegetable are also rich in potassium, a mineral that may help to control blood pressure and prevent irregular heart rhythms.

1 Serving: Calories 150 (Calories from Fat 0); Fat 0g; Saturated Fat 0g (0% of Calories from Saturated Fat); *Trans* Fat 0g; Cholesterol 0mg; Omega-3 0g; Sodium 160mg

Carbohydrate 32g (Dietary Fiber 2g); Protein 5g

% Daily Value: Vitamin A 4%; Vitamin C 6%; Calcium 8%; Iron 4%; Folic Acid 6%

Exchanges: 1 Fruit, 1/2 Milk, 1 Other Carbohydrates

Carbohydrate Choices: 2

"It is a special occasion for my family when I serve dessert. I always read the nutrition information before I make something, because I want to eat it, too. This is a great dessert that my kids like, and it's low in calories and fat."

NANCI D.

Fruited Bread Pudding with Eggnog Sauce

PREP: 15 MIN
BAKE: 45 MIN

8 SERVINGS

4 cups 1-inch cubes French bread

1/2 cup diced dried fruit and raisin mixture

2 cups fat-free (skim) milk

1/2 cup fat-free cholesterol-free egg product or 2 eggs

1/3 cup sugar

1/2 teaspoon vanilla

Ground nutmeg, if desired

Eggnog Sauce (below)

1 Heat oven to 350°. Spray pie plate, 9 x 1 1/4 inches, with cooking spray. Place bread cubes in pie plate; sprinkle with fruit mixture.

2 Beat milk, egg product, sugar and vanilla in small bowl with wire whisk until smooth. Pour milk mixture over bread. Press bread cubes into milk mixture. Sprinkle with nutmeg.

3 Bake uncovered 40 to 45 minutes or until golden brown and set.

4 Make Eggnog Sauce. Cut bread pudding into wedges, or spoon into serving dishes. Drizzle each serving with scant tablespoon sauce. Sprinkle with additional nutmeg if desired. Store pudding and sauce covered in refrigerator.

Eggnog Sauce

1/3 cup fat-free (skim) milk

1 container (3 to 4 ounces) refrigerated vanilla fat-free pudding

1/2 teaspoon rum extract

Mix all ingredients in small bowl until smooth.

a note from the Nutritionist

Because dried fruits have had most of their water removed, they are concentrated sources of nutrients. Raisins, for instance, are especially rich in iron and fiber. Add raisins to cereal, yogurt and low-fat granola for an on-the-run, high-energy snack, or stir them into low-fat muffins, breads and desserts.

1 Serving: Calories 145 (Calories from Fat 10); Fat 1g; Saturated Fat 0g (2% of Calories from Saturated Fat); *Trans* Fat 0g; Cholesterol 0mg; Omega-3 0g; Sodium 190mg

Carbohydrate 29g (Dietary Fiber 1g); Protein 6g

% Daily Value: Vitamin A 4%; Vitamin C 0%; Calcium 12%; Iron 6%; Folic Acid 6%

Exchanges: 1 Starch, 1/2 Fruit, 1/2 Milk

Carbohydrate Choices: 2

"When confronted with the foods I love but don't eat anymore, I say, 'I can't eat that.' There is no room for 'just a little,' because it's hard to stop. It is so great to get good-tasting desserts that are reasonable in fat and calories, like this bread pudding."

NANCI D.

PREP: **20 MIN**
BAKE: **30 MIN**

Peach and Blueberry Crisp with Crunchy Topping

6 SERVINGS

a note from the Nutritionist

You can still eat dessert and the foods you love, but perhaps a little different version of them. Typical fruit crisps can often be very high in fat, calories and carbohydrates. This one, with its topping of crushed cereal and nuts, gives you the same great crunch and taste, with much less fat and calories.

4 medium peaches, peeled and sliced (2 3/4 cups)

1 cup fresh or frozen (thawed and drained) blueberries

2 tablespoons packed brown sugar

2 tablespoons orange juice

1 teaspoon ground cinnamon

1/4 teaspoon ground nutmeg

1 cup Honey Nut Clusters® cereal, slightly crushed

1/3 cup chopped pecans

3/4 cup frozen (thawed) fat-free whipped topping

1 Heat oven to 375°. Spray bottom and sides of square baking dish, 8 x 8 x 2 inches, or rectangular baking dish, 11 x 7 x 1 1/2 inches, with cooking spray.

2 Place peaches and blueberries in baking dish. Mix brown sugar, orange juice, cinnamon and nutmeg in small bowl; drizzle over fruit.

3 Bake 15 minutes. Sprinkle with crushed cereal and pecans. Bake 10 to 15 minutes longer or until peaches are tender when pierced with a fork. Serve warm or cold with whipped topping.

"I make desserts only when company comes. This great-tasting crisp combines two of my favorite fruits and really fits the bill."

PAT R.

1 Serving: Calories 170 (Calories from Fat 55); Fat 6g; Saturated Fat 1g (4% of Calories from Saturated Fat); *Trans* Fat 0g; Cholesterol 0mg; Omega-3 0g; Sodium 50mg

Carbohydrate 27g (Dietary Fiber 3g); Protein 2g

% Daily Value: Vitamin A 2%; Vitamin C 8%; Calcium 2%; Iron 6%; Folic Acid 6%

Exchanges: 1 Starch, 1 Fruit, 1 Fat

Carbohydrate Choices: 2

Peach and Blueberry Crisp with Crunchy Topping

Fruit with Caramel Sauce

6 SERVINGS

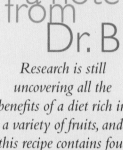

a note from Dr. B

Research is still uncovering all the benefits of a diet rich in a variety of fruits, and this recipe contains four varieties. Blueberries are a great source of antioxidants, naturally occurring components that have been found to reduce the risk of heart disease and help improve memory.

1 medium nectarine or peach, pitted and cut into wedges

1 kiwifruit, peeled and sliced

1 cup fresh strawberries, halved

1 cup fresh blueberries

2/3 cup caramel ice cream topping

1/4 teaspoon rum extract

1 Arrange fruit on individual dessert plates or in dessert dishes.

2 Mix ice cream topping and rum extract in 1-quart saucepan; heat over medium heat, stirring occasionally, until warm. Drizzle 1 heaping tablespoon topping mixture over each serving of fruit.

"Finally, a healthy dessert!
Something delicious with fruit that
I don't have to feel guilty about eating."

MARILYN B.

1 Serving: Calories 140 (Calories from Fat 0); Fat 0g; Saturated Fat 0g (2% of Calories from Saturated Fat); *Trans* Fat 0g; Cholesterol 0mg; Omega-3 0g; Sodium 130mg

Carbohydrate 34g (Dietary Fiber 2g); Protein 1g

% Daily Value: Vitamin A 2%; Vitamin C 52%; Calcium 2%; Iron 2%; Folic Acid 2%

Exchanges: 2 1/2 Fruit

Carbohydrate Choices: 2

Saucy Raspberry-Rhubarb

PREP: 10 MIN
COOK: 15 MIN
COOL: 30 MIN

6 SERVINGS

3 cups chopped fresh rhubarb or
1 bag (16 ounces) frozen cut
rhubarb, thawed

1/2 cup apple juice

3 tablespoons packed brown sugar

1 pint (2 cups) fresh raspberries

6 tablespoons reduced-fat sour cream

1 Heat rhubarb, apple juice, brown sugar and 1 cup of the raspberries to boiling in 1 1/2-quart saucepan; reduce heat. Simmer uncovered about 10 minutes, stirring occasionally, until rhubarb is soft. Cool about 30 minutes.

2 Stir in remaining 1 cup raspberries. Spoon into dessert dishes. Top with sour cream.

a note from Dr. B

Because they have high fiber and virtually no fat, the rhubarb and raspberry combination makes a wonderful dessert choice. To enjoy this dessert year-round, chop fresh rhubarb into 1/2-inch pieces, seal in an airtight freezer bag and freeze until ready to use.

"This is a really tasty dessert with a surprisingly low number of calories, low fat and high fiber. I treat myself every day to some sort of food like this that I can feel good about eating."

NANCY D.

1 Serving: Calories 85 (Calories from Fat 10); Fat 1g; Saturated Fat 1g (7% of Calories from Saturated Fat); *Trans* Fat 0g; Cholesterol 5mg; Omega-3 0g; Sodium 20mg

Carbohydrate 17g (Dietary Fiber 4g); Protein 2g

% Daily Value: Vitamin A 4%; Vitamin C 10%; Calcium 14%; Iron 4%; Folic Acid 4%

Exchanges: 1 Fruit

Carbohydrate Choices: 1

PREP: **20 MIN**

BAKE: **10 MIN**

COOL: **1 HR**

FREEZE: **6 HR**

Piña Colada Frozen Dessert

12 SERVINGS

a note from Dr. B

Play a winning hand in the heart-health game by knowing your options and taking control of what you eat. If you can't find no-sugar-added, reduced-fat ice cream, opt for ice milk or frozen yogurt, which are both lower in calories and fat than regular ice cream.

1 1/4 cups graham cracker crumbs (about 16 squares)

1/4 cup butter, melted or canola or soybean oil

1 tablespoon sugar

1 quart (4 cups) vanilla no-sugar-added, reduced-fat ice cream, slightly softened

1 can (8 ounces) crushed pineapple in juice, undrained

1/4 cup rum or 2 teaspoons rum extract

2 teaspoons coconut extract, if desired

1/4 cup flaked coconut, toasted*

*To toast coconut, bake uncovered in ungreased shallow pan in 350° oven 5 to 7 minutes, stirring occasionally, until golden brown.

1 Heat oven to 350°. Mix cracker crumbs, butter and sugar in small bowl. Press into ungreased square baking dish, 8 x 8 x 2 inches. Bake about 10 minutes or until dry. Cool completely, about 1 hour.

2 Beat ice cream, pineapple with juice, rum and coconut extract in large bowl with electric mixer on low speed just until blended. Spread in baked crust. Freeze about 6 hours or until firm.

3 Remove dessert from freezer about 5 minutes before serving. Sprinkle coconut over top.

1 Serving: Calories 165 (Calories from Fat 70); Fat 8g; Saturated Fat 5g (26% of Calories from Saturated Fat); *Trans* Fat 0g; Cholesterol 20mg; Omega-3 0g; Sodium 110mg

Carbohydrate 21g (Dietary Fiber 1g); Protein 2g

% Daily Value: Vitamin A 4%; Vitamin C 4%; Calcium 8%; Iron 2%; Folic Acid 2%

Exchanges: 1/2 Fruit, 1 Other Carbohydrates, 1 1/2 Fat

Carbohydrate Choices: 1 1/2

Frosty Margarita Pie

PREP: 15 MIN
FREEZE: 1 HR
30 MIN

8 SERVINGS

3/4 cup graham cracker crumbs
(10 squares)

1/2 cup finely chopped strawberries

1/2 cup sugar

1 quart (4 cups) vanilla fat-free
frozen yogurt

1 tablespoon grated lime peel

1/3 cup lime juice

2 to 4 tablespoons tequila, if desired

1 cup frozen (thawed) reduced-fat
whipped topping, if desired

Lime and strawberry slices, if desired

1 Mix cracker crumbs, chopped strawberries and
sugar in small bowl. Press in bottom and up sides of
pie plate, 9 x 1 1/4 inches; set aside.

2 Beat yogurt, lime peel, lime juice and tequila in
large bowl with electric mixer on high speed
just until blended. Spoon into crust. Freeze at least
1 1/2 hours or until firm enough to cut. Serve topped
with whipped topping; garnish with lime and
strawberry slices.

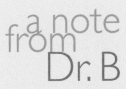

a note from Dr. B

*Holidays can present a
problem for staying on
your heart-health path.
To keep on track, follow
the basics: Keep up your
daily walk or other
exercise, plan ahead
what you will eat, keep
portion sizes small and
select desserts that are
low in calories and fat.
Make one of these
heart-healthy desserts
and bring it with you
to parties—you'll
know that you have a
dessert you can enjoy.*

*"Okay, so learning to take better care of myself and
my heart does mean changing a few things. But I won't give up pie!
This Frosty Margarita Pie is a creative way to keep some fun in my life."*

KEVIN W.

1 Serving: Calories 195 (Calories
from Fat 10); Fat 1g; Saturated Fat 0g
(1% of Calories from Saturated Fat);
Trans Fat 0g; Cholesterol 0mg;
Omega-3 0g; Sodium 95mg

Carbohydrate 43g (Dietary
Fiber 1g); Protein 3g

% Daily Value: Vitamin A 0%;
Vitamin C 20%; Calcium 8%;
Iron 2%; Folic Acid 2%

Exchanges: 1 Starch,
2 Other Carbohydrates

Carbohydrate Choices: 3

Mocha Cappuccino Pudding Cake

12 SERVINGS

a note from Dr. B

Everyone likes to indulge once in a while! This is a great dessert to indulge in, because one serving gives you that fabulous comfort-food taste but with lower fat and calories. You'll feel that you're taking care of yourself and eating well at the same time. If you are not a cappuccino lover, just leave out the coffee.

1 Serving: Calories 205 (Calories from Fat 20); Fat 2g; Saturated Fat 1g (6% of Calories from Saturated Fat); *Trans* Fat 0g; Cholesterol 5mg; Omega-3 0g; Sodium 190mg

Carbohydrate 44g (Dietary Fiber 1g); Protein 3g

% Daily Value: Vitamin A 2%; Vitamin C 0%; Calcium 8%; Iron 6%; Folic Acid 6%

Exchanges: 1/2 Milk, 2 1/2 Other Carbohydrates

Carbohydrate Choices: 3

1 1/4 cups all-purpose flour

1 3/4 cups sugar

1/4 cup baking cocoa

1 tablespoon instant espresso coffee (dry)

1 1/2 teaspoons baking powder

1/2 teaspoon salt

1/2 cup fat-free (skim) milk

2 tablespoons butter, melted or canola or soybean oil

1 teaspoon vanilla

1 teaspoon instant espresso coffee (dry)

1 1/2 cups very warm fat-free (skim) milk (120° to 130°)

1 Heat oven to 350°. Mix flour, 3/4 cup of the sugar, 2 tablespoons of the cocoa, 1 tablespoon espresso coffee, the baking powder and salt in medium bowl. Stir in 1/2 cup milk, butter and vanilla until well blended. Spread in ungreased square pan, 9 x 9 x 2 inches.

2 Mix remaining 1 cup sugar, remaining 2 tablespoons cocoa and 1 teaspoon espresso coffee in small bowl; sprinkle evenly over cake batter. Pour 1 1/2 cups very warm milk over sugar mixture.

3 Bake 35 to 45 minutes or until center is set and firm to the touch. Place sheet of aluminum foil or cookie sheet on lower oven rack under cake to catch any spills. Spoon warm cake into dessert dishes.

"This decadent dessert is low in fat and cholesterol."

WANDA S.

PREP: **25 MIN**

BAKE: **13 MIN**

COOL: **45 MIN**

CHILL: **2 HR**

Chocolate-Filled Cake Roll

12 SERVINGS

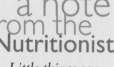

a note from the Nutritionist

Little things can make a big difference. Using a few mini chocolate chips makes it seem like a very chocolaty dessert without extra fat and sugar. And it's okay to eat eggs once in a while, as long as you keep your overall fat and cholesterol low. You can try the lower-cholesterol Omega-3 eggs offered in grocery stores.

1/4 cup powdered sugar

3 eggs

1 cup granulated sugar

1/3 cup water

1 teaspoon vanilla

1 cup all-purpose flour

1 teaspoon baking powder

1/4 teaspoon salt

2 tablespoons miniature chocolate chips

1 package (4-serving size) chocolate fat-free sugar-free instant pudding and pie filling mix

1 cup fat-free (skim) milk

1 cup frozen (thawed) fat-free whipped topping

1 Heat oven to 375°. Line jelly roll pan, 15 1/2 x 10 1/2 x 1 inch, with waxed paper. Grease waxed paper with shortening; lightly flour. Sprinkle powdered sugar evenly over clean dish towel in a rectangle the same size as the pan.

2 Beat eggs with balloon whisk or electric mixer with regular beaters on medium speed about 3 minutes or until thick and lemon colored. Beat in granulated sugar, water and vanilla. Beat in flour, baking powder and salt on low speed, mixing just until combined. Pour into pan. Sprinkle with chocolate chips.

3 Bake 11 to 13 minutes or until toothpick inserted in center comes out clean and top is just beginning to brown. Run knife around edges of pan to loosen cake. Immediately turn pan upside down onto sugared towel; remove pan and carefully peel off waxed paper. Place clean sheet of waxed paper over top of hot cake; gently roll up cake in towel starting with one long side. Cool at least 45 minutes.

4 Stir pudding mix (dry) and milk in medium bowl with wire whisk or fork 1 to 2 minutes or until thickened. Fold in whipped topping. Unroll cake and spread pudding mixture to within 1/2 inch of edges. Reroll cake. Wrap in plastic wrap; refrigerate at least 2 hours for filling to set. Store in refrigerator.

1 Serving: Calories 170 (Calories from Fat 20); Fat 2g; Saturated Fat 1g (5% of Calories from Saturated Fat); *Trans* Fat 0g; Cholesterol 55mg; Omega-3 0g; Sodium 210mg

Carbohydrate 34g (Dietary Fiber 1g); Protein 4g

% Daily Value: Vitamin A 2%; Vitamin C 0%; Calcium 6%; Iron 4%; Folic Acid 4%

Exchanges: 1 Starch, 1 Other Carbohydrates, 1/2 Fat

Carbohydrate Choices: 2

Double-Chocolate Chip Cookies

PREP: 30 MIN

BAKE: 8 TO 9 MIN
PER SHEET

2 DOZEN COOKIES

1/2 cup packed brown sugar

1/4 cup butter, softened

1/2 teaspoon vanilla

1 egg white

1 cup all-purpose flour

3 tablespoons baking cocoa

1/2 teaspoon baking soda

1/8 teaspoon salt

1/2 cup semisweet chocolate chips

1 Heat oven to 375°. Beat brown sugar and butter in large bowl with electric mixer on medium speed until light and fluffy, or mix with spoon. Beat in vanilla and egg white.

2 Stir in flour, cocoa, baking soda and salt. Stir in chocolate chips. Drop dough by teaspoonfuls about 2 inches apart onto ungreased cookie sheet.

3 Bake 8 to 9 minutes or until set (do not overbake). Cool 1 minute; remove from cookie sheet to wire rack.

a note from the Nutritionist

One way to increase the amount of whole grains you eat is to use whole grains in your baking. Whole wheat flour can be substituted for up to half of the all-purpose flour in most recipes. This is an excellent chocolate chip cookie with the great taste of chocolate in a lower-fat version.

"I can afford to have my daily chocolate fix with these delicious cookies at only 75 calories each! The chocolate chips and brown sugar are at reasonable amounts, and there's no egg yolk. All of these save on fat and calories, so you can treat yourself to one without the usual guilt."

LORI S.

1 Cookie: Calories 75 (Calories from Fat 25); Fat 3g; Saturated Fat 2g (23% of Calories from Saturated Fat); *Trans* Fat 0g; Cholesterol 5mg; Omega-3 0g; Sodium 60mg

Carbohydrate 11g (Dietary Fiber 1g); Protein 1g

% Daily Value: Vitamin A 0%; Vitamin C 0%; Calcium 0%; Iron 2%; Folic Acid 2%

Exchanges: 1 Other Carbohydrates, 1/2 Fat

Carbohydrate Choices: 1

Chewy Chocolate-Oat Bars

16 BARS

1/2 cup semisweet chocolate chips

1/3 cup fat-free sweetened condensed milk (from 14-ounce can) 1 cup whole wheat flour

1/2 cup old-fashioned or quick-cooking oats

1/2 teaspoon baking powder

1/2 teaspoon baking soda

1/4 teaspoon salt

3/4 cup packed brown sugar

1/4 cup canola or soybean oil

1 teaspoon vanilla

1/4 cup fat-free cholesterol-free egg product or 1 egg

2 tablespoons old-fashioned or quick-cooking oats

2 teaspoons butter, softened

1 Heat chocolate chips and milk in 1-quart heavy saucepan over low heat, stirring frequently, until chocolate is melted and mixture is smooth; set aside. Heat oven to 350°. Spray square pan, 8 x 8 x 2 or 9 x 9 x 2 inches, with cooking spray.

2 Mix flour, 1/2 cup oats, the baking powder, baking soda and salt in large bowl; set aside. Stir brown sugar, oil, vanilla and egg product in medium bowl with fork until smooth; stir into flour mixture until blended. Reserve 1/2 cup dough in small bowl for topping.

3 Pat remaining dough in pan (spray fingers with cooking spray or lightly flour if dough is sticky). Spread chocolate mixture over dough. Add 2 tablespoons oats and the butter to reserved dough; mix with pastry blender or fork until crumbly. Drop small spoonfuls of oat mixture evenly over chocolate mixture.

4 Bake 20 to 25 minutes or until top is golden and firm. Cool completely, about 1 1/2 hours. For bars, cut into 4 rows by 4 rows.

"One thing I do indulge in almost every night is popcorn made with olive oil and sprinkled with butter sprinkles and lemon pepper.

These delicious chocolate-oat bars are another great treat."

NANCY D.

Ginger-Orange Bars

48 BARS

1/2 cup sugar

1/2 cup butter, softened

1/2 cup molasses

1 egg

1 1/2 cups all-purpose flour

1/2 cup whole wheat flour

1 teaspoon baking soda

1/4 teaspoon ground ginger

2/3 cup buttermilk

2 teaspoons grated orange peel

Orange Frosting (below)

1 Heat oven to 350°. Spray jelly roll pan, 15 1/2 x 10 1/2 x 1 inch, with cooking spray.

2 Beat sugar and butter in large bowl with electric mixer on medium speed until light and fluffy. Beat in molasses and egg.

3 Mix all-purpose flour, whole wheat flour, baking soda and ginger in small bowl; add to sugar mixture alternately with buttermilk, beating on low speed until blended. Stir in orange peel. Spread in pan.

4 Bake 15 to 20 minutes or until toothpick inserted in center comes out clean. Cool completely, about 30 minutes.

5 Meanwhile, make Orange Frosting. Spread frosting over cooled bars. For bars, cut into 8 rows by 6 rows.

a note from Dr. B

Although butter contains saturated fat, you can still have some as long as you keep the amount low. For baking, use oil whenever you can, and try to eliminate shortening, the highest source of trans fat.

Orange Frosting

2 cups powdered sugar

1 tablespoon butter, softened

1/2 teaspoon grated orange peel

2 to 4 tablespoons orange juice

Mix all frosting ingredients in small bowl, adding enough orange juice for desired spreading consistency; beat until smooth.

1 Cookie: Calories 80 (Calories from Fat 20); Fat 2g; Saturated Fat 1g (16% of Calories from Saturated Fat); *Trans* Fat 0g; Cholesterol 10mg; Omega-3 0g; Sodium 45mg

Carbohydrate 14g (Dietary Fiber 0g); Protein 1g

% Daily Value: Vitamin A 2%; Vitamin C 0%; Calcium 0%; Iron 2%; Folic Acid 2%

Exchanges: 1/2 Starch, 1/2 Other Carbohydrates

Carbohydrate Choices: 1

Glazed Lemon-Coconut Bars

12 BARS

1 cup Reduced Fat Bisquick® mix

2 tablespoons powdered sugar

2 tablespoons firm butter

3/4 cup granulated sugar

1/4 cup flaked coconut

1 tablespoon Reduced Fat Bisquick mix

2 teaspoons grated lemon peel

2 tablespoons lemon juice

1/2 cup fat-free cholesterol-free egg product

Lemon Glaze (below)

1. Heat oven to 350°. Mix 1 cup Bisquick mix and the powdered sugar in small bowl. Cut in butter, using pastry blender or crisscrossing 2 knives, until crumbly. Press in ungreased square pan, 8 x 8 x 2 inches.

2. Bake about 10 minutes or until light brown. Meanwhile, mix remaining ingredients except Lemon Glaze in small bowl.

3. Pour coconut mixture over baked layer. Bake about 25 minutes longer or until set and golden brown. Loosen edges from sides of pan while warm. Make Lemon Glaze; spread over bars. Cool completely, about 1 hour. For bars, cut into 4 rows by 3 rows.

Lemon Glaze

1/2 cup powdered sugar

1 tablespoon lemon juice

Mix ingredients in small bowl until smooth.

1 Cookie: Calories 145 (Calories from Fat 25); Fat 3g; Saturated Fat 2g (12% of Calories from Saturated Fat); *Trans* Fat 0g; Cholesterol 5mg; Omega-3 0g; Sodium 150mg

Carbohydrate 27g (Dietary Fiber 0g); Protein 2g

% Daily Value: Vitamin A 2%; Vitamin C 0%; Calcium 0%; Iron 2%; Folic Acid 4%

Exchanges: 1 Starch, 1 Other Carbohydrates, 1/2 Fat

Carbohydrate Choices: 2

Jumbo Molasses Cookies

ABOUT 3 DOZEN COOKIES

a note from the Nutritionist

Molasses cookies are an old-fashioned favorite. These oversize cookies are cakelike and tender with the added bonus of being low in fat. Make a glaze by stirring 1/2 cup powdered sugar, 1 1/2 teaspoons fat-free (skim) milk, 2 drops of vanilla and, if desired, 2 drops butter flavor in a small bowl until smooth. Drizzle over cookies.

1 cup sugar

1/2 cup butter, softened

1 cup dark molasses

1/2 cup water

4 cups all-purpose flour

1 1/2 teaspoons salt

1 1/2 teaspoons ground ginger

1 teaspoon baking soda

1/2 teaspoon ground cloves

1/2 teaspoon ground nutmeg

1/4 teaspoon ground allspice

Sugar

1 Beat 1 cup sugar and the butter in large bowl with electric mixer on medium speed, or mix with spoon. Stir in remaining ingredients except sugar. Cover and refrigerate at least 3 hours until dough is firm.

2 Heat oven to 375°. Generously grease cookie sheet with shortening. Roll dough 1/4 inch thick on generously floured cloth-covered surface. Cut into 3-inch circles. Sprinkle with sugar. Place about 1 1/2 inches apart on cookie sheet.

3 Bake 10 to 12 minutes or until almost no indentation remains when touched lightly in center. Cool 2 minutes; remove from cookie sheet to wire rack.

1 Cookie: Calories 125 (Calories from Fat 25); Fat 3g; Saturated Fat 2g (12% of Calories from Saturated Fat); *Trans* Fat 0g; Cholesterol 5mg; Omega-3 0g; Sodium 150mg

Carbohydrate 24g (Dietary Fiber 0g); Protein 1g

% Daily Value: Vitamin A 2%; Vitamin C 0%; Calcium 2%; Iron 6%; Folic Acid 4%

Exchanges: 1/2 Starch, 1 Other Carbohydrates, 1/2 Fat

Carbohydrate Choices: 1 1/2

Be Good to Your Heart with Smart Fats

Studies show that some fat is essential for everyone, so dietary fats are now being perceived in a much more positive light. A good goal: Keep your calories from fat to between 20 to 35 percent of total calories, and keep saturated fat calories to no more than 10 percent of total calories.

The good news: Canola, olive and other vegetable oils can benefit your heart. Replacing some saturated-fat foods with poly- and monounsaturated fat foods to improve your ratio of "protective" cholesterol.

Add monounsaturated (good) fats to your diet by:

Snacking on walnuts, soy nuts, almonds, peanuts or adding nuts to salads, stir-fries, snacks and desserts.

Cooking, sautéing and baking with canola or olive oil.

Snacking on small amounts of avocados and olives or topping salads and casseroles with them.

Eating fatty fish once or twice a week, especially salmon, herring, mackerel, sardines, bluefish, pompano and albacore tuna.

Replacing some of the flour in baked goods with ground flaxseed (tablespoon for tablespoon) to increase good Omega-3 fatty acids. One teaspoon of ground flaxseed per day in a muffin, cookie or other baked good provides heart-protective benefits.

Simple ways to lower your overall fat and saturated fat:

- **Eat smaller portions.** As portions grow, so do calories and fat. Skip the super-size meals and snacks, and choose normal-size servings. Fill up on fruits and vegetables if you are still hungry.

- **Trim visible fat** from meat and remove skin from chicken and turkey before eating.

- **Cook lean.** Use cooking sprays instead of fat in nonstick pans. Also, broil, bake, roast, grill, poach, steam, stew or microwave foods whenever possible.

- **Select lean chicken, turkey, fish and meat.** Light-meat chicken and turkey are naturally low in fat, especially if you remove the skin. Most fish is also very lean.

- **Go meatless a couple of times each week.** Limiting the amount of meat and poultry you eat can help reduce saturated fat, while increasing fiber and complex carbohydrates. Instead of meat, try dishes made with dried beans and peas, grains, vegetables and fruits.

- **Choose reduced-fat mayonnaise, salad dressings and sour cream.** The amount of fat in creamy dressings can add up fast, so use reduced-fat whenever possible.

- **Use fat-free or reduced-fat dairy products.** Drink fat-free (skim) milk and use plain nonfat yogurt, cottage cheese, cheese, pudding and ice cream.

- **Go easy on butter, margarine and cream sauces.** Use tub margarine as a spread, canola oil or butter in baking and cream sauces once in a great while.

- **Cut back on "hidden" fats and trans fats** in foods like potato or other chips, French fries, high-fat cheeses and in baked goods such as doughnuts, muffins and cookies. Instead, eat lower-fat microwave popcorn, whole-grain tortilla chips, pretzels and other lower-fat snacks.

- **Be a label reader.** Nutrition labels tell you how much fat, saturated fat and trans fats each food contains.

- **Indulge in fresh fruits and vegetables.** Evidence indicates that eating a diet rich in many veggies and fruits can lower the risk of heart disease.

How much fat should I eat every day?

To estimate how many total grams of fat to aim for, multiply your daily calorie level by 30 percent and divide by 9. For example, if you need 2,000 calories per day, 2,000 calories x .3 = 600 calories. 600 calories/9 calories per gram of fat = 67 grams.

PREP: 20 MIN

BAKE: 10 TO 12 MIN
PER SHEET

Old-Fashioned Spiced Fruit Cookies

ABOUT 3 DOZEN COOKIES

1 medium tart red apple, unpeeled, cored and cut into wedges

1 medium orange, unpeeled and cut into wedges

1 cup chopped dates

3/4 cup packed brown sugar

1/2 cup canola or soybean oil

1 egg

1 cup all-purpose flour

1 cup whole wheat flour

1 cup plus 2 tablespoons ground flaxseed or flaxseed meal

1 teaspoon baking soda

1 teaspoon ground cinnamon

1/4 teaspoon salt

1/4 teaspoon ground nutmeg

1/4 teaspoon ground cloves

1 Heat oven to 350°. Place apple, orange and dates in blender or food processor. Cover and blend or process until well blended.

2 Mix brown sugar, oil and egg in large bowl. Stir in remaining ingredients and fruit mixture. Drop dough by tablespoonfuls onto ungreased cookie sheet.

3 Bake 10 to 12 minutes or until light golden brown. Immediately remove from cookie sheet.

Spiced Fruit Bars: Spread dough in ungreased rectangular pan, 13 x 9 x 2 inches. Bake 23 to 27 minutes or until toothpick inserted in center comes out clean. For bars, cut into 6 rows by 6 rows. 36 bars.

2 Cookies: Calories 220 (Calories from Fat 80); Fat 9g; Saturated Fat 1g (2% of Calories from Saturated Fat); Trans Fat 0g; Cholesterol 10mg; Omega-3 2g; Sodium 115mg

Carbohydrate 31g (Dietary Fiber 4g); Protein 4g

% Daily Value: Vitamin A 0%; Vitamin C 2%; Calcium 4%; Iron 20%; Folic Acid 20%

Exchanges: 1 Starch, 1 Other Carbohydrates, 2 Fat

Carbohydrate Choices: 2

"I like to snack. I always keep apples, bananas or dried fruit at my desk. I buy the best produce available because it is a treat. That keeps me from eating other, not as healthy, foods."

NANCI D.

Orchard Date-Apricot Bars

PREP: **20 MIN**

BAKE: **30 MIN**

COOL: **1 HR**

36 BARS

Date-Apricot Filling (below)

1 cup packed brown sugar

3/4 cup canola or soybean oil

3/4 cup all-purpose flour

1 cup plus 2 tablespoons ground flaxseed or flaxseed meal

1 teaspoon salt

1/2 teaspoon baking soda

1 1/2 cups quick-cooking oats

1 Make Date-Apricot Filling; cool. Heat oven to 400°. Spray rectangular pan, 13 x 9 x 2 inches, with cooking spray.

2 Mix brown sugar and oil in large bowl. Stir in remaining ingredients; mixture will be moist and crumbly. Press half of the crumb mixture evenly in bottom of pan. Spread with date-apricot filling. Top with remaining crumb mixture; press lightly.

3 Bake 25 to 30 minutes or until lightly browned. Cool in pan on wire rack about 1 hour. For bars, cut into 6 rows by 6 rows.

Date-Apricot Filling

1 1/4 cups dates (8 ounces pitted)

1 1/2 cups dried apricots, cut up (8 ounces)

1/2 cup sugar

1 1/2 cups water

Mix all ingredients in a saucepan until well blended. Cook over medium-low heat, stirring constantly, until thickened, about 10 minutes.

a note from Dr. B

This wonderful, old-fashioned recipe now contains flaxseed. Buying whole flaxseed and grinding it into meal with a coffee grinder is less expensive than buying ground flaxseed. Because flaxseed is high in fat (good fat) and fats do not keep very long, grind only the amount you need and keep it covered in the refrigerator for up to two weeks.

1 Cookie: Calories 155 (Calories from Fat 55); Fat 6g; Saturated Fat 0g (3% of Calories from Saturated Fat); *Trans* Fat 0g; Cholesterol 0mg; Omega-3 1g; Sodium 90mg

Carbohydrate 23g (Dietary Fiber 2g); Protein 2g

% Daily Value: Vitamin A 4%; Vitamin C 0%; Calcium 2%; Iron 10%; Folic Acid 10%

Exchanges: 1/2 Starch, 1 Other Carbohydrates, 1 Fat

Carbohydrate Choices: 1 1/2

Molasses Lover's Carrot-Raisin Cookies

ABOUT 3 DOZEN COOKIES

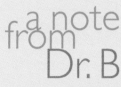

a note from Dr. B

You can experiment with flaxseed meal to increase your consumption of Omega-3 fatty acids. In recent studies, 1 gram, or about 1 teaspoon, of ground flaxseed per day was shown to reduce cholesterol and triglyceride levels. You'll get that amount by eating two of these cookies a day.

2/3 cup dark molasses

1/2 cup canola or soybean oil

1 egg

1 cup all-purpose flour

1 cup plus 2 tablespoons ground flaxseed or flaxseed meal

1/2 cup wheat germ

1/2 teaspoon baking powder

1/2 teaspoon baking soda

1 cup shredded carrots

1/2 cup golden raisins

Glaze (below)

1 Heat oven to 375°. Mix molasses, oil and egg in medium bowl. Stir in remaining ingredients. Drop dough by tablespoonfuls onto ungreased cookie sheet.

2 Bake 6 to 9 minutes or just until set. Let stand 1 minute; remove from cookie sheet to wire rack. Cool completely, about 30 minutes. Make Glaze; drizzle about 1/2 teaspoon over each cookie.

Glaze

1 cup powdered sugar

4 to 5 teaspoons fat-free (skim) milk

1/2 teaspoon vanilla

Mix ingredients in small bowl until smooth.

1 Cookie: Calories 110 (Calories from Fat 45); Fat 5g; Saturated Fat 0g (4% of Calories from Saturated Fat); *Trans* Fat 0g; Cholesterol 5mg; Omega-3 1g; Sodium 30mg

Carbohydrate 14g (Dietary Fiber 1g); Protein 2g

% Daily Value: Vitamin A 10%; Vitamin C 0%; Calcium 2%; Iron 10%; Folic Acid 12%

Exchanges: 1 Other Carbohydrates, 1 Fat

Carbohydrate Choices: 1

"The midnight raid on the kitchen is satisfied with this healthy, tasty cookie."

PAT R.

Chewy Chocolate-Oat Bars (page 220), Molasses Lover's Carrot-Raisin Cookies and Old-Fashioned Spiced Fruit Cookies (page 226)

A Menu Plan with Your Heart in Mind

To help you get started, try our week's worth of heart-healthy eating suggestions. You can think of them as ideas for healthy, quick meals and snacks that contain moderate calories, fat and saturated fat and higher fiber.

A good way to begin is to determine your calorie needs. See page 24 for a quick way to estimate your calories. If you are trying to lose weight, you will want to decrease your calorie and fat intake and increase your activity level. These daily menus vary from about 1,700 to 1,800 calories, 25 to 33 grams of total fat, about 10 grams of saturated fat and less than 300 milligrams of cholesterol. Feel free to mix and match meals from different days to add variety and tailor the plan to your liking. Do keep track of calories, fat and saturated fat and cholesterol to make sure you're not eating too much or too little. Here's to your heart health!

Based on your individual calorie needs, shoot for these daily goals:

- **Total fat**—30 percent or less of total calories

- **Saturated fat**—10 percent or less of total calories

- **Dietary cholesterol**—300 milligrams or less per day

Monday

Breakfast
1 serving Cheerios® cereal
1 cup fat-free (skim) milk
1 medium banana or 1/2 cup blueberries
1 cup decaf coffee or herbal tea
Calories 305 • Total Fat 0g • Saturated Fat 0g • Cholesterol 4mg

Lunch
1 serving Turkey-Wild Rice Soup (page 112)
1 slice whole wheat bread or dinner roll
1 teaspoon squeeze or soft tub margarine
Carrot and celery sticks
2 tablespoons reduced-fat vegetable or ranch dip
1 medium nectarine
Calories 400 • Total Fat 13g • Saturated Fat 2g • Cholesterol 28mg

Dinner
1 serving Apple-Rosemary Pork and Barley (page 124)
1 serving 1 cup steamed green beans or
Sweet Potato Wedges (page 200)
1 small whole-grain dinner roll
1 teaspoon squeeze or soft tub margarine
1 serving Sherbet and Melon
1 cup fat-free (skim) milk
Calories 830 • Total Fat 11g • Saturated Fat 2g • Cholesterol 65mg

Snack
(can be eaten any time during the day)
1 medium orange or clementine
6 ounces low-fat yogurt or 1/2 cup sugar-free,
fat-free pudding chocolate made with fat-free (skim) milk
2 tablespoons fat-free whipped topping
Calories 245 • Total Fat 2g • Saturated Fat 1g • Cholesterol 8mg

DAILY TOTAL: Calories 1780 • Total Fat 26g • Percent Calories from Fat 13% • Percent Calories from Sat Fat 1.5% • Saturated Fat 5g
Carbohydrate 172g • Cholesterol 110mg • Protein 73g • Fiber 33g • Sodium 2130mg

Tuesday

Breakfast
1 Flaxseed Morning Glory Muffin (page 34)
1 cup fat-free (skim) milk
1/2 cup orange juice

Calories 370 • Total Fat 10g • Saturated Fat 0g • Cholesterol 24mg

Lunch
1 serving Barbecued Chicken Pizza (page 146)
1 cup grapes
1/2 cup bell pepper strips or cucumber slices
1 cup fat-free (skim) milk

Calories 495 • Total Fat 10g • Saturated Fat 4g • Cholesterol 55mg

Dinner
1 serving Glazed Beef Tenderloin with
Herbed New Potatoes (page 115)
1 serving Easy Fresh-Fruit Salad (page 182) or mixed-greens salad
with 2 tablespoons reduced-fat Caesar dressing
1 serving Mocha Cappuccino Pudding Cake (page 216)
1 cup fat-free (skim) milk

Calories 750 • Total Fat 4g • Saturated Fat 6g • Cholesterol 89mg

Snack
(can be eaten any time during the day)
1 serving Roasted Sesame and Honey Snack Mix (page 66)
1 medium apple

Calories 245 • Total Fat 4g • Saturated Fat 0g • Cholesterol 0mg

DAILY TOTAL: Calories 1860 • Total Fat 38g • Percent Calories from Fat 19% • Percent Calories from Saturated Fat 2% • Saturated Fat 11g
Carbohydrate 295g • Cholesterol 168mg • Protein 91g • Fiber 19g • Sodium 2855mg

Wednesday

Breakfast
Cornmeal-Berry Scone (page 77)
1/2 cup sliced strawberries
1 cup fat-free yogurt (any flavor)

Calories 335 • Total Fat 6g • Saturated Fat 4g • Cholesterol 20mg

Lunch
1 serving Curried Tuna Salad with Toasted Pecans (page 98)
1 slice whole-grain bread or dinner roll
1 teaspoon squeeze or soft tub margarine
1/2 cup baby carrots, corn or peas
1/2 cup pineapple chunks

Calories 480 • Total Fat 9g • Saturated Fat 1g • Cholesterol 25mg

Dinner
1 serving Glazed Chicken over Couscous Pilaf (page 105)
1 serving Fresh Spinach, Orange and Red Onion Salad (page 195) or
Wilted Spinach Vinaigrette (page 198)
1 Chewy Chocolate-Oat Bar (page 220)
1 cup fat-free (skim) milk

Calories 705 • Total Fat 11g • Saturated Fat 3g • Cholesterol 89mg

Snack
(can be eaten any time during the day)
1 medium pear
3 cups light popcorn
1 cup fat-free (skim) milk

Calories 265 • Total Fat 3g • Saturated Fat 1g • Cholesterol 4mg

DAILY TOTAL: Calories 1785 • Total Fat 29g • Percent Calories from Fat 15% • Percent Calories from Sat Fat 4.5% • Saturated Fat 9g
Carbohydrate 291g • Cholesterol 138mg • Protein 99g • Fiber 30g • Sodium 2125mg

Thursday

Breakfast
1 serving Canadian Bacon and Potato Frittata (page 38)
2 slices whole-wheat bread, toasted
2 teaspoons jam or jelly
1/2 cup cranberry juice
Calories 460 • Total Fat 5g • Saturated Fat 2g • Cholesterol 15mg

Lunch
1 serving Loaded Potatoes (page 132)
1 cup baby-cut carrots
1 medium banana
1 cup fat-free (skim) milk
Calories 470 • Total Fat 6g • Saturated Fat 3g • Cholesterol 29mg

Dinner
1 serving Broiled Dijon Burgers (page 118)
1 serving Swiss Potato Patties (page 203)
1 cup steamed broccoli with lemon
1 serving Créme Caramel (page 208)
Calories 535 • Total Fat 11g • Saturated Fat 5g • Cholesterol 60mg

Snack
(can be eaten any time during the day)
1 serving Harvest Bread (page 75) or
2 Molasses Lover's Carrot-Raisin Cookies (page 228)
1 cup fat-free (skim) milk
Calories 270 • Total Fat 7g • Saturated Fat 1g • Cholesterol 5mg

DAILY TOTAL: Calories 1735 • Total Fat 29g • Percent Calories from Fat 15% • Percent Calories from Saturated Fat 6% • Saturated Fat 11g
Carbohydrate 281g • Cholesterol 119mg • Protein 96g • Fiber 28g • Sodium 2780mg

Friday

Breakfast
1 serving Berry-Banana Smoothie (page 32)
1 whole-wheat English muffin
2 teaspoons peanut butter
Calories 445 • Total Fat 10g • Saturated Fat 2g • Cholesterol 9mg

Lunch
1 serving Curried Tuna Salad with Toasted Pecans (page 98)
1 serving Triple-Cabbage Slaw (page 196)
1 medium apple
1 cup fat-free (skim) milk
Calories 500 • Total Fat 3g • Saturated Fat 1g • Cholesterol 29mg

Dinner
1 serving Barley, Corn and Lima Bean Sauté (page 161)
1 serving Nutty Greens with Ranch Dressing (page 185)
1 slice French bread
1 serving Peach and Blueberry Crisp with Crunchy Topping (page 210)
Calories 675 • Total Fat 14g • Saturated Fat 5g • Cholesterol 0mg

Snack
(can be eaten any time during the day)
1 serving Campfire Popcorn Snack (page 69)
1 cup chocolate fat-free (skim) milk
Calories 210 • Total Fat 1g • Saturated Fat 0g • Cholesterol 0mg

DAILY TOTAL: Calories 1830 • Total Fat 29g • Percent Calories from Fat 14% • Percent Calories from Saturated Fat 4% • Saturated Fat 8g
Carbohydrate 345g • Cholesterol 38mg • Protein 91g • Fiber 42g • Sodium 2830mg

Saturday

Breakfast
1 serving Baked Apple Oatmeal (page 36)
1/2 cup cherries or 1 medium banana
1 serving Sugar 'n Spice Green Tea (page 31)
Calories 382 • Total Fat 8g • Saturated Fat 1g • Cholesterol 0mg

Lunch
1 serving Rush-Hour Tuna Melts (page 148)
1 serving Quinoa-Almond Salad (page 157) or
Harvest Salad (page 179)
1 cup fat-free (skim) milk
Calories 555 • Total Fat 13g • Saturated Fat 3g • Cholesterol 24mg

Dinner
1 serving Grilled Salmon with Hazelnut Butter (page 151)
1 Wild Rice–Corn Muffin (page 76)
1 serving Sweet Potato Wedges (page 202)
1 teaspoon squeeze or soft tub margarine
1 cup cooked bell pepper strips
1 cup fat-free (skim) milk
Calories 710 • Total Fat 29g • Saturated Fat 7g • Cholesterol 95mg

Snack
(can be eaten any time during the day)
1/4 cup cottage cheese
2 tablespoons sunflower nuts or
1/2 cup reduced-fat frozen yogurt or ice cream
1 tablespoon fat-free chocolate fudge topping
Calories 150 • Total Fat 10g • Saturated Fat 3g • Cholesterol 0mg

DAILY TOTAL: Calories 1795 • Total Fat 60g • Percent Calories from Fat 29% • Percent Calories from Saturated Fat 7% • Saturated Fat 14g
Carbohydrate 116g • Cholesterol 135mg • Protein 97g • Fiber 22g • Sodium 1845mg

Sunday

Breakfast
1/2 cup high-fiber cereal
1 cup fat-free (skim) milk
1 cup fresh raspberries or blueberries
Calories 200 • Total Fat 1g • Saturated Fat 0g • Cholesterol 14mg

Lunch
1 serving Chunky Vegetable Chowder (page 141)
6 whole-grain crackers with 1 to 2 ounces mozzarella cheese
1 hard roll
1 teaspoon squeeze or soft tub margarine
1 cup cherry tomatoes or grape tomatoes
1 cup fat-free (skim) milk
Calories 745 • Total Fat 24g • Saturated Fat 7g • Cholesterol 29mg

Dinner
1 serving Plum-Glazed Turkey Tenderloins (page 106)
1/2 cup cooked brown rice
1 serving Dilled Corn with Popped Amaranth (page 199)
1 serving Frosty Margarita Pie (page 215)
1 cup hot herbal tea or coffee
Calories 720 • Total Fat 10g • Saturated Fat 3g • Cholesterol 75mg

Snack
(can be eaten any time during the day)
1 whole-grain granola bar or 1/2 cup Hiker's Trail Mix (page 68)
1/2 cup apple juice or apple cider
Calories 170 • Total Fat 2g • Saturated Fat 1g • Cholesterol 0mg

DAILY TOTAL: Calories 1835 • Total Fat 37g • Percent Calories from Fat 18% • Percent Calories from Saturated Fat 5% • Saturated Fat 11g
Carbohydrate 308g • Cholesterol 108mg • Protein 73g • Fiber 27g • Sodium 2010mg

Additional Resources

Heart and Health Web Sites

American Heart Association
www.americanheart.org

Centers for Disease Control and Prevention
www.cdc.gov/health

Mayo Clinic
www.mayoclinic.com

National Heart, Lung, and Blood Institute
www.nhlbi.nih.gov

WomenHeart:
The National Coalition for Women with Heart Disease
www.womenheart.org

Texas Heart® Institute
www.texasheart.com

Nutrition and Healthful Eating Web Sites

American Dietetic Association
www.eatright.org

Beltsville Human Nutrition Research Center
www.barc.usda.gov/bhnrc

Glossary of Heart-Healthy Terms

Below you'll find definitions of the nutrition and medical terms used in this cookbook.

Angina Pectoris: A disease characterized by brief attacks of crushing pain in the chest.

Antioxidant: Substances that inhibit oxidation in plant and animal cells. Found in fruits and vegetables, antioxidants may be important in preventing cholesterol from damaging your arteries.

Arteries: The blood vessels that deliver oxygen and other nutrients to your body's cells.

Atherosclerosis: A chronic disease characterized by abnormal thickening and hardening of the *arterial* walls; plaque builds up on these walls, making them thicker and less flexible.

Blood Vessels: The network of tubes that carry blood throughout your body.

Body Mass Index (BMI): A method of measurement, used to determine whether a person is obese, that takes your weight and height into account.

Cardiovascular Disease: The catch-all term for diseases of the heart and blood vessels.

Carotenoid: A category of nutrients that produce colors—usually yellow to red—in foods, such as carrots, and may be important for health. Carotenoids include beta-carotene, a precursor to Vitamin A.

Cholesterol: A fatlike substance found in animal fat that is important for cell structures, hormones or nerve coverings. LDL (low-density lipoprotein), or "bad" cholesterol, increases the risk of heart disease. HDL (high-density lipoprotein), or "good" cholesterol, protects against heart disease.

Circulatory System: The organs that move blood through the body, including the heart, lungs, arteries and veins.

Congenital Heart Disease: Heart defects that are present at birth. These can include improperly formed blood vessels or heart valves or problems with the walls between different sections of the heart.

Congestive Heart Failure: Commonly known as heart failure, it is the result of the heart—which may be damaged by heart diseases, heart attacks or other problems—working too long, too hard.

Coronary Artery Disease: See Coronary Heart Disease, below.

Coronary Heart Disease (CHD): A buildup of fatty, cholesterol-filled deposits in the arteries that block the normal flow of blood and can cause a heart attack. In America, this is the most common heart disease.

DASH Diet: The acronym for the Dietary Approaches to Stop Hypertension diet study. The DASH diet included more fruits and vegetables, low-fat dairy products and less saturated fat than a typical American diet. During the study, participants who followed the diet found their blood pressures dropped.

Diabetes: A disease that occurs when the body is not able to use glucose (a form of sugar produced from the digestion of carbohydrate foods) for energy.

Fat: A necessary nutrient, fat helps build new cells, shuttles vitamins through the body and makes particular hormones that regulate blood pressure.

Fiber: The material in plant foods that the body does not digest; it passes through to be eliminated.

Folic Acid (Folate): An important B vitamin found in leafy green vegetables, in citrus fruits and in legumes. Folic acid protects the heart by helping to lower the body's levels of homocysteine, produced when the body breaks down proteins.

Heart Attack: A disabling or life-threatening condition that occurs when blood flow to the heart is cut off.

Heart Failure: A condition that is the result of the heart—which may be damaged by heart diseases, heart attacks or other problems—working too long, too hard.

Hemorrhagic Stroke: A type of stroke caused by bleeding in the brain.

High Blood Pressure (Hypertension): When the force of a heartbeat pushes blood into your arteries, it exerts pressure on the walls of the blood vessels. Blood pressure is classified as "high" when it is equal to or greater than 140/90 millimeters of mercury.

High-Density Lipoprotein (HDL): "Good" cholesterol, HDL carries cholesterol to the liver where it is broken down and removed from the body. The higher your HDL, the lower your risk of cholesterol building up in your arteries, and the lower your risk of developing coronary heart disease.

Homocysteine: A substance produced when the body breaks down proteins. High blood levels of homocysteine are associated with an increased risk of coronary artery disease.

Hypertension: See High Blood Pressure, above.

Insoluble Fiber: Fiber that doesn't dissolve in water; it helps add bulk to stools and keeps the bowels moving regularly. It is found primarily in whole-grain cereals and bread, bran and in the skins of fruits and vegetables.

Isoflavones: Hormone-like substances, found in plant sources such as soybeans, that may have heart-protective and cancer-preventive effects.

Lipid Profile: An analysis of the fats (lipids) present in your blood.

Lipoprotein: The combination of the lipids and protein in your blood.

Low-Density Lipoprotein (LDL): "Bad" cholesterol, LDL carries cholesterol through the bloodstream to your cells. The higher your LDL, the higher your risk of cholesterol building up in your arteries, and the greater your risk of developing coronary heart disease.

Meditation: A quiet form of contemplation and mindfulness used to establish a sense of peace, inner calm and relaxation.

Metabolic Syndrome: A cluster of conditions that place you at greater risk of heart disease. These include insulin resistance, high blood pressure, high blood levels of triglycerides, low levels of HDL and an increased tendency for blood to clot.

Monounsaturated Fat: "Good" fats found in canola oil, olive oil, nuts and avocados. Liquid at room temperature, these fats tend to raise heart-healthy HDL cholesterol while lowering "bad" LDL cholesterol.

Nutrients: Substances used by the body to build, repair and maintain cells. Protein, carbohydrates, fats, water, vitamins and minerals all are examples of essential nutrients.

Obese: The medical designation for people who have a body mass index (BMI) of 30 or above.

Omega-3 Fatty Acids: Unsaturated fats, found in fatty fish such as salmon, herring, mackerel, sardines, bluefish, pompano and albacore tuna and in plant sources such as flaxseed and walnuts.

Overweight: The medical designation for people who have a body mass index (BMI) of 25 to 29.

Phytonutrients: Nutrients found in plant foods that help strengthen our bodies' defenses against heart disease.

Polyunsaturated Fat: "Good" fats, liquid at room temperature, found in corn, soybean, sunflower and other salad oils.

Protein: This nutrient helps the body build new cells. In addition, proteins work with hormones and enzymes to help the body function and generate infection-fighting antibodies.

Saturated Fat: "Bad" fats that tend to elevate blood cholesterol levels and that are solid at room temperature. These fats are found mostly in animal foods such as meat, cheese, butter, whole milk and poultry. Other highly saturated fats are found in coconut and palm oil, as well as in cocoa butter.

Soluble Fiber: Fiber that can be dissolved in water. It helps lower cholesterol in the blood. The best sources of soluble fiber are oats, barley, rye, beans, seeds and nuts, brown rice and most fruits and vegetables.

Stroke: The sudden reduction or loss of consciousness, sensation and voluntary motion caused by a rupture or obstruction of an artery in the brain.

Syndrome X: See Metabolic Syndrome, above.

Trans Fatty Acids: Fats produced when hydrogen is added to liquid vegetable oil, turning it into a solid fat. Found in shortening, stick margarine, French fries, doughnuts and baked goods. These fats may raise blood cholesterol.

Triglycerides: A transportable type of fat found in the blood. Triglycerides are used as a form of energy by the body; high blood triglyceride levels add to the risk of developing heart disease.

Unsaturated Fat: "Good" fats, liquid at room temperature, that do not tend to elevate blood cholesterol levels. These fats usually come from plant sources and include olive oil, sunflower oil, corn oil, nuts and avocados.

Veins: The system of blood vessels that carries deoxygenated blood back to the heart to be reoxygenated.

Vitamins: A group of vital nutrients, found in small amounts in a variety of foods, that are key to cell development, controlling body functions and helping release energy from fuel sources.

Whole Grains: The entire edible part of any grain: the bran, endosperm and germ. Wheat, corn, oats and rice are the most common whole grains. Experts recommend eating at least three servings of whole grains every day.

Yoga: An ancient practice based on deep breathing, stretching and strengthening exercises that is believed to balance the mind, body and spirit.

The Doctor Explains Heart Tests

Several tests or series of tests can diagnose possible heart disease. The choice of which test and how many tests to perform depends upon a patient's risk factors, history of heart problems and current symptoms and the doctor's interpretation of these factors.

At first, a doctor starts with simple tests. More complicated ones may be used if needed. More specific tests depend on the patient's particular problem and the cardiologist's assessment of that problem.

Some of the tests are **noninvasive** and don't involve inserting needles, instruments or fluids into the body. Other tests are **invasive** and do involve inserting needles, instruments or fluids into the body. The top tests used to diagnose heart disease are:

Angiogram—Shows the amount of blockage in the vessels around the heart and is used to determine whether bypass open-heart surgery or percutaneous coronary intervention (angioplasty or stenting) is needed. To perform the test, a thin plastic tube (catheter) is used to inject dye into the coronary arteries.

Coronary Calcium Imaging by Electron Beam Tomography (EBT)—This noninvasive test determines the amount of plaque burden in the arteries and can detect atherosclerosis before the person notices symptoms. Each person's score is compared to that of others their age, and a coronary calcium percentile is determined. Scores that are less than 75 percent for one's age indicate premature aggressive coronary atherosclerosis.

Cardiac Catherization—Measures blood pressure within the heart and how much oxygen is in the blood and gives information about the pumping ability of the heart muscle. A catheter is inserted into an artery or vein in the arm or leg and advanced into the chambers of the heart or into the coronary arteries.

Echocardiogram—Sends sound waves (like sonar) into the chest to rebound from the heart's walls and valves. The recorded waves show the shape, texture and movement of the valves, the size of the heart chambers and how well they're working.

Electrocardiogram—Used to find out if the heart rate and rhythm are normal or if heart damage has occurred, it is a graphic record of the heart's electrical impulses. A 12-lead electrocardiogram uses several wires, or leads, that are attached to the arms, legs and chest. Each lead records the same electrical impulse, but from a different position in relation to the heart.

Holter Monitor—Detects heart rhythm or ischemia (inadequate blood flow to the heart muscle); a 24-hour portable monitor of the electrocardiogram.

Signal-Averaged Electrocardiogram (SAECG)—Identifies people at risk of a dangerous rhythm in the heart's lower (pumping) chambers. This rhythm, called "ventricular tachycardia," can lead to sudden cardiac death. In this high-resolution ECG, computers are used to amplify and enhance the ECG signal. Small electrical currents, called "ventricular late potentials," can be recorded with a signal-averaged ECG.

Stress Echocardiography—Done before, during or immediately after some form of physical stress (such as bicycle or treadmill exercise), this test is useful to diagnose coronary heart disease.

Transesophageal Echocardiography (TEE)—A special type of echocardiogram; a tube with an echocardiogram transducer on the end of it is passed down a person's throat and into the esophagus (the tube connecting the mouth to the stomach). The esophagus is right behind the heart, and images from TEE can give very clear pictures of the heart and its structures.

Pantry Planner for Heart Health

Having a wide variety of ingredients on hand offers tremendous flexibility for preparing fresh, easy and great-tasting heart-healthy recipes. This pantry list covers the basics of good-for-your-heart cooking. And, feel free to add your own favorites to have on hand.

Fresh Produce

Any vegetable or fruit in season

Broccoli

Cabbage

Carrots

Cucumbers

Garlic

Onions

Potatoes

Salad greens (any variety)

Spinach and other leafy greens

Sweet potatoes

Apples

Bananas

Grapes

Melons

Oranges, Tangerines

Dairy

Fat-free (skim) or low-fat (1%) milk

Fat-free sour cream

Plain fat-free yogurt

Flavored fat-free yogurt

Tub margarine

Light cream cheese

Low-fat or fat-free cheese

Meats/Poultry/Fish

Well-trimmed beef, pork and lamb cuts (e.g., "loin")

Skinless chicken and turkey

All types of shellfish and fish, especially fatty types (salmon, tuna)

Lean cold cuts (e.g., sliced roast turkey or beef)

Low-fat sausages

Cereals/Pastas

Whole-grain cereals

Oatmeal

Whole-grain pasta

Quinoa, other grains

Snacks

Whole-grain crackers or flatbreads

Rice crackers

Whole-wheat pretzels

Plain popcorn or low-fat microwave popcorn

Fig bars

Graham crackers

Canned and Bottled Goods

Reduced-sodium broths

Reduced-sodium tomato soup

Canned beans

Canned no-salt-added tomatoes

Fat-free bean dip

Canned fruits (in water or fruit juice)

Oils and Dressings/Sauces

Canola oil

Olive oil

Soybean Oil

Natural peanut butter

Low-fat or fat-free salad dressings

Sherry, balsamic and/or flavored vinegars

Reduced-sodium marinara sauce

Salsa

Frozen Foods

Soy burgers and crumbles (look for low-fat brands)

Frozen orange juice

Low-fat frozen yogurt

Whole-fruit freezer pops

Bakery

Whole-grain breads and rolls

Whole-grain English muffins

Whole-grain pitas

Corn tortillas

Fat-free flour tortillas

Angel food cake

Beverages

Flavored sparkling water

100 percent fruit juices

Helpful Nutrition and Cooking Information

Nutrition Guidelines

We provide nutrition information for each recipe that includes calories, fat, cholesterol, sodium, carbohydrate, fiber and protein. Individual food choices can be based on this information.

Recommended intake for a daily diet of 2,000 calories as set by the Food and Drug Administration

Total Fat	Less than 65g
Saturated Fat	Less than 20g
Cholesterol	Less than 300mg
Sodium	Less than 2,400mg
Total Carbohydrate	300g
Dietary Fiber	25g

Criteria Used for Calculating Nutrition Information

- The first ingredient was used wherever a choice is given (such as 1/3 cup sour cream or plain yogurt).

- The first ingredient amount was used wherever a range is given (such as 3- to 3-1/2–pound cut-up broiler-fryer chicken).

- The first serving number was used wherever a range is given (such as 4 to 6 servings).

- "If desired" ingredients and recipe variations were not included (such as sprinkle with brown sugar, if desired).

- Only the amount of a marinade or frying oil that is estimated to be absorbed by the food during preparation or cooking was calculated.

Ingredients Used in Recipe Testing and Nutrition Calculations

- Ingredients used for testing represent those that the majority of consumers use in their homes: large eggs, 2-percent milk, 80 percent lean ground beef, canned ready-to-use chicken broth and vegetable oil spread containing not less than 65 percent fat.

- Fat-free, low-fat or low-sodium products were not used, unless otherwise indicated.

- Solid vegetable shortening (not butter, margarine, nonstick cooking sprays or vegetable oil spread as they can cause sticking problems) was used to grease pans, unless otherwise indicated.

Equipment Used in Recipe Testing

We use equipment for testing that the majority of consumers use in their homes. If a specific piece of equipment (such as a wire whisk) is necessary for recipe success, it is listed in the recipe.

- Cookware and bakeware without nonstick coatings were used, unless otherwise indicated.

- No dark-colored, black or insulated bakeware was used.

- When a pan is specified in a recipe, a metal pan was used; a baking dish or pie plate means ovenproof glass was used.

- An electric hand mixer was used for mixing only when mixer speeds are specified in the recipe directions. When a mixer speed is not given, a spoon or fork was used.

Cooking Terms Glossary

Beat: Mix ingredients vigorously with spoon, fork, wire whisk, hand beater or electric mixer until smooth and uniform.

Boil: Heat liquid until bubbles rise continuously and break on the surface and steam is given off. For rolling boil, the bubbles form rapidly.

Chop: Cut into coarse or fine irregular pieces with a knife, food chopper, blender or food processor.

Cube: Cut into squares 1/2 inch or larger.

Dice: Cut into squares smaller than 1/2 inch.

Grate: Cut into tiny particles using small rough holes of grater (citrus peel or chocolate).

Grease: Rub the inside surface of a pan with shortening, using pastry brush, piece of waxed paper or paper towel, to prevent food from sticking during baking (as for some casseroles).

Julienne: Cut into thin, matchlike strips, using knife or food processor (vegetables, fruits, meats).

Mix: Combine ingredients in any way that distributes them evenly.

Sauté: Cook foods in hot oil or margarine over medium-high heat with frequent tossing and turning motion.

Shred: Cut into long thin pieces by rubbing food across the holes of a shredder, as for cheese, or by using a knife to slice very thinly, as for cabbage.

Simmer: Cook in liquid just below the boiling point on top of the stove; usually after reducing heat from a boil. Bubbles will rise slowly and break just below the surface.

Stir: Mix ingredients until uniform consistency. Stir once in a while for stirring occasionally, often for stirring frequently and continuously for stirring constantly.

Toss: Tumble ingredients (such as green salad) lightly with a lifting motion, usually to coat evenly or mix with another food.

Metric Conversion Guide

VOLUME

U.S. Units	Canadian Metric	Australian Metric
1/4 teaspoon	1 mL	1 ml
1/2 teaspoon	2 mL	2 ml
1 teaspoon	5 mL	5 ml
1 tablespoon	15 mL	20 ml
1/4 cup	50 mL	60 ml
1/3 cup	75 mL	80 ml
1/2 cup	125 mL	125 ml
2/3 cup	150 mL	170 ml
3/4 cup	175 mL	190 ml
1 cup	250 mL	250 ml
1 quart	1 liter	1 liter
1 1/2 quarts	1.5 liters	1.5 liters
2 quarts	2 liters	2 liters
2 1/2 quarts	2.5 liters	2.5 liters
3 quarts	3 liters	3 liters
4 quarts	4 liters	4 liters

WEIGHT

U.S. Units	Canadian Metric	Australian Metric
1 ounce	30 grams	30 grams
2 ounces	55 grams	60 grams
3 ounces	85 grams	90 grams
4 ounces (1/4 pound)	115 grams	125 grams
8 ounces (1/2 pound)	225 grams	225 grams
16 ounces (1 pound)	455 grams	500 grams
1 pound	455 grams	1/2 kilogram

MEASUREMENTS

Inches	Centimeters
1	2.5
2	5.0
3	7.5
4	10.0
5	12.5
6	15.0
7	17.5
8	20.5
9	23.0
10	25.5
11	28.0
12	30.5
13	33.0

TEMPERATURES

Fahrenheit	Celsius
32°	0°
212°	100°
250°	120°
275°	140°
300°	150°
325°	160°
350°	180°
375°	190°
400°	200°
425°	220°
450°	230°
475°	240°
500°	260°

Note: The recipes in this cookbook have not been developed or tested using metric measures.
When converting recipes to metric, some variations in quality may be noted.

The Ciccarone Center for the Prevention of Heart Disease

A Center with Heart

The Ciccarone Center for the Prevention of Heart Disease at Johns Hopkins provides a comprehensive program geared toward the prevention of coronary heart disease. The center, located in Baltimore, MD, was created in 1989 through the efforts of Dr. Roger S. Blumenthal in memory of his close friend Henry Ciccarone, a legendary athlete and lacrosse coach at Johns Hopkins who died at age 50 after his third heart attack. Dr. Blumenthal has been Clinical Director of the Center since 1997.

Prevention, Management and Care

Heart disease prevention is the primary goal of the Ciccarone Center, as is providing care for patients who currently have vascular disease. The center specializes in helping adults who are at high risk for future cardiovascular disease due to multiple risk factors (e.g., hypertension, high cholesterol, diabetes, cigarette smoking, sedentary lifestyle and overweight) or a history of known cardiovascular disease. Physicians specializing in endocrinology and cardiology foster a comprehensive approach to patient care. Experienced nurse practitioner health educators provide lifestyle counseling related to all issues of preventive cardiology. Of special interest to the Ciccarone Center are women, persons who have cardiovascular disease before the age of 65 or those with a family history of premature cardiovascular disease.

Education

In addition to clinical activities, the center also educates health care providers about heart disease. The physicians and nurses at the center are active clinical investigators in one or more of the following fields: hypertension, familial-clustered coronary disease, high cholesterol, diabetes, thrombosis, accelerated atherosclerosis, estrogen replacement therapy and non-invasive cardiovascular imaging.

Research

A leading goal of the Ciccarone Center is to conduct cutting-edge research on atherosclerosis and risk factors for heart disease. Dr. Charles Lowenstein, an expert in vascular biology, directs the basic science research of the Ciccarone Center, while Dr. Roger Blumenthal directs the clinic and clinical research of the Ciccarone Center. In 2003, Ciccarone Center investigators published articles in *Cell, JAMA, Circulation, Archives of Internal Medicine, Journal of the American College of Cardiology and Annals of Internal Medicine.*

Visit Us Online

To learn more about the Ciccarone Center for the Prevention of Heart Disease at Johns Hopkins, visit www.hopkinsmedicine.org/CardiacSurgery/excellence/ciccarone or call (410) 955-7376.

Index

Note: *Italicized* page references indicate photographs.

Complete your cookbook library
with these *Betty Crocker* titles

Betty Crocker Baking for Today
Betty Crocker Basics
Betty Crocker's Best Bread Machine Cookbook
Betty Crocker's Best Chicken Cookbook
Betty Crocker's Best Christmas Cookbook
Betty Crocker's Best of Baking
Betty Crocker's Best of Healthy and Hearty Cooking
Betty Crocker's Best-Loved Recipes
Betty Crocker's Bisquick® Cookbook
Betty Crocker Bisquick® II Cookbook
Betty Crocker Bisquick® Impossibly Easy Pies
Betty Crocker Celebrate!
Betty Crocker's Complete Thanksgiving Cookbook
Betty Crocker's Cook Book for Boys and Girls
Betty Crocker's Cook It Quick
Betty Crocker Cookbook, 10th Edition— *The* **BIG RED** *Cookbook*®
Betty Crocker's Cookbook, Bridal Edition
Betty Crocker's Cookie Book
Betty Crocker's Cooking Basics
Betty Crocker's Cooking for Two
Betty Crocker's Cooky Book, Facsimile Edition
Betty Crocker's Diabetes Cookbook
Betty Crocker Dinner Made Easy with Rotisserie Chicken
Betty Crocker Easy Family Dinners
Betty Crocker's Easy Slow Cooker Dinners
Betty Crocker's Eat and Lose Weight
Betty Crocker's Entertaining Basics
Betty Crocker's Flavors of Home
Betty Crocker 4-Ingredient Dinners
Betty Crocker Grilling Made Easy
Betty Crocker Healthy Heart Cookbook
Betty Crocker's Healthy New Choices
Betty Crocker's Indian Home Cooking
Betty Crocker's Italian Cooking
Betty Crocker's Kids Cook!
Betty Crocker's Kitchen Library
Betty Crocker's Living with Cancer Cookbook
Betty Crocker Low-Carb Lifestyle Cookbook
Betty Crocker's Low-Fat, Low-Cholesterol Cooking Today
Betty Crocker More Slow Cooker Recipes
Betty Crocker's New Cake Decorating
Betty Crocker's New Chinese Cookbook
Betty Crocker One-Dish Meals
Betty Crocker's A Passion for Pasta
Betty Crocker's Picture Cook Book, Facsimile Edition
Betty Crocker's Quick & Easy Cookbook
Betty Crocker's Slow Cooker Cookbook
Betty Crocker's Ultimate Cake Mix Cookbook
Betty Crocker's Vegetarian Cooking